DATE DUE FOR RETURN

Modernizing Infrastructure in Transformation Economies

Modernizing Infrastructure in Transformation Economies

Paving the Way to European Enlargement

Christian von Hirschhausen

Lecturer in Economics, Berlin University of Technology (TU Berlin) and Senior Researcher, DIW Berlin (German Institute for Economic Research), Germany

Edward Elgar
Cheltenham, UK • Northampton, MA, USA

Published by
Edward Elgar Publishing Limited
Glensanda House
Montpellier Parade
Cheltenham
Glos GL50 1UA
UK

Edward Elgar Publishing, Inc.
136 West Street
Suite 202
Northampton
Massachusetts 01060
USA

1003918496

A catalogue record for this book
is available from the British Library

Library of Congress Cataloguing in Publication Data

Hirschhausen, Christian von, 1964–
    Modernizing infrastructure in transformation economies: paving
the way to European enlargement/by Christian von Hirschhausen.
      p. cm.
    Includes bibliographical references and indexes.
    1. Infrastructure (Economics)—Europe, Eastern. 2. Infrastructure
(Economics)—Former Soviet republics. 3. European Union—
Europe, Eastern. 4. European Union—Former Soviet republics.
5. Europe—Economic integration. I. Title.
HC244.Z9 C335   2002
388'.0947—dc21   2002026393

ISBN 1 84376 113 0

Printed and bound in Great Britain by MPG Books Ltd, Bodmin, Cornwall

Contents

Figures

Tables

Abbreviations

bbl	barrel (159 liters)
bcm	billion cubic meters
BfAI	Bundesstelle für Außenhandelsinformationen
bn.	billion (10^9)
BOT	build-operate-transfer
c.i.f.	cost-insurance-freight
CEE	Central and East European economies (countries)
CENTREL	Central European Electricity Association
CIS	Commonwealth of Independent States
CMEA	Council of Mutual Economic Assistance
EBRD	European Bank for Reconstruction and Development
ECMT	European Conference of Ministers of Transport
EEK	Estonian Crown (national currency)
EIB	European Investment Bank
EU	European Union
EUR	Euro
FDI	foreign direct investment
GDP	gross domestic product
GW	Gigawatt (10^6 kW)
GWh	Gigawatt hour (10^6 kWh)
HUF	Hungarian Forint
IEA	International Energy Agency
IFO	international financial organization
ISPA	Instrument for Structural Policies for Pre-Accession
kV	kilo Volt
kW	kilo Watt
kWh	kilo Watt hour
LIBOR	London Interbank Offered Rate
LPVR	least-present-value-of-revenue (auction)
mn.	million
MW	Megawatt (10^3 kW)
MWh	Megawatt hour (10^3 kW)
p.a.	per annum

PHARE   Poland-Hungary Assistance and Reconstruction Program
PIP   Public Investment Programs
R&D   research and development
S&T   science and technology
t   (metric) ton (1,000 kg)
tce   tons of coal equivalent
tcm   trillion cubic meters
TEN   Trans-European Networks
th cm   thousand cubic meters
TINA   Transport Infrastructure Needs Assessment Agency
TPA   third party access
trn.   trillion (10^{12})
UCTE   Union for the Coordination of Transmission of Electricity
USD   US dollar

1. Introduction

... I believe to be the basic problem facing public and private policy: the design of institutional arrangements that provide incentives to encourage experimentation (including the development of new products, new knowledge, new reputations, and new ways of organizing activities) without overly insulating these experiments from the ultimate test of survival.
Harold Demsetz (1969, 20): *Information and Efficiency: Another Viewpoint.*

1. THE ISSUE: HOW TO CONDUCT SUCCESSFUL INFRASTRUCTURE REFORMS IN EAST EUROPEAN TRANSFORMATION COUNTRIES

The design of infrastructure policies is a controversial issue both in developed industrial countries and in emerging and developing countries. Politicians and public investment banks generally argue that 'the extension of infrastructure ... makes a significant contribution to economic growth and employment' (European Investment Bank, 1995), while, by contrast, economic research has nothing conclusive to say on that matter (Gramlich, 1994). A subject of particularly heated debate was the role of *infrastructure policies in the transformation countries* of Eastern Europe and the Commonwealth of Independent States (CIS),[1] where the often dismal state of infrastructure was sometimes presented as one of the most serious obstacles to economic recovery and sustained growth in the 1990s. Often the following question was posed: had not the East German example, as a very particular case of transformation, shown that hundreds of billions of EUR invested into building new infrastructure, almost exclusively publicly financed, were a prerequisite

---

[1]   Throughout this book, the term Central and Eastern Europe comprises mainly the EU accession countries (Poland, Czech Republic, Slovak Republic, Hungary, Slovenia, Estonia, Latvia, Lithuania) plus Bulgaria and Romania; in some cases it also includes other East or South-East European countries (Croatia, Yugoslavia, Bosnia-Hercegovina, Montenegro, Albania); the other EU accession candidates, Cyprus, Malta, and Turkey are not covered in this book. The CIS countries include the Russian Federation, Ukraine, Belarus, Kazakhstan, Azerbaijan, Armenia, Turkmenistan, Uzbekistan, Kyrgistan, Tadjikistan). In some instances the generic term 'Eastern Europe' is used to designate all countries in the region.

for economic recovery? And had not the international donors given infrastructure development the highest priority for Eastern Europe, with estimated investment needs of over a thousand billion EUR? While no second Marshall Plan has been put in place, financial institutions, national governments and private investors have indeed put many resources into development plans, advice and political support for specific infrastructure initiatives. Eastern Europe, it was sometimes argued, could even become a pacesetter of market-oriented infrastructure reform, liberalization and privatization; it could thus follow the reform path established by Anglo-Saxon countries such as the UK and the US or Latin America, and hence avoid the dragging reform process that plagued continental Europe during the 1980s and 1990s.

More than a decade into economic transformation in Eastern Europe and with only a few years to go until the eastward enlargement of the European Union (EU), the evaluation of infrastructure reforms in the region is more sober. Radical reforms have in general failed to deliver the expected results. Thus, just to cite the most prominent examples, the 20 or so projects for private highway financing in Eastern Europe in the early 1990s have not brought about the expected results; power sector reform towards a market system has been less successful than hoped for in Poland, Russia, Kazakhstan, and Ukraine. On the other hand, gradual but consistent approaches to reform, supported by a stabilizing institutional environment, are beginning to bear fruit in the Central and East European countries scheduled for accession to the EU. Also, it now turns out that the level of infrastructure investment and the lack of state-of-the-art infrastructure do *not* seem to have been an insurmountable obstacle to economic recovery and growth in most transformation countries.

This book takes a look at a decade of infrastructure policy reforms in Eastern Europe in the context of European integration; in particular it analyzes attempts to introduce market-oriented restructuring in the institutional context of systemic transformation. Based upon a comparative institutional analysis, the book discusses different approaches of East European transformation countries to introducing reforms in infrastructure sectors, and whether these reforms have led to the expected results: for example, fiscal relief, private investment, increased efficiency, and convergence toward EU standards. One particularly important issue to be examined is the relation between systemic transformation and the *sequencing* of reforms. For example, it may be argued that given the substantial institutional instability surrounding the first years of the transformation period, a *gradual* but time-consistent approach to liberalization was a more promising path towards a market economy than an overambitious approach that was bound to fail very early, due to numerous formal and informal obstacles. If this were so, the Eastern European experience would increase the scope of reform options available to other emerging and developing economies, rather than to confirm the existence of one 'first-best' approach.

The questions posed in this book are linked to one main topical issue of *economic policy* in and for Eastern Europe transformation countries, and they address one central *theoretical* issue:

– The *economic policy* issue is what could have been done to manage the transformation process more efficiently, and whether there still is a need for specific infrastructure policies in the process of European enlargement. Although many Central and Eastern European countries are about to join the EU, the reform of their infrastructure sectors has not been accomplished, and the European integration process may suffer from this. The hesitant liberalization in EU countries (think of railways, power, gas) may be hampered further by reform-resistant accession countries. One additional policy issue for the European Union and other donor countries is how to assist the accession process in *Central and Eastern Europe* (for example, through the Trans-European-Networks TEN program, PHARE/ISPA, the structural funds). A concrete question *vis-à-vis CIS countries* is what kind of reforms should be supported in their infrastructure sectors where in some cases the transformation crisis and a lack of political willingness to reform have caused them to suffer badly;

– the *theoretical* issue is whether the institutional specifics of system transformation in Eastern Europe warrant a specific approach to infrastructure policy in these countries: that is, a policy that differs from the market- and competition-oriented approach generally recommended for developed industrial countries. Arguments in favor of specific infrastructure policies for development, following Rostow's (1960) reasoning, were indeed voiced early on in the transformation process. Similar arguments in favor of a transformation-specific infrastructure policy were also developed at the micro-level (Aghion and Schankerman, 1999, Thimann and Thum, 1999) and with regard to the optimal speed of liberalizing network industries (Armstrong and Vickers, 1998). At an institutional level, it was argued that the outcome of infrastructure policy reforms depended primarily on the institutional environment in place, which differed significantly between East European transformation countries and developed, institutionally stable industrialized countries. The reform process in Eastern Europe thus allows for an empirical analysis of the relation between institutions and infrastructure policy, an issue of interest not only for European integration, but also for other emerging regions in the world.

2. A POSITIVE COMPARATIVE INSTITUTIONAL ECONOMIC APPROACH

2.1 The Quest for Specific Analysis and Concrete Policy Conclusions

The research presented in this book is based on the assumption that in order to produce results relevant to theory and policy, the *specific* institutional and technical conditions prevailing in the country or sector under consideration have to be considered. Schematically speaking, one can distinguish two different approaches to analyzing infrastructure policies in transformation and developing countries:

– The first, more traditional one, is to put forward normative prescriptions for first-best infrastructure policy reform based on traditional static welfare economics ('one-size-fits-all'). This approach considers reforms to be a linear process that should guide the sector in question towards a pre-defined structure, independently of the technical and institutional conditions. An example is the proposal to liberalize and privatize the infrastructure in East European transformation countries as quickly as possible, to separate the infrastructure from the superstructure ('unbundle'), and so on, and thus in essence to adopt a model applied in the UK since the late 1980s. This approach has the advantage of giving clear guidelines to policy makers in the respective countries, eventually to give political support to reform-oriented politicians, and to produce a broad consensus among foreign experts. But the approach has one fundamental drawback: *it does not work* in institutional settings that are substantially different from those of developed industrial countries. For example, there is now plenty of evidence that this big-bang approach did not work in the first several years of systemic transformation in Eastern Europe. Today, there is a consensus among the research community *and* politicians that the neglect of the specific economic and institutional situation in the transformation countries was a major cause of the transformation crisis (for example, Stiglitz, 1999);

– the second approach, positive institutional economics, seeks to integrate the *institutional environment* of transactions; that is, the exchange of property rights, into the policy analysis, and thus to take into account the diversity of institutional settings that exist in reality.[2] The *comparative institutional approach* rejects the *nirvana* approach that postulates the possibility of identifying and implementing a first-best, welfare optimizing state of the world. Instead, the comparative institutional approach seeks a solution among alternative *real* institutional arrangements' (Demsetz, 1969, 1, italics added).

---

[2] Furubotn and Richter (2000) have called this approach the 'microeconomic foundation of microeconomics'.

While it does not reject certain fundamental assumptions of economic behavior (such as bounded rationality and opportunism), the positive institutional approach aims at integrating the country-, sector- and system-specific aspects of any given situation into the policy analysis. In particular, the institutional approach takes into consideration the rules governing the exchange of property rights and the sanctions related thereto (North, 1990, 3), to which it attaches the notion of *transaction costs* that traditional approaches neglect. Among the six branches that Furubotn and Richter (2000, 29 sq.) distinguish within the new institutional approach, we consider three to be particularly relevant to the study of infrastructure policies in transformation countries: transaction-cost economics proper (in the sense of extended industrial economics, such as Coase, 1937 and Williamson, 1975, 1985); constitutional economics and the new institutional approach of collective action (for example, Buchanan, 1975; Buchanan et.al., 1980; Olson, 1965, 1982, 1999); and the new institutional approach to economic history explaining long-run economic development (North, 1981, 1990).[3]

The thrust of institutional economics for infrastructure policy analysis is that there is no (longer) such a thing as a best way to restructure and privatize a formerly state-owned, vertically integrated monopoly. Instead, both the choice of the reform model and the sequencing of reform steps should take into account the institutional endowment of a country and the technical state of the infrastructure that determines the transaction costs. Also, political and judicial peripheral conditions (such as EU legislation) have to be taken into consideration. The role of institutions in the restructuring of infrastructure sectors is increasingly attracting policy makers' and researchers' interest, both in highly developed industrial countries and in developing countries; yet, empirical evidence is scarce thus far. Over the last decade, the institutional approach has moved from general to sectoral analyses (for example, Kumkar, 1999 for the power sector). Spiller (1993, 1996), Levy and Spiller (1994), Spiller and Vogelsang (1997), and Spiller and Tommasi (2000) have developed an inductive case-study-oriented approach identifying the institutional characteristics specific to certain countries and sectors in infrastructure policy, mainly with reference to Latin America. Ménard and Clarke (2000a, b) were among the first to apply positive institutional economics to African utility restructuring, where they find a relation between the institutional environment and the success of deregulation (in the water sector). Recent experience with infrastructure liberalization in Western industrialized countries shows abundantly that reforms result in a *variety* of regulatory models, the results of which are difficult to compare (examples are

---

[3]   We thus leave aside the three other branches, which are property rights, contract theory (principal-agent theory), and the new institutional approach to political economics (in the terms of political organization), see Furubotn and Richter (2000, 31 and 32).

the regulation of network access in telecommunication, power and gas, vertical unbundling in the railway sector or highway financing; among others, see Glachant, 1998). Currently no comprehensive analysis is available for the countries of Eastern Europe and the CIS that are not yet established advanced market economies yet are attempting market-oriented infrastructure sector reforms. Thus, one aim of this book is to test the theoretical foundations of institutional economics against empirical evidence from the East European transformation countries.

2.2 Specifics of East European Transformation Countries

The choice of a positive institutional economic perspective also takes into account the fact that as of today few emerging or developing countries have succeeded in *radical* liberalization and privatization of their infrastructure sectors. The transformation countries of Eastern Europe can be classified in this group of countries. A specific analysis of the infrastructure policies in this region in itself is justified by at least three characteristics distinguishing the East European reform process from others:

– The system-wide nature of the *systemic transformation process*, which goes far beyond a mere structural reform. Infrastructure policy reform in Eastern Europe was subject to systemic change at *all* economic and political levels, from the enterprises, the sectors, regions, up to the national level. Not only were the formal institutions of socialism abandoned rapidly, but the informal institutions, too, had to adapt to the opening of the economies and the changing of relative prices. In a time as unstable as the period of post-socialist systemic reform, it is difficult to separate the analysis of infrastructure policy from the reshaping of the surrounding institutional framework. In particular, system transformation implies a degree of risk and uncertainty of economic decisions uncommon in established market economies and gradually changing emerging countries;

– the *structural similarities* of the economies entering the transformation process in the early 1990s. Indeed, never in modern economic history had such a large number of countries (26) entered a reform process with similar starting conditions. Whereas some differences did exist between the transformation countries regarding their socialist past (for example, between countries of Eastern Europe and the Soviet Union), at least four decades of Soviet socialism had created similar economic systems within the Soviet block and its infrastructure. The case of the East European transformation countries is therefore a rare occasion where a real-time, comparative analysis is possible;

– a third specific aspect to be taken into account is *European enlargement and integration* as the major politico-economic development of the 1990s, in which the Central and Eastern European countries participated directly, for example, as future members of the EU. Conversely, the European CIS countries also had to take an enlarged Europe into account in the definition of their infrastructure policies (physically, for example, in the design of TEN, or institutionally, such as in the definition of regulatory structures not too dissimilar from EU legislation). The European perspective imposed certain political and technical policy choices on the transformation countries (examples are environmental standards and network specification), whereas the upcoming EU accession also provided a clear policy perspective for many transformation countries.

3. STRUCTURE OF THE BOOK

The book is divided into *three parts*: the *conceptual issues*; an *empirical analysis* of infrastructure policies across Eastern Europe including in-depth case studies; and *conclusions*.

3.1 Part I: Conceptual Issues on Infrastructure Policies in Eastern Europe

Part I provides a conceptual framework and identifies the specific features of infrastructure policy reform in Eastern Europe. Chapter 2 defines the concept of *infrastructure* and identifies the different approaches to infrastructure policy in socialism and in a market economy. In a market economy, infrastructure should be thought of as a *service* that can be provided by *private* enterprise and is subject to competition and, where natural monopolies prevail, some sort of state regulation. We show that the very nature of socialist infrastructure development was incompatible with the requirements of a market economy; this incompatibility also explains the problems of adapting the socialist infrastructure in the early years of the transformation process, and the need to redesign new infrastructure development schemes in the EU accession countries.

Chapter 3 analyzes the process of *systemic transformation* in Eastern Europe. Transformation is considered to be a process of formal and informal institutional change, whereby the socialist system was replaced by other institutions geared toward implementing the principles of a market economy. Two distinct phases within the transformation process can be identified: whereas in *phase I*, the transformation crisis (early 1990s), all transformation countries embarked on similar reform programs, *phase II* was characterized by increasingly divergent paths of reform, both at the macro level and at the structural level (mid- to late-1990s). Around the turn of the century, the transformation process has led to divergent outcomes, where most Central and East European countries have achieved EU-compatibility, whereas the CIS economies of the former Soviet Union have established mixed economies.

Chapter 4 links the two preceding chapters and discusses options for infrastructure policies for transformation countries on the way to European integration. Specifically, the chapter ponders arguments in favor of a *transformation-specific infrastructure* policy in Eastern Europe during the 1990s. Calls for a second 'Marshall Plan' for East European countries were indeed voiced early in the transformation process; in essence, the Rostow (1960) vs. Hirschman (1958) controversy of the late 1950s reappeared, the former arguing for state-financed infrastructure as a precondition for economic upswing, the latter considering on the contrary a development strategy based on infrastructure scarcity. In addition, microeconomic arguments were also cited in defense of an argument that a competition-oriented infrastructure policy might *not* be optimal under the specific conditions of transformation. Among the factors put forward were the poor technical state of infrastructure in the EU accession countries, the unexpected decline of production, the economic recession, and a high degree of uncertainty limiting private investment. We discuss different theoretical approaches in favor of transformation-specific infrastructure policies, covering macroeconomic, industry structure and regulatory aspects. From this discussion we derive concrete working hypotheses to be tested in the empirical Part II.

3.2 Part II: Empirical Analysis

Part II provides a survey of infrastructure policies across Eastern Europe during the decade of systemic transformation (1991–2001). It combines aggregate analysis covering the essential developments in all 26 transformation countries with empirical analyses of selected programs, sectors, or individual instruments of infrastructure policy. Empirical studies come from a variety of sectors – transport, power, gas, R&D – and countries (EU-accession countries and CIS countries), that can be considered a representative sample (comprehensive coverage of *all* sectors and countries would be beyond the scope of such a book as this). A particular focus is placed on the reforms necessary for a smooth integration of Eastern Europe with the material and institutional infrastructure of the European Union. Chapter 5 presents quantitative and qualitative evidence on infrastructure sector developments in Eastern Europe. We also discuss the evaluation of infrastructure reform carried out by international organizations such as the European Bank for Reconstruction and Development (EBRD) and the

European Union. The latter part of the chapter derives a methodology for empirical tests and case studies that is applied throughout the rest of the book in Chapters 6–11.

Chapter 6 looks for evidence that the *public investment programs* (PIP) carried out in several transformation countries had a positive impact on the reform process and that they accelerated the convergence process. They were developed to spur public and private infrastructure investments. The empirical test consists of an in-depth analysis of public investment programs in the three Baltic countries (Lithuania, Latvia, Estonia) between 1994–99. It turns out that none of the large-scale state infrastructure development plans have achieved their objectives, due to over-dimensioned and unrealistic demand projections, bureaucratic obstacles and a lack of complementary private commitment to investment.

Chapter 7 analyzes approaches to and results of infrastructure policy towards *innovation*. Public support in the form of proactive national innovation and technology policies was considered to be particularly important for the modernization of East European S&T systems and their catching up with Western Europe. However, an analysis of the socialist innovation system shows that a gradual transformation towards market structures was difficult, due to the different international technological trajectories to which the former socialist countries had to adhere. The chapter also summarizes previous empirical research at the sectoral level implying that the *internationalization* of innovation, production and sales networks was the major force driving technological catching-up of East European enterprises.

Chapter 8 discusses the attempts at introducing a major innovation in post-socialist infrastructure policy, namely *private project financing*. We ask whether the observed difficulties encountered in implementing this instrument in the transport sector in Eastern Europe can be explained by the specific conditions of the transformation countries, such as institutional instability, low time consistency of public policy and low purchasing power. Empirical evidence comes from different projects of private highway finance all over Eastern Europe. In particular, we highlight financial, technical and institutional difficulties of the pilot project M1, the introduction of the first toll-financed highway in Hungary in the mid-1990s. We conclude that should the EU accession countries wish for a rapid development of highway infrastructure (for example, to reach an average EU level) and private investment, then the state has to assume a portion of the risk.

The following Chapters 9–11 report empirical evidence from energy sector restructuring (power and gas), where experience from recent reforms in Western countries provides a certain point of reference for comparison. Chapter 9 analyzes the process of *power utility re-regulation* in Eastern

Europe during the decade of systemic transformation, and the perspectives thereof. One observes that countries attempting radical reforms towards a market-based system have faced significant problems (for example, Poland), whereas countries opting for a conservative reform approach (for example, Hungary) seem to show better medium-term results. Quantitative indicators are wholesale and retail prices, cost coverage ratios and the degree of unbundling and privatization. The chapter concludes with concrete policy suggestions of how to design the reform process from here on, in particular the integration of the EU-accession countries into the institutional framework defined by the EU.

A more political economy-oriented perspective is provided in Chapter 10 on *gas sector restructuring*. Despite attempts by some governments to introduce competition in the sector, results have been poor thus far, particularly concerning structural transformation. This is particularly true for the large CIS gas industries. We discuss to what extent resistance to reform is a matter of political unwillingness, or of an *inability* to introduce reforms in the absence of a market environment. Chapter 11 focuses more on the resource aspects of gas sector reform. We show that the process of systemic transformation also has consequences for the economic value of East European *gas reserves*. In fact there is a fundamental difference between the former socialist notion of (physical) reserves and the market economic notion of (profitable) reserves. Taking the example of Russia, Western Europe's largest gas supplier, we show that this re-evaluation might have significant consequences for domestic policies, but also for exports.

3.3 Part III: Summary and Conclusions

Chapter 12 *summarizes* the main findings of the book and derives *conclusions* for economic research and infrastructure policies in and for the East European countries and for the process of European enlargement. It is argued that after ten years of transformation, very different situations prevail between countries and sectors. For example, in most Central and Eastern European countries, there is no longer any reason *not* to pursue market-oriented infrastructure policies. On the other hand, however, the CIS countries are still further away from having market economy regulation and, therefore, market-oriented infrastructure reforms are less likely to succeed soon. External financial support, such as a second Marshall Plan, does not seem to be conducive to enhancing the reform process.

4. ACKNOWLEDGEMENTS

This book is the result of six years of research on infrastructure policies in Eastern Europe, carried out by the author within a variety of research projects (1996–2001). Accordingly, thanks go primarily to the colleagues with whom the projects were carried out and who in part co-authored earlier publications and reports: Jürgen Bitzer, Hella Engerer, Petra Opitz and Thomas Waelde. Together with them, I thank discussion partners – enterprises, politicians and economists throughout Eastern and Western Europe – who have provided the essential ingredient of a bottom-up comparative institutional approach. The research took place in three different organizations: the scientific thrust was obtained while working as Visiting Professor at WIP, the Workgroup for Infrastructure Policy at TU Berlin University of Technology (School of Economics and Management, F VIII), whereas most of the empirical work was carried out in projects at DIW Berlin (German Institute for Economic Research) and the German Advisory Group to the Government of Ukraine (that has now merged with the IER, the Institute for Economic Research in Kiev). Thanks go also to the many colleagues in these organizations for productive cooperation and to their respective leaders for scientific guidance: Professor Hans-Jürgen Ewers,[†] Chair of the Workgroup for Infrastructure Policy (WIP) at Berlin University of Technology and the scientific mentor of this book;[4] Professor Lutz Hoffmann, former President of DIW Berlin and Co-Head of the German Advisory Group, now President of the Institute for East European Studies (Munich); Dr. Axel Siedenberg, Director of Deutsche Bank Research and Co-Head of the German Advisory Group; and Professor Wolfram Schrettl, Head of the Department of International Economics at DIW Berlin and Chair of East European Economics at the Free University Berlin.

A slightly more extended version of this book has been accepted as 'Habilitationsschrift' by the School of Economics and Management (F VIII) of Berlin University of Technology (TU Berlin). I am particularly grateful to Professor Meran, Professor Henke, Chair of Public Economics at TU Berlin and Director at the European Center for Comparative Government and Public Policy, for participating in the scientific jury, and to Professor Hoffmann for providing his expertise on the book.

Sponsoring for the more empirically oriented projects was obtained mainly from the German Ministry of Economy (TRANSFORM program) and the KfW Kreditanstalt für Wiederaufbau, the European Commission (GDs Economic and Financial Affairs, Enterprise, R&D, Energy) and various

---

[4] Professor Ewers passed away in April 2002, just after the submission of the manuscript. I am grateful for the time spent with him and will keep him in good memory.

business enterprises; the usual disclaimer applies. Some of the research has already been published in journal articles, which are in part reproduced in Chapters 3, 6, and 10.

Further thanks go to the 'dream team' consisting of Berit Meinhart, Deborah Bowen and Wolfgang Härle for research and statistical support, layout, proofreading, and finishing the book; to Uta Kreibig, Yvonne Tang, and Grit Hannemann for research assistance; and to many others for the critical reading of parts of the manuscript. Cordial thanks for secretarial support also go to Iris Semmann, Giesela Tietke and Heidrun Becker at DIW Berlin, Christel Gölling at TU Berlin and Svitlana Shokina at IER, Kiev. Last but certainly not least, special thanks are due to the personal and family infrastructure that has supported this work, in particular Béatrice, Clara and Gregor; I dedicate this book to them.

Part I

Conceptual Issues

2. Infrastructure Policy in Socialism and in the Market Economy

Socialism is the throughway to Leviathan. ... Free relations among free men – this precept of ordered anarchy can emerge as principle when successfully renegotiated social contract puts 'mine and thine' in a newly defined structural arrangement and when the Leviathan that threatens is placed within new limits.

Buchanan (1975, 180): *The Limits of Liberty.*

The expansion of [socialist] infrastructure is driven by political and ideological factors. This is particularly the case for infrastructure in education, health, and social affairs, aiming at the intensive reproduction of the labor force.

Tjulpanov ([1969] 1975, 351): *Political Economy and its Application to Developing Countries.*[5]

1. INTRODUCTION

Infrastructure is generally considered as an important requirement for economic development (World Bank, 1994). However, opinions differ widely on the question of the right infrastructure policy to promote development. This chapter contrasts the market economy concepts of infrastructure and infrastructure policies against the socialist concepts and thus develops the conceptual basis upon which the analysis of infrastructure policies in East European transformation countries will be based. The chapter is structured in the following way: Section 2 defines the concept of infrastructure and discusses various definitions in the literature. Section 3 presents an ideal-typical functioning of infrastructure policy in a *market economy* and considers the question under what conditions infrastructure might *not* be supplied by market competition. Furthermore we discuss the institutional requirements of a competition-oriented infrastructure policy. Section 4 then presents the *socialist* concept of infrastructure policy. In particular, we

---

[5] Translated from the German version.

interpret the evolution of infrastructure in Eastern Europe over the last decades that lead to the state observed in the early 1990s, a difficult point of inception for reform on the way to EU accession both in a physical and an organizational sense. Section 5 concludes.

2. THE CONCEPT OF INFRASTRUCTURE

Infrastructure is a term that is used in many fields of economics, for example, regional economics, public finance, and growth theory. However, there is no easy definition. There may be a popular consensus that 'bridges, streets and tunnels' are infrastructure. Among economists, there is a broad consensus that the term 'infrastructure' designates areas where a state economic policy may be required (for example, due to significant market failure).[6] In an attempt to identify factors of economic development, Jochimsen (1966, 100) defined infrastructure as 'the sum of material, institutional and personal capacities available to economic agents that contribute to the normalization of factor payments for similar inputs, thus leading to a complete economic integration and the highest possible level of economic activity.' In other words, in a market economy infrastructure works against the frictions and discontinuities in space and between inputs. Thus, Jochimsen already argued in the terminology of the new institutional economics. The main task of infrastructure is to reduce *transaction costs*. Infrastructure reduces the intransparencies of markets, where identical factor inputs receive different payments. Infrastructure thus leads to a reduction of these differences, ideally the differences in factor payments disappear completely.[7]

Jochimsen (1966, 103 sq.) distinguished three categories of infrastructure:

– *Material* infrastructure is that part of the physical capital stock of an economy which is used as a fundamental input into other directly productive activities. This has been called (physical) *social overhead capital* in development economics (Hirschman, 1958). Examples are equipment and structures in telecommunication, transport, energy, water and sewage;

– *personal infrastructure* comprises the entrepreneurial, mental and other skills of the people; it refers to the quantity and quality of skills that contribute directly to increased integration and a higher level of economic output;

---

[6] In the economic literature, the infrastructure debate (then called social overhead capital) emerged in the late 1950s, with the works of Hirschman (1958), Rostow (1960), and Tinbergen, Jan (1959, *Selected Papers*. Amsterdam).

[7] Sections 2. and 3.1 of this chapter summarize a corpus of research and teaching developed jointly in the Institute of Transport Economics at Muenster University, and the Workgroup for Infrastructure Policy at TU Berlin, under the guidance of Professor Ewers.

– the *institutional infrastructure* corresponds to what new institutional economics calls the *institutional environment*; it is the non-physical environment of economic action which is specific to a given society. Institutional infrastructure includes internal and external norms (or formal and informal institutions) that shape economic behavior and thus have a direct impact on the societal decision-making process. To a certain degree, institutional infrastructure takes the form of the constitutional framework (choice of rules); on the other hand, it is developed within society through partial decisions, the 'choice within rules'. Examples are the legal system, the economic constitution, banking and finance regulation, the bureaucracy, but also informal institutions such as trust, culture, and so on.

To this basic definition of infrastructure, dating back to the 1960s, one could add two more concepts that were brought up in the course of the infrastructure debate in the early 1990s, in which infrastructure once again was put on top of the policy and research agenda (for example, Aschauer, 1989): *technological infrastructure*, and *information infrastructure*.[8]

Independently of the definition of infrastructure, there is a broad consensus upon certain typical *characteristics* of infrastructure:

– *Technical* characteristics: infrastructure is generally an input into production, is often technically indivisible, has a long life, is not traded, and its exclusion is in most cases technically demanding;

– *economic* characteristics: infrastructure leads to a reduction of transaction costs, it usually has a subadditive cost function, a tendency towards natural monopoly, high sunk costs, network externalities and little rivalry in consumption (examples are sectors that are generally called 'network' sectors, such as telecommunication, power, gas);

– *socio-economic* and *organizational* characteristics: some infrastructure goods are considered to be a citizen's right, thus the state has to assure a minimum supply to everybody (for example, health care). In most cases, there is a necessity for centralized planning and coordination, and an intensive private-public cooperation. The traditional public finance literature assumes that 'infrastructure' is a generally applicable and universal concept. This implies that infrastructure policy conclusions can be drawn independently of the system, and in particular that they can be applied to non-market

---

8   Technological infrastructure was defined as 'the set of specific, industry-relevant capabilities which have been supplied collectively and which are intended for several applications in two or more firms or user organizations; ... TI is embodied in a variety of forms: human capital (formal education, tacit capabilities resulting from both training and experience), physical capital (instrumentation), knowledge (design methodologies), and organization (e.g. networks linking users of technological services with a technological center supplying them.' (Teubal et al., 1996, 10 sq.). Information infrastructure designs the interaction between technical, personal and material infrastructure that is the basis for the so-called knowledge-based, information economy (sometimes called *new economy*).

economies as well.[9] However, this assumption contradicts the comparative institutional approach according to which any policy prescription depends on the *specific* institutional environment; it also contradicts the notion of *path dependent* policy conclusions. Hedtkamp (1995) adopted a systemic *comparative* perspective, and argued *against* the universal application of the concept of infrastructure.[10] His differentiation of time- and system-dependent infrastructure is only relevant in the context of large system transformation (which is precisely what we are dealing with in this book).

3. INFRASTRUCTURE POLICY IN A MARKET ECONOMY

3.1 Reference Model for Efficient Supply of Infrastructure

3.1.1 Market competition
Following Hayek (1945, 1969), market competition can be described as a form of coordination with intrinsic advantages over political representation or bureaucratic organizational forms, as it allows *decentralized* decisions and thus leads to more efficient results (Hayek's market as a search process, '*Markt als Entdeckungsverfahren*'). The market is superior to a system of political decision about the assumed preferences of the constituency; it is all the more superior to the bureaucratic organizations' decision making which is subject to a double principal-agent problem (consumer/voter – politician – bureaucrat) (Cullis and Jones, 1998).

Normative welfare economics assumes the existence of one 'optimal' institutional setting, i.e. a free market economy with private property and a high degree of decentralized, individual freedom of economic choices. In this model, infrastructure policy can be evaluated by using traditional welfare measures. The social optimum is given when the Pareto conditions are fulfilled: that is, when for all goods and consumers the marginal rate of substitution equals the marginal rate of transformation. In this state, the economy achieves allocative and productive efficiency and also triggers innovation and thus generates additional knowledge.

New institutional economics proposes a less complex, but also more feasible instrument for comparing different policies. It complements the traditional welfare economic analysis with the analysis of *institutional specifics* and thus institutional differences between different settings in which

---

9   For example, Jochimsen (1966, 4) argued that his theory of market economy development could be transferred without any methodological difficulty onto other economic systems, for example, centrally planned economies.

10   Hedtkamp's approach is *subject*-oriented: infrastructure is everything that is *not* provided by the private sector, and that constitutes a necessary condition for private production.

economic policy is taking place. Institutional economics proposes a *qualitative* comparison of the results of institutional and organizational behavior, and suggests application of rather loose efficiency criteria (for example, only a broad distinction between 'efficient' and 'inefficient' outcomes of a regulatory process). The aim of this approach, *comparative institutional analysis* (Demsetz, 1969), is not to evaluate individual decisions (such as the construction of a road between point A and point B), but to evaluate the constitutional *process* leading to economic policy decisions (for example, the institutional and organizational framework for the supply of road infrastructure).

3.1.2 Arguments against competition in infrastructure policies

In this section, we discuss whether *market competition* can be used as a mechanism of allocation in infrastructure sectors. Three levels of infrastructure policy need to be distinguished (see Wink, 1995; Ewers and Rodi, 1995):

– *Network planning* (this means long-term planning of infrastructure at central and regional levels);

– *financing*, and

– *operation* (construction, operation, maintenance, and so on).

It is often argued that infrastructure supply cannot follow market principles, either for normative political reasons, or because the markets are considered to be insufficiently contestable. In addition, the following political arguments are advanced *against* the market- and competition-oriented supply of infrastructure:

– Conflicts with general political objectives such as the creation of equal living conditions across a country;

– conflicts with distribution issues, such as the supply of an adequate public service, or a minimal infrastructure supply to every citizen (for example, health services);

– security and strategic aspects (for example, the necessity for the state to assure internal and external security).

The main weakness of these arguments is that they confuse issues of distribution and allocation. At least for *financing* and *operation* of infrastructure, the above arguments can be rejected on the grounds of the fundamental law of public economics: that allocative decisions should be separated from distribution aspects (Musgrave and Musgrave, 1996). Distribution conflicts can be appeased by efficient market allocation, in that the latter generally achieves better results, upon which decisions regarding distribution (according to Musgrave the 'Distribution Ministry') can rely. Security-oriented goals, for example, the construction of uneconomical infrastructure along national borders, does indeed require a coordination at the level of network planning. However, financing and a part of the operation of these infrastructures may as well follow market principles, as long as the technical requirements and security aspects are fulfilled. *Network planning*, on the other hand, cannot be left completely to the forces of a free market: the high probability that network effects will be foregone by decentralized network planning necessitates some form of coordination.

Market failure arguments against a decentralized, private supply of infrastructure may include high transaction costs, low excludability and low rivalry in consumption, positive externalities and a tendency towards natural monopoly. However, in the areas of *financing* and *operation*, there are no conclusive market-failure arguments against a competition-oriented supply of infrastructure. High sunk costs make direct competition less likely, but do not prevent it completely, as long as the economic policy framework remains competition-oriented – such as repeated competition *for* the market (Demsetz, 1968). A limit of market allocation may appear in the area of *network planning*. The state may have a comparative advantage in some sovereign responsibilities, such as long-term corridor planning and expropriation, and due to this advantage, its participation in network planning will generally reduce transaction costs. Externalities (for example, negative environmental effects) may also require some sort of state coordination. However, the participation of the state in network planning does not exclude the private supply of the infrastructure itself.[11]

The application of this market-oriented reference model causes *transaction costs*, mainly by transforming existing institutional and organizational structures in conformance with the market-oriented model. The private operation of infrastructure, too, may in some cases lead to higher transaction costs than the present ones (depending upon the coordination costs between private agents and the state regulator). However, the important point is that market processes and competition *can* be used efficiently to supply infrastructure. Anyone excluding these decentralized mechanisms should prove why, given a certain institutional situation, market principles and the introduction of competition should *not* lead to better results than administrative procedures.

---

[11]   An entirely private supply of network infrastructure has been proposed by Buchanan (1965) in a club model. Network planning, according to this model, is organized in private user clubs, whereas the state maintains its sovereign functions and assures the continuity of the legal framework (see Sandler and Tschirrhardt, 1980, 1997). Applications are discussed by Brenck (1993) for the railway sector, and by Ewers and Rodi (1995) for highways.

3.2 Institutions and Infrastructure Policy

3.2.1 Institutions

Whereas the previous section has argued that market-oriented policy is *possible* in infrastructure sectors, this section discusses some institutional *conditions* for an efficient market-oriented infrastructure policy. Jochimsen (1966) discussed the institutional component as a key to understanding the efficiency of a regulatory process – an assessment shared more or less explicitly by almost all authors on infrastructure policy issues. Among the various definitions available, we shall use the most commonly agreed one, coined by Douglas North (1990).[12] According to North, institutions define the incentive structures of and within societies. Further, 'institutions can be *formal*, such as written rules (laws) or *informal*, such as conventions and codes of behavior' (North, 1990, 4, italics added). Conceptually different from institutions (the rules) are the *organizations* (the players) that develop as a reaction to the institutional framework and that are the units which *apply* the institutions.[13]

The role of institutions within the infrastructure policy and their role in the regulatory process are treated differently in the literature. The quantitative industrial economic approach considers institutions merely to result from incomplete constitutions, or more generally from incomplete contracts (Laffont and Tirole, 1993, 612).[14] On the basis of this assumption, the industrial economic approach constructs models to identify optimal institutional settings, that is, the system of checks and balances for a regulatory agency, or the optimal ownership structure of a utility. The approach is limited to the set of *formal* institutions; informal institutions are discarded from the analysis. By contrast, the qualitative, 'soft' approach pursued by new institutional economics is to consider the interaction between institutions and public policy as an iterative process that cannot be planned or designed ex-ante. In this model, institutions are endogenized as 'integral elements of a general economic model' (Furubotn and Richter, 2000, 7).[15]

---

[12] 'Institutions are the rules of the game in a society, or, more formally, are the humanly devised constraints that shape human interaction. ... [institutions] structure incentives in human exchange, whether political, social, or economic. Institutional change shapes the way societies evolve through time and hence is the key to understanding historical change.' North (1990, 3).

[13] 'Organizations include political bodies (political parties, the Senate, a city council, a regulatory agency), economic bodies (firms, trade unions, family farms, cooperatives), social bodies (churches, clubs, athletic associations) and educational bodies (schools, universities, vocational training centers).' North (1990, 5).

[14] Institutions matter 'because the ultimate principles – the people – cannot design a complete contract or grand mechanism governing the behavior of regulated firms, regulators, politicians, or interest groups.' Laffont and Tirole (1993, 665).

[15] One classical example on which no final judgment can be made is the trade-off between the

The hypothesis according to which institutions can be shaped to obtain economic efficiency is dropped (North, 1981, 1990, 7): institutions are devised by organizations in their own interest, which generally results in 'typically inefficient property rights prevailing' (North, 1990, 7). Institutions only determine the opportunities in a society; *organizations* determine how these opportunities are taken advantage of.[16] This latter approach seems more appropriate for the analysis of specific cases of infrastructure policy and also corresponds to the comparative institutional approach that we have suggested as the guideline for a policy-oriented, real-world analysis of infrastructure policy in Eastern Europe.

3.2.2 The institutional endowment
In order to be operational, the set of infrastructure-relevant institutions has to be limited. Levy and Spiller (1994, summarized by Spiller, 1996, 428) have defined the notion of 'institutional endowment' of a country as the sum of five elements:
 – The country's legislative and executive institutions;[17]
 – the judicial institutions;[18]
 – custom and other informal but broadly accepted norms that are generally understood to constrain the action of individuals;
 – the character of the contending social interests within a society; and
 – the administrative capabilities of the nation.

Whereas the first two elements correspond to the traditional category of *formal* institutions, custom and social interests are generally considered as part of the *informal* institutional environment. Administrative capabilities are situated somewhere in between formal and informal institutions. In the following, we identify some specific formal and informal institutions that may

---

costs of vertically integrated monopolies, and the potential benefits of 'operational and investment coordination within vertically and horizontally integrated industrial hierarchies' (Joskow, 1996, 341). Whether the competition-oriented approach will be welfare enhancing depends on the comparison of the deadweight-losses from monopolistic price setting on the one hand, and the potentially higher productive efficiency of vertically and horizontally integrated structures on the other ('Williamson-Harberger conflict').

[16] 'The resultant path of institutional change is shaped by (1) the lock-in that comes from the symbiotic relationship between institutions and the organizations that have evolved as a consequence of the incentive structure provided by those institutions and (2) the feedback process by which human beings perceive and react to changes in the opportunity set.' North (1990, 7).

[17] 'These are the formal mechanisms for appointment of legislators and decision makers, for making laws and regulations, apart from judicial decision making; for implementing these laws, and that determines the relation between the legislature and the executive.' (Spiller, 1996, 428).

[18] 'These comprise its formal mechanisms for appointing judges and determining the internal structure of the judiciary; and for resolving disputes among private parties, or between private parties and the state.' (Spiller, 1996, 428).

favor a competition-oriented infrastructure policy, mainly by reducing transaction costs and restraining discretionary power of the state and the regulator.

3.2.3 Formal institutional conditions

Jochimsen (1966, 117 sq.) first formulated the *formal* institutional requirements of a market-oriented infrastructure policy, which he defined as a part of the 'institutional infrastructure'. According to Jochimsen, the fundamental principles of a competition-oriented economic constitution are very similar to the ordo-liberal concepts for a free market economy, as defined by Eucken ([1952] 1990, 254 sq.):

– *Private property*, allowing for decentralized negotiations, based on economic assessment, which is a requirement for generating new knowledge and innovation;

– *freedom of contract* goes hand in hand with private property. Without freedom of contract, private property loses its function in decentralized economic exchange;

– the principle of *liability* obliges the economic agent to bear the private *and* – as far as possible – the social costs of his or her action.[19]

These fundamental principles of a market economy provide a guideline with regard to which a given set of formal institutions at the constitutional and the working level can be evaluated. Going beyond the constitutional principles, Eucken formulated a set of *regulative* principles that are also relevant for infrastructure policies, such as the creation of a monopoly office responsible only to the law (Richter, 1999, 5). The implementation of these principles in a system of divided powers (legislative, executive, judiciary) may take *different* forms.[20]

---

[19] Three more general institutions suggested by Eucken are the existence and the *stability of money* as the universal equivalent of value (or primacy of monetary policy), a certain *continuity of economic policy* based upon the institutionalization of decision-making processes, and the principle of *open markets*, which is once again correlated to the principles of private property and freedom of contract.

[20] Spiller (1996, 450) contends that 'countries with electoral and legislative systems that bring about decentralized government have stronger chances of development equilibria where government discretion is restrained.' This translates the traditional view that decentralization of decision making is a requirement for efficient private economic activity (principle of subsidiarity). On the other hand, North (1990, 103) shows that decentralization is not a panacea, as it may be contradictory to existing formal and informal structures as in the case of the failed decentralization of administration in Latin America in the early nineteenth century. More recent evidence collected by Estache (1995) also shows no decisive advantage of decentralized decision making in infrastructure policy.

3.2.4 Informal institutional conditions

The *informal* requirements of a competition-oriented infrastructure policy are still more difficult to characterize. The importance of informal institutions is evident: on the one hand, they determine how the formalized rules and sanctioning mechanisms are implemented at the working level; on the other hand, informal institutions can even dominate economic behavior beyond formalization. North (1990, chapter 5) identified two main informal determinants of institutional change: *cultural change*, which is largely beyond the scope of economic analysis, and the change of *relative prices*, which he considered to be the home territory of economists. Whereas cultural change is largely exogenous to public policy, the driving force of institutional change at the working level, *relative prices*, is not. This applies to factor prices (for example, the relative prices of labor, capital and ground prices), but also to the prices of information and technology.[21]

It is not possible to identify a set of informal institutions necessary for an efficient competition-oriented infrastructure policy. Although not comprehensive, the following aspects can be considered to be necessary parts of an informal institutional setting for competition-oriented infrastructure policy (see Waelde and Hirschhausen, 1999):

– *Trust* in society, both regarding the functioning of the political and legal system, the independence and monitoring of the regulator, and also between individual economic agents within society;

– a broad *consensus* regarding the interpretation of general legal and economic terms necessary to implement infrastructure policy, for example, 'reasonable', 'public well-being', 'fair' return on investment, and so on;

– broad *knowledge* in society on the technical, political and economic aspects of infrastructure policy; a critical, independent press, which in turn leads to a conscious, critical public opinion;

– a far-reaching *separation* of state action (politics), which should provide a level playing field, from 'economic' decision making, that is, private decision making concerning production and consumption;

– finally, a low degree of *corruption* in politics and in the private sector.

3.2.5 Examples of the importance of formal and informal institutions

There is a growing body of empirical analyses on the relationship between the institutional framework and the success of an infrastructure policy; for example, measured by the degree to which competition-oriented deregulation is implemented (see Spiller, 1993; Spiller and Vogelsang, 1997; Ménard and

---

[21] Changes of relative prices result not only from above, through public policy, but also from below, that is, endogenously, 'reflecting the ongoing maximization efforts of entrepreneurs (political, economic and military) that will alter relative prices and in consequence induce institutional change' (North, 1990, 84).

Clarke, 2000a and b; and Glachant, 1998). This section provides selected examples for three important issues in infrastructure (de-)regulation: credibility, control and administrative capacities.

a) Institutional environment and credibility of the regulator
In a nutshell the institutional creed can be summarized as follows: 'Independent of *how* an industry is regulated, what counts is that it is regulated in a *credible* way.' The fundamental problem here is that opportunism and incomplete contracts abound in both infrastructure policy making and regulation, and they also affect the action of the regulatory agency itself (Spiller, 1996). According to Stigler's positive institutional approach, the regulator – like private enterprise – acts to maximize its *own* utility. Thus, the regulator, too, has to be constrained ('who regulates the regulator?'). Therefore, the credibility of the regulator itself is not exogenous, but depends upon the formal and informal environment of *checks and balances*. The abuse of discretionary power by the regulator is defined as the *regulatory risk*; usually it aims at the expropriation of quasi-rents of the regulated enterprise.

Spiller (1996) and Kumkar (1998b, 27 sq.) suggest different institutional and organizational approaches to limit the opportunistic behavior of the regulator towards the regulated infrastructure enterprise:

– A potential means of increasing the credibility of the regulator is to oblige it to make *public declarations* regarding the objectives and the steps to be taken in the process of regulation. The regulated enterprises and the general public thus obtain free information which can later be used to monitor the regulator;

– a long-term measure is the development of an *organizational structure* of vertical and horizontal relations spun around the regulator;

– *legal constraints* can also be constructed to reduce regulatory discretion. This can be done, for example, by integrating general clauses regarding the status of the regulated enterprise such as a survival protection clause for regulated enterprises;

– *reputation building* is a strategy by which the regulator and/or the state can decrease the regulatory risk, and thus convince potential investors and other economic actors of the stability of the regulatory setting (Spiller, 1993, 404).[22]

The means of constraining the regulator and building credibility also depend upon the credibility of the surrounding institutions. This is all the more important when there is no established *track record* on the credibility of

---

[22] One way to create a good reputation is to introduce a new regulatory regime *before* privatization, and thus prove the ability of the regulator to adhere to newly defined rules (see Spiller, 1993, for the case of the Chilean power sector).

the regulator. In this case, expectations regarding the behavior of the regulator have to be based on an assessment of the credibility of the institutional environment.

b) The importance of a critical public
Spiller and Vogelsang (1997) stress the role of an informal institution which, according to their analysis, has significantly contributed to the stabilization of the regulatory process in the telecommunication sector in the UK: a *critical public*. This institution dwells mainly on informal norms, such as a wide-spread concern for the public interest, a high level of information, a generally positive attitude to competition and a critical opinion regarding the centralized execution of power. For example, the stable relationship between a very powerful regulator and the privatized telecommunication enterprise British Telecom (BT) is explained by the fact that the discretionary power of the regulator was constrained by formal *and* informal norms. On the formal side, no less than three administrations participate in the regulatory process (see Figures 2.1 and 2.2): the former Branch Ministry (Department of Trade and Industry, *DTI*) has the right to block the call of the sectoral regulator (OFTEL's Director General, *DG*) to the anti-monopoly commission (Monopolies and Mergers Commission, *MMC*) and thus to re-establish the old state of regulation (x_0, which in general is favorable to the old monopolist). Figure 2.1 shows the most likely distribution of preferences of the players along the X-factor axis (MMC being in favor of a high X-factor, the incumbent monopolist BT voting for a low X-factor). The vertical axis measures the utility of the DTI. In case of a clear violation of the public interest, for example, by choosing a low X-factor, the DTI suffers from a loss of reputation (T), for example, by a weakened position in future negotiations, or even by losing votes in future elections. The upper triangle in Figure 2.1, u_1, shows a utility for different X-factors without reputation loss, u_2 includes the potential reputation loss T.

Figure 2.2 shows the full set of possibilities of the regulatory process and the respective outcomes: x_0, that is, the initial state of regulation, or P, the new X-factor set by the sectoral regulator DG. It can now be shown that this institutional setting restricts the discretionary power of the Branch Ministry (DTI) through potentially significant losses of reputation. The higher the potential loss of reputation, the less the DTI will be inclined to act in favor of the monopolist BT. If the reputation loss T is sufficiently high, the outcome of regulation will correspond to the objective of the sectoral regulatory agency OFTEL (DG), which itself is controlled through the MMC. Spiller and Vogelsang (1997) conclude from the British example that as long as the action of the regulator can be observed at relatively low costs, the deviation of the pre-announced policy path depends upon the loss of reputation that the regulator suffers from this deviation.[23]

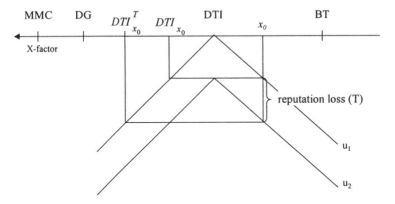

Source: Spiller and Vogelsang (1997, 616)

Figure 2.1 Interests of the participating organizations in the regulation of British telecommunication

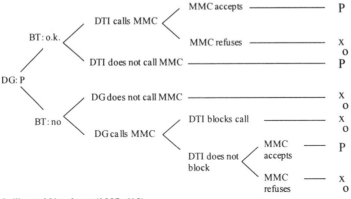

Source: Spiller and Vogelsang (1997, 618)

Figure 2.2 Decision-making process in the regulation of British telecommunication

---

[23] Thus, over the last 20 years of British re-regulation and privatization, an efficient, more or less formalized institutional structure has emerged (executive, legislative, judiciary, public opinion), which severely limits the discretionary power of the regulatory organizations. This may also explain the fact that to this day, no significant drop in investment in these capital-intensive infrastructure sectors (telecommunication, power, gas, water) has been observed in the UK.

It can be concluded that regulatory processes are likely to differ between different countries, in part due to different attitudes of the *critical public* vis-à-vis a competition-oriented infrastructure policy. The attitude may depend upon the costs of obtaining information, the ability to organize specific interest groups and the transparency of the regulatory process; it also depends on the ability of interest groups to internalize potential gains from lobbying activities (Olson, 1965). Different attitudes of the general public may then be one factor explaining the observed difference between the regulatory process in the UK (active general public) and in the early East European transformation countries (absence of a critical public).

c) Efficient administration
It is generally agreed that efficient administration (or bureaucracy) plays a crucial role in the implementation of economic policy, in particular competition policy. According to Jochimsen (1966, 124), the development of a universally applicable rule of law will not work without administration at all levels of the executive functioning smoothly, including 'competent and unselfish civil servants.'[24] The formal structure of the administration has to be consistent with the informal norms and values of the society in which it is supposed to work. Mummert (1995, 52) remarks that beyond consistency, formal and informal institutions also have to increase efficiency in order to foster sustainable development. Thus, while administration cannot trigger development on its own, it is a *necessary* institution; on the other hand, the absence of adequate administration may block economic development, no matter what the surrounding conditions are.

Empirical evidence supports the hypothesis of a link between administrative capabilities and the efficiency of a regulatory process. North (1990, 96 sq.) observed that the economic dynamic in the USA after 1789 can partly be explained by the consistency of the legal foundations (Northwest Ordinance) and the administrative capabilities in the definition and execution of property rights. By contrast, the transfer of this administrative structure to Latin American countries in the nineteenth century failed: the informal institutions there were oriented towards centralized, hierarchical decision making, and were thus incompatible with the proposed decentrally-oriented administrative procedures. More recent evidence comes from liberalization and re-regulation of infrastructure in South America (Spiller, 1993; Levy and Spiller, 1994; Spiller and Tommasi, 2000). It has been observed that reforms are more likely to succeed in small countries with small administrations. A

---

[24] Reference is made to Max Weber's book *Wirtschaft und Gesellschaft* (first edition: 1925).

too-powerful administration can block reforms by neutralizing the role of the legislator (example: telecommunication reforms in Argentina).

3.3 Stylized Actors and Interest Groups – A Political Economy Perspective

The fact that aside from sectoral planning, all activities in an infrastructure sector *can* be organized by market competition does not imply that this reference scenario is really applied in practice, be it in Western Europe, Eastern Europe, or elsewhere. The result of a regulatory process also depends upon the underlying logic of collective action. Positive institutional economics assumes that neither the organizations implied in the regulatory process nor the regulator itself pursues the general economic interest, but instead, by participating in the regulatory process, they seek to maximize their own utility. The institutional approach to understanding collective action is useful to explain the significant discrepancy between the theoretical competition-oriented reference model, and the real-world outcomes; this discrepancy is particularly intense in monopolistic infrastructure sectors. In this section, we identify ideal types of actors and vested interests that participate in the regulatory process in a democratic market economy (following Olson, 1965; Stigler, 1971; Wink, 1995). This classification will be applied later to concrete cases of infrastructure policy in Eastern Europe:

– *Private households* should, theoretically, be in favor of competition-oriented infrastructure policies, because an efficient supply of infrastructure reduces prices. However, one observes that in reality private households are particularly fierce opponents of privatization and a competition-oriented infrastructure policy. This can be explained by the fact that governments have a natural preference for public service provision and income-proportional taxes for public goods, that is, a cross-subsidization from richer to poorer income groups; this increases the votes in favor of an extensive infrastructure supply by the state. Public households then generally consume more infrastructure than they are willing to pay for. This leads in *most* countries, and in particular in the transformation countries of Eastern Europe, to a marked political sensitivity towards infrastructure service pricing (Spiller, 1996, 424);

– a similar argument holds for the demand of *enterprises* with intensive infrastructure use which tend to benefit from cross-subsidies from other tax-payers with lower infrastructure use;

– the *supplier* of infrastructure as the regulated, usually monopolistic enterprise has a particular interest in a favorable regulatory setting, and thus against a competition-oriented infrastructure policy. By contrast, *potential* service suppliers that may suffer from regulatory barriers to entry usually play a minor role in the regulatory process;

– *specialized administrations* that participate in the regulatory process face a conflict of interests: on the one hand, a certain proximity to the dominating regulatory agency can assure participation in the regulatory rent; and on the other, in the case of competition for regulatory activities, the administration can develop a strategic position by criticizing the dominant regulator and thus try to obtain a dominant role for itself in future regulation.[25]

In a democratic *market* economy, the outcome of the regulatory process and the divergence from the above ideal-typical reference scenario can be roughly explained by an institutional analysis of the actors and their vested interests. This analysis closes the theoretical part on infrastructure policy in a market economy. The next section will describe the very different decision-making process for infrastructure policy from which the East European transformation countries emerged: the *socialist* one.

4. INFRASTRUCTURE IN SOVIET SOCIALISM

The socialist notion of infrastructure as well as socialist infrastructure policy were diametrically opposed to the aforementioned market economy principles, as analysis thereof demonstrates. The retrospective of infrastructure in Soviet socialism is necessary for two reasons. First, it explains how the infrastructure that existed up to the early 1990s in the East European transformation countries has emerged in the last few decades, both in physical and organizational terms. Second, it shows why socialist infrastructure was incompatible with the requirements for infrastructure in the emerging market economies of Eastern Europe in the 1990s.

4.1 The Socialist Concept of Infrastructure

Soviet socialism was a system in which decisions touching upon the production and distribution of goods did not depend upon monetary criteria, but were made instead by political decisions of the Socialist Party and the state. In a nutshell, Soviet socialism can be characterized by the following principles:[26]

---

[25] Other interest groups can consist of state or private organizations (for example, communal administrations, consumer groups, non-governmental organizations, domestic and foreign investors). Their interests and impact on the regulatory process have to be identified case-by-case.

[26] This section does not include a system-theory discussion of socialism, but is restricted to the

- Abandonment of the money-commodity relationship and the 'capitalist' principles of 'value added';
- dominance of the Socialist Party in important questions regarding the production of goods (plan) and their distribution (through pricing policies, direct distribution, etc.);
- absence of a separation between the Party and economic activity;[27]
- absence of money as a universal equivalent of value.[28]

The socialist interpretation of the concept of infrastructure was in clear opposition to that of the 'capitalist' foreign countries. Tjulpanov ([1969] 1975, 351), a major Soviet development economist, drew the following distinction between the socialist and the capitalist notions of infrastructure: in socialism, the development of infrastructure was *not* subordinated to the requirements of the (profit-oriented) production process for the sake of producing value-added, but its objective was to improve the functioning of the socio-economic superstructures. The ultimate objective here was the *reproduction of the labor force* (Tjulpanov, 1975, 351). By contrast, in capitalist countries, the development of infrastructure was determined by the needs of 'capital'.[29]

The socialist concept of infrastructure comprised the following categories:[30]

1. *Technical infra-sectors:* Transportation system; energy management; water and wastewater management; postal service and telecommunications; electronic data processing; land improvement; emergency services; land, air and water protection; street-cleaning, refuse disposal and recycling, lighting systems, parts of the construction industry;

2. *Material and financial service infra-sectors:* Wholesale and retail trade, catering trade, domestic services, repair work, banking and savings banking, insurance business;

---

understanding of infrastructure policy. For a broader analysis of (Soviet) socialism see Mises ([1920] 1930, [1932] 1951), Kornai (1992), Stiglitz (1994).

[27] This unity was realized by the unlimited power of the Socialist Party (such as the KPDSU in the Soviet Union, the SED in the GDR, etc.). A distinction between the State and the Party did not exist in socialism; thus, these terms are synonymous, a more precise expression would be State/Party.

[28] This objective was obtained through three distinct monetary circuits: paper money (for the purchase of few consumer goods), fiduciary money (for internal calculation within the State planning system), and foreign currency money (for carrying out foreign trade).

[29] An East German Handbook of Socialism defined infrastructure as follows: 'Part of the territorial structure of the economy ... The infrastructure characterizes the basic equipment of a territory in qualitative and quantitative terms. As a fixed basis (according to Marx 'Hüllen und Trassen'), ... the infrastructure serves the process of reproduction.' *Wörterbuch der Ökonomie: Sozialismus.* Berlin, Dietz Verlag, 1973, 415, translated from the German original.

[30] *Wörterbuch der Ökonomie: Sozialismus.* Berlin, Dietz Verlag, 1973, 415.

3. *Educational infra-sectors, including cultural and social work:*
Educational system (from kindergarten to high school); libraries; museums;
archives; academies and institutes; radio and television; theater; concert and
film industries (including other places of entertainment and recreation);
housing services; public health services; child care; youth services; sports and
tourism, vacation industry;[31]

4. *Infra-sectors of political organizations and administrations:* buildings
and facilities of the state and of social organizations

Thus, in socialism, infrastructure included all activities that contribute to
the process of reproduction in society (in a larger sense) or of material
production (in a narrower sense). This notion of infrastructure was very broad
and included categories that would not belong to infrastructure in a market
economy, for example, (Koziolek et al., 1986, 22 sq., Lunina, 1997):

– The *rolling stock* of transport systems;

– electronics, new technology, production of new products, microchips to
automate the construction of nuclear power plants including construction of
heavy machinery and factories and other facilities, opencast mining
equipment, coal refining and production of coal dust;

– products for the rationalization of transportation, handling and storage
processes, social infrastructure (for example, formation of political elites and
culture);

– 'everyday infrastructure' (such as shoe repair shops, hairdressers, tailors,
photographers).

4.2 Infrastructure Policy in Soviet Socialism

4.2.1 A political process
According to its ideological importance, infrastructure occupied a special
position within the socialist planning process. Some sectors were given
permanent priority; for example, transport, energy, non-civil communication.
Furthermore, particular temporary goals of infrastructure were integrated in
the long-term and the five-year planning process within the economy at the
national, regional and local level.

Following the above differentiation of infrastructure policy into *network
planning, finance* and *operation*, socialist infrastructure policy can be
characterized as follows:

– *Network planning* was carried out at the highest political level. Absolute
priority was given to strategic military aspects. Needs of the population
beyond the most basic economic needs were neglected (for example,

---

[31] Point 3, and points 2 and 4 comprise what are usually referred to as *social* infra-sectors.

telecommunication). Economic criteria, such as cost-benefit-analysis, were virtually non-existent; decisions depended mainly upon *political* bargaining;

– *financing* did not constitute an individual activity within the socialist system. Every infrastructure project that was decided upon politically automatically obtained the required financial means (at least theoretically – in reality, however, this was often not the case);

– the *operation* of infrastructure policy was mainly the task of the industrial combines, in coordination with the local state organs.[32] The social infrastructure, too, was in many cases supplied directly by the enterprise.[33] As in the rest of the economy, problems of controlling the production of infrastructure services led to an overestimation of *quantitative* objectives. The tonnage ideology was particularly developed in infrastructure sectors (Lunina, 1997, 2).[34]

The state of infrastructure in Eastern Europe in the early 1990s has to be considered as the result of the implementation of socialist infrastructure ideology to sectoral or regional infrastructure policies. Just as in many other areas, there were substantial difficulties *implementing* centrally fixed plans at the decentralized working level. The relation between socialist infrastructure ideology and policy is discussed in the following three sectors to which the socialist literature of the 1970s and 1980s accorded an important role in socialist economic development: transport, science and technology, and energy.

4.2.2 Transport

The development of the transport sector as a technical and material condition of socialist society was dealt with extensively by socialist theoreticians.[35] The

---

[32] Industrial and agricultural combines often had at their disposal better material conditions to construct and operate infrastructure. In many cases, they even had a dominant position vis-à-vis the state organs. In some cases, the entire infrastructure of a region was assured by a few or even one large industrial enterprise. For example, in the Soviet Union, the construction, operation and maintenance of local roads were often assured by agricultural combines, state farms, and industrial enterprises (Lunina, 1997, 4).

[33] One-third of housing in Soviet Ukraine was administered by industrial enterprises and Ministries (Lunina, 1997, 3).

[34] For example, the construction of material infrastructure was evaluated according to the *quantity* of material used (such as concrete) or the *quantitative* capacities created (for example, kilometers of rail, telephone cables, and so on). Lunina (1997, 3) explained a very peculiar development of socialist infrastructure: the creation of highly centralized infrastructure corridors and the parallel underdevelopment of regional and local infrastructure networks. Thus, the most important orientation for the Soviet Ministry of Transport was the absolute figure for the transport of goods and persons, expressed in person-kilometers or ton-kilometers. The higher the absolute amount of transport, the more investment means were provided.

[35] According to Lenin, the transport sector had to execute the production and distribution processes decided by the Party. The rapid development of transport in the Soviet Union in the 1920s was considered a crucial condition 'to supply factories with grain, coal and fuel,

transport sector also corresponded in organizational terms to the ideal type of standardized socialist organization and planning. It was a real-world presentation of the socialist planning system itself: highly centralized, planned in the finest detail (quantities, relation to upstream production, etc.) and totally subordinated to the control of the Socialist Party.[36] The *railway system* played a pivotal role within the transport sector. It was organized as a 'party within a party', having at its disposal parallel party organizations.[37] The necessity of nationwide and even internationally centralized coordination led to a strictly hierarchical organizational structure.

Socialist transport policy resulted in a highly developed transport network for industrial goods and, to a lesser extent, a network for public passenger transport. Railways had absolute priority, whereas motorized individual transport was treated as secondary, both for the transport of goods and of persons. This resulted in a very peculiar modal split between rail and road. For example, statistical yearbooks for 1988 show the split (in t-km): Soviet Union: 88/12, GDR: 79/21, Poland: 76/24, Czechoslovakia: 76/24. Railway infrastructure was mainly designed for mass transport of heavy industrial goods (such as coal, ores, oil, metals). For this purpose, high-density corridors were developed between the raw material sources, industry and the centers of consumption. A heavy-goods 'tourism' developed, transporting industrial goods over thousands of kilometers back and forth, just to assure the principle of socialist work sharing, independent of any cost considerations.[38]

4.2.3 Science and technology

Within Soviet socialism a particular social value was attributed to S&T. The development of S&T systems was considered a precondition to fulfill the Marxist-Leninist doctrine of societal development. Socialist ideology accorded to science the role of a *directly* productive force. S&T was

---

[36] to assure the reconstruction of industry and to end the famine of factory and railway workers' (cited in Koziolek, et al., 1986, 189).

[37] 'Neither the railway system nor the entire transport system ... can function properly, if there is no unitary will that unites all workers within one organization, an organization that works with clockwork precision ... For the successful functioning of work according to modern principles of large indusry, it is necessary that every worker submit himself – without any objection – to one unified will. For the proper functioning of the railway system, this submission is all the more necessary.' *Lenin: Werke*, Bd. 27, Dietz Verlag, Berlin (Ost). 1974, 202 and 260.

[38] See Autorenkollektiv der Hochschule für Verkehrswirtschaft Friedrich Liszt (1978): *Lehrbuch der Transportwirtschaft*. Berlin (Ost).

The average transport of coal within CMEA is said to have been 3,000 km. Thus, the mere transport costs of coal are already at the level of the world market prices (in a market economy, transport costs for coal are estimated at 10 USD/1,000 km; economically justifiable transport is estimated at about 500–1,000 km).

organized within a separate development plan, like other industrial branches such as metallurgy or chemistry. The state industrial combines, enterprises and institutes were integrated into this large-scale plan (Kinze, et al., 1983, 410). The S&T system was evaluated mainly in quantitative terms. On the *input* side, categories such as expenses or employment were considered an important indicator of societal utility. On the *output* side, the quantity of research results was the most important criterion. By contrast, questions of the applicability of results were neglected (see Chapter 7 for detailed case studies).

4.2.4 Energy

Lenin also dwelled extensively on the development of the energy sector as a condition for the socialist reproduction of labor. He stressed the *societal* aspects of energy sector development at least as intensively as the technical aspects. In particular, he insisted on the necessity of power supply to every factory and to every household.[39] Thanks to its highly centralized structure, the energy sector was also well suited as a catalyst for the introduction of mass organization of labor, education and culture.[40] The development of the energy sector was also a direct result of *regional* and *geopolitical* objectives. Thus, the development of Western Siberian oil and gas resources was justified by the political objective of expanding the accessible territory of the Soviet Union into formerly untouched areas (e.g., the Far East). Thus, the political center of Moscow was connected by thousands of kilometers of oil and gas pipelines with Siberia, while, according to economic criteria, a large part of these oil and gas resources cannot be considered economically feasible, because of the high fixed and variable transport costs.[41]

Treating socialist infrastructure development as a homogeneous block and mainly on the basis of ideological statements may be unfair. Certainly, the large infrastructure programs pursued by socialist countries had significant development effects, in particular in the formerly undeveloped regions of Russia and Central Asia. Also, infrastructure development in the West European market economies was largely driven by political programs and

---

[39] In 1906, Lenin developed a thesis on the cultural *and* social implications of energy sector development, followed later by his theory of communism as 'Soviet power plus the electrification of the whole country'.

[40] Lenin regularly stressed the synergies of scientific, technical, economic and societal objectives within the development of long-term energy plans. The acceleration of technical and scientific progress in strategic sectors such as the energy sector would contribute to educational and cultural development at least as much as theoretical training programs.

[41] The sharp drop of energy production, in particular oil and coal, after the beginning of transformation confirms the low international competitiveness of Russian energy sources (gas being an exception).

ideology, rather than by economic considerations (e.g. railroad development in the nineteenth century.

5. CONCLUSIONS

This chapter has analyzed different concepts of infrastructure. Our aim has been to characterize the point of departure of sector reform in Eastern Europe, *socialist* infrastructure, and to identify an ideal type of a *market-oriented* infrastructure policy. Infrastructure policy has been seen here in a broad sense, including not only regulation aspects of network industries, but also regional policy, distribution, economic growth and security aspects.

In market economies, infrastructure can be defined as 'the sum of material, institutional and personal capacities available to economic agents that contribute to the normalization of factor payments for similar inputs, thus leading to full integration and the highest possible level of economic activity' (Jochimsen, 1966, 100). This approach is close to new institutional economics, which also considers transaction costs as an important determinant of organizational structures and economic development. The ideal-typical vision of a market economy according to Hayek (1945, 1969) sees competition and decentralized bargaining and exchange as the optimal way to foster economic and technical development. We have asked whether market competition can assure the three different functions of infrastructure policies, that is, network planning, financing and operation: *Financing* as well as *operation* of infrastructure can be carried out by the private sector according to market criteria. In the area of *network planning* some form of state participation in the hierarchical organization is likely to lead to lower transaction costs, as the state has a comparative advantage in the execution of sovereign responsibilities.

The *institutional environment* of a country or sector determines the possible approaches to and outcomes of infrastructure policy. The institutional endowment of a country consists of formal and informal elements. Among the *formal* institutional and organizational requirements of a competition-oriented infrastructure policy are private property, freedom of contracts, liability, and open markets. The importance of *informal* institutions for market- and competition-oriented infrastructure policies lies in the way in which formal rules are translated into practice at the working level. This includes aspects such as a functioning administration and legal system, the level of trust in society and a minimal consensus regarding the interpretation of generic legal terms (such as 'reasonable', 'economic well-being', 'fair' rate of return). Empirical evidence confirms the close interdependence of the institutional environment and the infrastructure policy. If this is so, the traditional welfare economic search for first-best solutions can be usefully complemented by a positive, case-specific analysis in an institutional framework (*comparative institutional approach*).

In Soviet socialism, infrastructure policy was an important element of the development strategy. The main objective of infrastructure policy was to optimize the '*reproduction* process' of the labor force (in other words: improvements to the quality of life). Infrastructure policy was a highly centralized affair. *Network planning* was carried out at the highest political level; it was dominated by strategic and military considerations, whereas the needs of the population were largely neglected (an example being telecommunication). Questions of *financing* were irrelevant. The supply of infrastructure was dominated by the *tonnage ideology*, that is, quantitative measures of evaluation.

The two extremes of infrastructure policies, that is, market-oriented policy at one extreme and socialist policy at the other, have been presented in this chapter in a *stylized* form. The infrastructure policies observed in Western market economies in most cases do not correspond to the market economy reference model. This discrepancy can be explained by the theory of collective action, according to which the implementation of a competition-oriented infrastructure policy has significant short-term political costs but relatively modest political returns. However, this market economic reference model is necessary to evaluate infrastructure policy reform approaches of East European countries in the process of European enlargement.

3. The Process of Systemic Transformation

We tried to do our best ... but then things proceeded as usual.
Victor Chernomyrdin, Prime Minister of the Russian Federation, 1996.

1. INTRODUCTION

This chapter analyzes the conditions under which infrastructure sector reforms took place in Eastern Europe in the 1990s; that is, the *systemic transformation* in the former socialist countries. The aim of the chapter is to describe the characteristics of the transformation process and its specific institutional aspects. This analysis will later be used to check whether a transformation-specific infrastructure policy was justified in Eastern Europe in the early 1990s, or may still be justified today. Section 2 reviews the theoretic debate on transformation in the 1990s, Section 3 identifies two distinct phases of transformation, referred to in the following as phase I and phase II. Section 4 presents stylized evidence of differences among economic systems throughout Eastern Europe that have emerged in the wake of the transformation process. Section 5 concludes.[42]

2. THE TRANSFORMATION DEBATE OF THE 1990s

2.1 Four Levels of System Transformation

In the literature on systemic change in Eastern Europe, the term 'transformation' refers to the reshaping of socialist countries into some form of a market economy.[43] The main feature common to all transformation countries in Eastern Europe and the CIS was the reshaping of the formal and,

---

[42] Parts of this chapter are based on Hirschhausen and Waelde (2001).
[43] See Stahl (1998, 15). Note that there is a difference in notion between the Anglo-Saxon term of 'transition' (Latin root: *trans-ire*) and 'transformation' (Latin root: *trans-formare*), which is more generally applied in the tradition of Max Weber, the latter designating a more *open* process of active systemic change. We use the notion of 'transformation' throughout this text.

in many cases, informal infrastructure, away from the former socialist system towards some form of a market economy. The specificity of system transformation in Eastern Europe stemmed from the fact that not a single area of political, economic, or societal life was spared from a fundamental restructuring. Four levels of transformation can be distinguished:[44]

– At the political or *constitutional* level (*choice of rules*) the socialist one-party system was abolished and replaced by other forms, ideally by a parliamentary democracy;

– at the *economic* level, the non-monetary, centrally coordinated socialist mechanisms of production and distribution were replaced by other forms of economic exchange, ideally a market economy dominated by private ownership and competition;

– at a societal level, individual patterns of behavior changed, due to the fact that consumption behavior could now largely be based on monetary evaluation;[45]

– at the level of technological developments, the socialist S&T system, which was oriented towards autarchy in military technology, was replaced by the integration of domestic enterprises in international innovation and production networks.

System transformation in Eastern Europe thus posed a singular challenge requiring specific and unconventional economic policy responses. Streit (1997, 3812) insisted on the *singularity* of the transformation process, resulting not only from the initial historical conditions of each transformation country, but also from a heterogeneous distribution of resources, interest groups and political strategies that had led to the end of socialism. Streit and Mummert (1996, 4) warned quite early on that the transfer of reform concepts from other regions in the world (such as from Latin America) would be insufficient to address the specific challenges of system transformation in Eastern Europe.[46]

---

[44] See also Eger (2000) who distinguishes five dimensions of transformation as a process of comprehensive institutional change: retreat of the state (privatization, liberalization), reallocation of resources, reorganization of production and productive capacities, redistribution, and decentralization.

[45] This has effects, for example, on the organization of social life, away from the former system of mutual barter.

[46] The conceptual debate on the nature of transformation goes far beyond a mere issue of wording. It also touches upon the question of which economic policies are suited to succeed the introduction of a market economy. An example is the debate on the priorities of the reform process; for example, between the more macroeconomically-oriented economists and the proponents of an institutional approach. Thus, the controversy between the International Monetary Fund and the World Bank after the failed transformation of.the Russian economy was also grounded in different initial positions regarding the nature of the transformation process. Thus, the Chief Economist of the IMF, Stanley Fischer, described transformation in Russia as a 'return to a system that is well understood in the rest of the world.' This vision implied a straightforward approach of structural adjustment: stabilization, liberalization and

2.2 Constitutional and Partial Decisions

The institutional perspective on transformation emerged only after the traditional macroeconomic recipes had failed to bring about the expected results. The early days of transformation were indeed dominated by a *macroeconomic* debate on the optimal sequencing of reform steps. It has entered the literature as the debate on 'gradualism-vs.-shock-therapy' and related macroeconomic issues (Melo and Gelb, 1996; Funke, 1993; Bofinger et al., 1996). However, the economic results of the first post-socialist years were unexpected and largely disappointing in all countries: among them were the collapse of production, high inflation, low foreign direct investment and the slow speed of privatization; combined, this led to the 'transformation crisis' (Schmieding, 1993). Only afterward did institutionally oriented and political economy oriented approaches enter the debate more frequently (Streit and Mummert, 1996). A distinction drawn by political economics (Buchanan, 1975) was introduced between two layers of transformation: the building of an institutional infrastructure ('choice of rules') and the day-to-day policy-making process ('choice within rules').

With regard to the institutional aspects, the major fields of action in the transformation process should have been the *constitutional* decisions. In essence, transformation required two large fields of reform: i) the introduction of *law* as a stable system of legally and judicially protected entitling 'rights', in contrast to temporary and volatile governmental commands; and ii) the institutionalization of an *economic* constitution based on clearly attributable property rights, providing incentives for individuals to set up independent enterprises in a monetized environment. It also required collective action to promote the evolution of markets, to introduce competition (by freeing markets from price control and production commands and by introducing competition laws), to set up bankruptcy as a sanction for business failure and to introduce modern systems of direct and indirect taxation.[47]

The role of institutional factors in the transformation process was considered more and more important as the reforms proceeded and faced difficulties. In fact, following attempts to introduce standard reform packages used in structural adjustment programs throughout the world, it was observed

---

privatization. By contrast, Joseph Stiglitz (1991, 1), as Chief Economist at the World Bank, argued against this interpretation, by developing an institutional approach: 'I argue that the failures of the reforms in Russia and most of the former Soviet Union are not just due to sound policies being poorly implemented. I argue that the failures go deeper, to a misunderstanding of the foundation of a market economy as well as a misunderstanding of the basics of an institutional reform process.'

[47] See for a detailed catalogue of required reforms Schrader (1999, 6, 21, 77, 145) or the summary of the 'Washington Consensus' on stabilization, liberalization and privatization by Lipton and Sachs (1990).

that the success of any transformation country depended much more on the institutional infrastructure than on short-term macroeconomic policies (Ahrens, 1994, 1996; Cornia and Popov, 1998; World Bank, 1996, 1997; Raiser, 1997, 1999). Various studies also tended to confirm a positive link between the development of institutional infrastructure and the development of the economy (Havrylyshyn, et al., 1999; Heybey and Murrell, 1997; Wagener, 2000, Raiser, et al., 2001). This understanding was supported by empirical case studies showing that the transformation of socialist systems went beyond simple technical questions such as those of privatization and trade liberalization (Bomsel, 1995).

A critical analysis of decision making in the transformation process reveals that given the pressure to proceed with partial decisions, *constitutional* decisions were largely neglected by the transformation countries. For most actors, choices *within* rules dominated the very definition of the choices *of* rules. This contradicts the normative institutional interpretation, according to which transformation policies should target primarily the definition of new rules, but not intervene too much with the economic choices within these rules, which should be left to individuals (Streit and Mummert, 1996, 3).

Subsequently, several authors started to classify different categories of transformation countries, according to, for example, macroeconomic performance (Havrylyshyn et al., 1999), structural indicators, or simply the political process of EU integration.

3. PHASE I AND PHASE II OF TRANSFORMATION

An *ex-post* analysis of the transformation process in Eastern Europe reveals two distinct phases. They can be characterized by the degree of convergence and divergence among the transformation countries (see for other criteria Voigt and Engerer, 2000, 34 sq.; Gros and Suhrcke, 2000; Gregory, 1999; Roland, 2000).

3.1 Phase I: Collapse of Production and Transformation Crisis

Whereas the outcome of transformation is open to debate, there is a broad consensus on its beginnings: the process of economic transformation, and the scientific debate on this topic, began when the preceding period, socialism, ended. The break between the two periods was brought about by *monetization*, that is, the introduction of money as a universal equivalent of value, and the end of the Communist Party as the main coordinator of production and distribution (Hirschhausen, 1996). *Phase I* of transformation is the period in which the Eastern European countries tried to implement structurally similar reform programs, and had shared many of the same difficulties implementing these reforms at the working level, mainly due to a lack of institutional infrastructure.

The most characteristic development within phase I of transformation was the sharp drop in industrial and aggregate production (for statistical data see the Annex). With the collapse of socialist coordination and production networks, the production of goods and services shrank to unprecedented and unexpected dimensions. Not a single transformation country could avoid a sharp drop in production, accompanied by a profound reorganization of productive activities: the cumulative drop in industrial production exceeded one-fourth for all countries. Macroeconomic and fiscal instability and growing unemployment were additional and largely unexpected results of phase I. The data in the Annex provide extensive statistical coverage of macro-indicators for most transformation countries.

Figure 3.1 provides some quantitative evidence of the output decline: it compares the drop in industrial production at the moment when monetary reforms and price liberalization were introduced. The curves are 'normalized' with regard to the year of monetization, indicated as t_0. In other words, the development of industrial production is shown for each country relative to the year in which profound reforms were started (t_0). Three common characteristics emerge quite clearly (Hirschhausen and Bitzer, 2000, 48 sq.):

– first, output reductions were only moderate in the periods t_{-1}, t_{-2} and so on, that is, in the final years of socialism;

– second, a large depression in output occurred after t_0, that is, after the monetization of the economy. No country was spared from the decline of output, which reached at least a fourth of the former production level (Hungary, Poland) and up to over 50 per cent (in most republics of the former Soviet Union);

– third, the output curves then followed a J-curve, with output picking up about three years after monetization: in Figure 3.1 t_1, t_2 and, occasionally, t_3 continue the production decrease. Starting approximately from t_4 and t_5, production then witnessed the upward section of the J-curve, with slopes differing between countries.

A variety of arguments were advanced to explain the recession observed in phase I of transformation:

– Some authors explained the 'transformation crisis' by the difficult *initial conditions* in the former socialist countries that had not been sufficiently taken into account during the initial years of reforms (Heybey and Murrel, 1997; Havrylyshyn et al. 1999). They observed that the lowest drop in production was observed in countries that had already started some reforms in the latter days of socialism, or that had less distorted economies (for example, Poland, Hungary, Czechoslovakia);

– macroeconomists established a link between macro-instability of the early years of reform (inflation, exchange rates, slump in investment) and the slump in production (Melo and Gelb, 1996; Fischer and Gelb, 1991; Brücker et al., 1995);

– the slow pace of real privatization was also held responsible for the transformation crisis. Though formal privatization proceeded quite rapidly, even in less reform-oriented countries (such as Lithuania or Russia), neither a significant transfer of property rights to the private sector nor the emergence of efficient corporate governance were observed in most countries (Engerer, 2001);

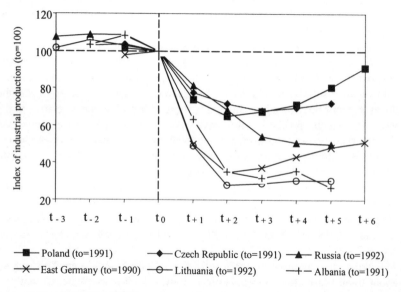

—■— Poland (to=1991)   —◆— Czech Republic (to=1991) —▲— Russia (to=1992)
—✕— East Germany (to=1990)   —⊖— Lithuania (to=1992)   —+— Albania (to=1991)

Source: National Statistics, EBRD

Figure 3.1 Industrial production in selected Central and Eastern European countries (1989–2000)

– a microeconomic and institutional approach explains the slump in production with a left-hand shift of the production possibility frontier, following the substantial disorganization of post-socialist economies (Blanchard and Kremer, 1997; Marin and Schnitzer, 1999);[48]

---

[48] Technical production capacities shrank due to a devaluation of physical and human capital and an increase in labor and raw material costs; the organizational production frontier

– another unresolved issue of the transformation crisis was related to the optimal sequencing of reform (shock therapy vs. gradualism). Proponents of *shock therapy* argued that fundamental reforms would only be possible during a short period of time, the 'window of opportunity', until the political pendulum would swing back towards more conservative policies (Lipton and Sachs, 1990; Streit and Mummert, 1996, 16). The window of opportunity opened because certain coalitions of lobbying groups from socialist times were destroyed with the end of socialism, whereas new coalitions against reform had not yet had a chance to emerge. This political economy approach argued in favor of a rapid creative destruction of the former political and economic structures to assure the sustainability of reforms. By contrast, *gradualists* argued for step-by-step reform, in which socialist production networks were *gradually* put under hard budget constraints. Gradualists also argued that their approach would lead to a higher political acceptance of reforms. In turn, they accepted a certain continuity of post-socialist governance structures in the political and the economic system (Ees and Garretsen, 1994; Dewatripont and Roland, 1995; Aslund, 2002. See also Lau et al., 2000, on reform in China).

The heterogeneity of arguments for the transformation crisis implies that no simple explanation is possible. Given the systemic nature of the changes, partial analysis is insufficient. Traditional economic models, such as Keynesian or neoclassical business cycle models or the endogenous growth theory, also fail to provide an explanation, because they assume a more or less constant, exogenous institutional framework. However, it is precisely the formal *institutional void* that characterizes phase I of transformation (Schmieding, 1993).

3.2 Phase II: Increasing Divergence of Transformation Paths

The common denominator of phase I for *all* transformation countries was the missing institutional framework for market economic development. By contrast, *phase II* of transformation was characterized by a *growing divergence* of transformation paths among the former socialist countries, as observable in institutional and economic indicators. Not all East European countries were able or willing to proceed on a pre-defined reform path. Even with similar reform packages put in place, the institutional reforms proceeded quite differently thereafter, leading to diverging transformation processes across the countries of Eastern Europe. Few similarities were still observed, for example, between truly reforming countries of Central and Eastern Europe

---

shrank due to the collapse of former mechanisms of coordination and the exponential increase in transaction costs.

and some non-reforming CIS countries. This growing heterogeneity of transformation paths, and thus the (gradual) shift from phase I to phase II, can be dated in the mid-1990s (approximately 1994–1996), and it can be exemplified by different indicators:

– From a *macroeconomic* perspective, a divergence of growth rates was observed after 1994, between growing transformation countries (mainly in Central and Eastern Europe) and continuous GDP decline (mainly in European CIS countries);[49]

– a *political* divide between transformation countries could be observed with regard to the relationship of the transformation countries to the EU. From around the winter of 1994 (EU Council Summit at Essen), a clear separation existed between the potential EU member countries (Estonia, Latvia, Lithuania, Poland, the Czech Republic, the Slovak Republic, Hungary, Slovenia, Romania, Bulgaria) and the 'other' transformation countries;

– Meske (1998) and Radosevic (1999) used *structural indicators* of the S&T system to identify different transformation paths (such as the degree of structural fragmentation and internationalization and the role of the state). Radosevic (1999, 8) defined three groups: group I included so-called 'leading' countries with largely finished structural reforms (examples: Poland, the Czech Republic, Hungary, Estonia, Slovenia); group II, the 'middle' group, with countries in the process of structural transformation (examples: Latvia, Croatia, Slovakia, Lithuania, Romania, Serbia, Montenegro); and group III, the 'least advanced', only a very gradual restructuring of the former socialist system (examples include Moldova, Bulgaria, Russia, Belarus, Ukraine);

– the development of the formal *institutional framework*, too, indicated a growing divergence between transformation countries. Quantitative evidence of this is provided by the EBRD transition indicators (for example, the overall indicator of market-oriented reforms; see Annex). Qualitatively, Johnson et al. (2000) explained differences in private sector development between Poland and Russia/Ukraine with different degrees of development of formal and informal rules of property rights. Self-organization and informal rules

---

[49] Havrylyshyn et al. (1999) distinguished three groups of countries with regard to their structural transformation and growth patterns (see Annex): a) *sustained growth* was achieved in countries with a high level of market-oriented reform and structural change, and a decreasing (albeit still important) role of the government. This was the case in most Central and Eastern European countries, as well as in Armenia and Georgia; b) *reversed growth*, that is, several years of growth followed by another recession, was caused by too little enterprise reform accompanied by too loose monetary and fiscal policies in the early phase of transformation (that is, Romania and Bulgaria); c) *no growth* for eight years (1992–99) was the result of attempts to preserve unpreservable socialist industrial structures by means of state planning, protectionist trade policies and the absence of structural reform (for example, Ukraine and Belarus) (cited from Hirschhausen and Bitzer, 2000, 47).

continued to dominate in post-Soviet countries, whereas Central and Eastern European countries had largely succeeded in formalizing property rights. Johnson et al. (1997) identified a divergence between Central and Eastern Europe and the CIS more generally in the differences in transaction costs that led to different growth rates and a decreasing informal sector in CEE countries.[50]

4. THE END OF TRANSFORMATION AND STYLIZED OUTCOMES

4.1 From Phase II Towards the End of Transformation

The *end* of transformation was reached when the development of macro-, micro- and institutional characteristics of an economy was no longer determined by the structures inherited from socialism, but instead became country-, region- or sector-specific. The socialist legacy did not disappear, but it diminished in such a way that links could no longer be identified between the socialist period and current economic development. In other words, the 'transformation' of socialism into another economic system was over, and a new development phase beyond transformation opened up. The question of the dynamics of transformation goes beyond a mere issue of wording; it also touches upon concrete policies to be applied in these countries, for example, optimal methods of privatization, the pace of price liberalization, the treatment of the inter-enterprise arrears issue, and infrastructure policies (see Pittman, 2001, for concrete examples). Along these lines, some authors have suggested turning the transformation debate into a more general debate on comparative economic systems (Ahrens, 1996; Nuti, 1999; Dallago, 1999).

The thesis on the end of transformation, when first put forward in 1998,[51] was controversial. This can be explained, on the one hand, by different theoretic approaches to social science,[52] and on the other hand, by the

---

[50] Note that the results of these classifications are not identical: thus, according to the macro-criterion, countries like Armenia and Georgia would join EU accession countries like Poland in the group of 'high-growth' countries. Clement and Jungfer (1998) identified three different transformation stages on the move from a centrally planned economy to a 'real' market economy. Cornia and Popov (1998) insisted on structural and institutional conditions that determined differences in output performance; they came up with four broad clusters of transitional economies, corresponding to 'highly different economic models which have vastly dissimilar potentials for growth.'

[51] Hirschhausen, Christian von and Thomas Waelde (1998, *The End of Transition*. Paper presented at the Annual Conference of the Verein für Socialpolitik, Rostock, September).

[52] For example, an evolutionary economist would reject the idea of structural breaks in time,

opposition of some groups of economists to the idea of an end of transformation. However, since the celebrations of the tenth anniversaries of the beginning of systemic transformation (between 1999 and 2001), a broad consensus has emerged both in the scientific and the public debate that the economic problems faced by former socialist countries have only a little left in common.[53] Former transformation countries no longer pursue specific economic reform programs under the direct guidance of international financial organizations as they did during transformation. The end of transformation also implies the end of certain reform options. The key decisions concerning constitutional and operational change have been made and have become largely irreversible. The common characteristics of post-socialist systemic change have disappeared and new, different forms of economic systems are stabilizing, creating a systemic irreversibility. Path dependency and day-to-day politics have taken over, partial decisions now dominate constitutional considerations.

4.2 Different Institutional Layers

Contrary to the initial idea of a unitary transformation process, a variety of models of legal and economic reform have emerged in Eastern Europe and the CIS. The empirical evidence highlights the differences in outcomes of the transformation process among countries that had adopted similar reform approaches. What indicators can be used to trace the differences among transformation countries? The specificity of any country's approach to transformation and the outcomes thereof, cannot be identified by comparing macroeconomic data, as the latter are affected by institutional change only indirectly and in the long term. Instead, we distinguish three *institutional* layers to characterize the transformation process in Eastern Europe:

i) The set of *formal institutions,* which includes the legal framework and the technical prerequisites to operate and control markets, the monetization of the economy (that is, money being used as the dominant means of

---

and analyzes institutional dynamics in an evolutionary way; for him or her, *every* socio-economic development is but a gradual transformation (Stahl, 1998).

53 The restructuring of two major journals of transformation research is also representative of this movement: The journal *Economics of Transition* stated that '... in some important respects these countries [Central European countries undergoing transition towards a market economy, especially those on track for early accession to the EU] can be studied in the same terms as one would study the relatively developed countries of Western Europe. ... Other countries, especially in the CIS, are much further behind in their reforms...' (*Economics of Transition*, vol. 7(1) p. i). The journal *Communist Economies & Economic Transformation* has even dropped the 'transformation' aspect from its title, to become simply *Post-Communist Economies*, 'because of a growing feeling that the major processes into which transformation has generally been divided – stabilisation, liberalisation and privatisation – have in substantial measure been completed' (journal announcement, early 1999).

transactions) and budget constraints on independently operating enterprises (for example, bankruptcy procedures, banking and financial sector regulation). The introduction and functioning of the formal institutions can be observed and even quantified (for example, with the EBRD transition indicators);

ii) the *informal institutions,* which include the non-codified legal, economic and cultural conventions; the level of trust in economic transactions substituting for formal regulations;[54] the comprehension and approval of market mechanisms by the population; the civil service culture with more or less explicitly defined incentive structures; the culture of political, professional and academic debate; and the public control of this debate as well as of the press and other mass media. In the absence of clearly identifiable and quantifiable indicators, the evaluation of informal institutions depends largely upon subjective empirical observations;

iii) the *societal consensus* about the economic system which encompasses both the normative aspect ('what system *should* govern?') and the positive aspect ('what system *does* in fact govern?'). What is more, the societal understanding of core economic concepts was quite different in post-socialist countries than in established Western market economies (for example, 'contract', 'legislation', 'money', 'property', 'state', 'profit') (Waelde and Hirschhausen, 1999, 102 sq.).

4.3 Three Stylized Outcomes of Systemic Transformation

The economic and institutional developments in the former socialist countries have shown that there is no prescribed path of system transformation, nor are there similar outcomes. On the contrary, in the early twenty-first century, a variety of economic systems following quite different paths of development can be observed in Eastern Europe, and not all of them are compatible with EU accession. Based upon the different institutional layers defined above and at the risk of oversimplification, we propose a classification of three ideal-typical outcomes of system transformation:[55]

a) The reforming *Central and Eastern European market economy* has largely adopted the formal institutions of a market economy or has at least made a binding commitment to do so in the near future. The upcoming accession to the EU provides a stable framework for further reform. At the

---

[54] On the role of trust in transition, see the theoretical and empirical work of Raiser (1997, 1999) and Raiser, et al. (2001), including a quantification of trust and first econometric evidence.

[55] On the discussion of systemic divergence in Eastern Europe, see also the special issue of *Economic Systems* (1999, 'Convergence and Divergence of Economic Systems'. Vol. 23, No. 2 (June), 127-76).

non-codified level, an adaptation of informal institutions can be observed, which, if not fully in favor of a market economy, nevertheless poses no major obstacles to the gradual introduction of a market culture in many spheres of public life. The societal consensus is an outright rejection of the socialist system and a binding commitment to a market economy. This consensus is stable and time consistent. Countries representing this group are Poland, Hungary and Estonia;

b) the *post-Soviet mixed economy* is a blend of incoherently functioning elements of a market economy and some elements of state intervention. This type of country has made an initial, formal attempt to introduce market-oriented institutional reform, but was not able or willing to carry it out fully and bear the political and social consequences. Reforms have therefore been half-hearted. Though some formal institutions of a market economy were put into place (for example, privatization procedures, legal framework, monetary policies, bankruptcy law), they have not developed much normative power at the level of execution (Ahrens, 1994; Welfens, 1998; Thanner, 1999). On the informal level, there is some rejection of attempts to monetize and formalize civic relations (Stiglitz, 1999; Raiser, 1999). Examples for this group of countries comprise Russia, Ukraine, to some extent also Belarus, though the latter also has characteristics of the next group;

c) the *Caspian state economy* has not seriously considered introducing market-oriented institutions, but has opted to use its newly gained independence to transform Soviet socialism into an autocratic, clan-based regime based upon strong state involvement in the economy. The formal institutions of Soviet socialism have been abandoned, but they have not been replaced by market institutions. In the absence of an established legal framework, let alone the rule of law, important decisions are made by leading politicians at their own discretion. The societal consensus, if any, gives priority to the consolidation of the new-born republics, with little consideration to economic efficiency. Instead, the transformation process seems to lead from socialism towards some form of rentier governance structure, similar to those of the Arab oil countries in the Gulf. Examples of the Caspian state economy are Azerbaijan, Turkmenistan and Uzbekistan.

Table 3.1 (see end of chapter) synthesizes the main institutional characteristics of the three stylized outcomes of system transformation.

5. CONCLUSIONS

The aim of this chapter is to provide some insight into the process of system transformation in Eastern Europe during the 1990s, leading in most Central and East European countries to the path of EU accession. *Ex-post*, two distinct phases can be identified within the transformation process: in *phase I* (the transformation crisis), all transformation countries embarked on similar reform programs and faced similar obstacles; the new formal institutions (private property, competition laws, and so on) did not work the way they do in established market economies; simultaneously with the emerging institutional void came an unprecedented drop in output. *Phase II* was characterized by increasingly divergent paths of transformation which can be traced in macroeconomic and institutional indicators. Different institutional capabilities to define and carry out consistent economic policies could be observed. Based upon an institutional analysis and empirical evidence, we identify three ideal types of transformation outcomes: the reforming Central and Eastern European market economy, the post-Soviet mixed economy, and the Caspian state economy.

The specifics of transformation and different development paths determine the countries' potential EU compatibility, and they have an impact on the infrastructure policies to be applied in these countries. This applies particularly to phase I and the institutional void, for which (ex-post) the efficiency of an orthodox, competition-oriented infrastructure policy with immediate liberalization and privatization might be questioned. Furthermore, it appears that in phase II, similar reform approaches were likely to lead to widely diverging results, depending upon the institutional endowment and the state of development of the respective country. In the following chapter, we shall make use of the analysis of the transformation process when it comes to comparing different options for infrastructure policies in Eastern Europe.

Table 3.1 Three stylized outcomes of system transformation

		i) Reforming Central and Eastern European market economies (e.g. Poland, Hungary, Estonia)	ii) Post-Soviet mixed-economies (e.g. Russia, Ukraine, Belarus)	iii) Caspian state economies (e.g. Azerbaijan, Turkmenistan, Uzbekistan)
FORMAL INSTITUTIONS	**Legal framework**	A revision of socialist legislation has been carried out and a legal basis for a market economy introduced, largely following the EU model (acquis communautaire)	Formally, a vast body of new legislation has been adopted; but low level of knowledge and acceptance of new legislation at working level	Absence of a culture of formal law; strong informal component in case-by-case problem solving
	Ownership change	Largely completed; many enterprises remain state-owned (e.g. Poland), but they, too, are subject to capital constraints	Large-scale privatization is more advanced on paper than in reality; ownership is dispersed; mysterious privatization of the few cash cows (e.g. Gazprom)	Little privatization in the strategic sectors (e.g. energy), state holds controlling stakes
	Budget constraints/ enterprization	Budget constraints have solidified, bankruptcy law is in place; relatively large number of factory closures; abandoning of multifunctionality (production intertwined with social sphere)	Budget constraints weak; few factory closures; rise in inter-enterprise arrears; multifunctionality remains strong, in particular in rural areas	No hard budget constraints applied
	Money	Introduced and accepted as the dominant agent of economic transactions; monetary policies are applied and effective	(Partially) convertible, real money introduced, but domestic economies rely heavily on barter; rise of inter-enterprise arrears	Many economic transactions take place in US dollars or without money (barter)
	Banking system, financial markets	Increasing importance of financial markets; competition within the banking sector is intensifying; modest real interest rates	Formally introduced, but a competitive banking system does not yet exist; small investments are auto-financed from retained earnings	Little institutionalization of banking system and financial markets; important role of the state in allocating investments
	Role of the state	More and more a 'state-regulator', with attempts to emulate the EU model of economic regulation; active regional policies	Selective pursuit of vertical industrial policies and selective protectionist trade policies	Autocratic, clan-based state structures dominate and control public life; little separation between state and economic sphere

Table 3.1 Three stylized outcomes of system transformation (continued)

		i) Reforming Central and Eastern European market economies (e.g. Poland, Hungary, Estonia)	ii) Post-Soviet mixed-economies (e.g. Russia, Ukraine, Belarus)	iii) Caspian state economies (e.g. Azerbaijan, Turkmenistan, Uzbekistan)
INFORMAL INSTITUTIONS	Approval of market mechanisms	Widespread comprehension and dominant approval of market mechanisms; collective memory of pre-World War II national market economies and comparatively high living standards	Little acceptance of market mechanisms, only slowly growing	Criticism of market economy principles; significant share of informal transactions
	Role of external references	The institutional setting of the EU is widely accepted and considered as a benchmark; this provides a stable framework for expectations	Reference to foreign institutional models is traditionally rejected, latent ex-post approval of some institutions of Soviet socialism (mainly social benefits)	Focus on consolidation of new-born Republic rather than foreign models
	Perception of unemployment	Unemployment at a level similar to EU countries; unemployment benefits and social security have been (at least formally) put in place	Official unemployment figures are kept artificially low (10–15 percent, real underemployment estimated at 20–30 percent)	Few attempts to cushion socio-economic effects of unemployment, no labor market policies
SOCIETAL CONSENSUS		Wide consensus on rejection of socialist experience, commitment to market economy; consensus is stable and time-consistent	Weak consensus in favor of some kind of reform, but absence of a constructive public debate on different options; any consensus is likely to be unstable	Some consensus on the consolidation of the new-born Republic, but hardly any debate on options for the future economic system; absence of public debate

Source: Based on Hirschhausen and Waelde (2001, 104–105)

4. Specific Infrastructure Policies for Eastern Europe?

... we argue that in the CEE region – in contrast to more developed countries – a reasonable case can be made for allowing a temporary period of monopoly for basic services.

Mark Armstrong and John Vickers (1996, 295): *Regulatory Reform in Telecommunications in Central and Eastern Europe.*

1. INTRODUCTION

This chapter discusses arguments in favor of a specific infrastructure policy in Eastern Europe during the 1990s. The objective is to identify those aspects within the process of systemic reform that differ significantly from infrastructure reform in other regions of the world and to assess whether those differences justify particular infrastructure policies. Indeed, calls for a second 'Marshall Plan' were voiced very early on in the transformation process, and a standard argument for explaining the transformation crisis was that (public) infrastructure investment was neglected in the early years of transformation. Different strands of economic theory were developed to show why, under the conditions of radical systemic change, traditional market-oriented approaches to infrastructure policy might not be appropriate. This chapter lays out these theoretical arguments that will be tested empirically in the subsequent Part II.

The chapter is structured in the following way: Section 2 describes the point of inception of post-socialist infrastructure policies, the collapse of 'socialist' infrastructure. At this point in time, a gradual market-oriented transformation of the inherited organizational and physical infrastructure of Eastern Europe was largely impossible. Section 3 identifies the specific conditions under which infrastructure policies in Eastern Europe were developed; among them are the drop in production and obstacles to growth, monopolistic industrial structures and a particularly high degree of uncertainty. In Section 4 we present different theoretical approaches in favor of a specific infrastructure policy, covering macroeconomics, industry structure and regulatory aspects. The main controversies are whether there was a particular need for public investment in infrastructure during systemic transformation and what the optimal timing and sequencing for liberalization might have been. Section 5 concludes.[56]

2. POINT OF INCEPTION: COLLAPSE OF SOCIALIST INFRASTRUCTURE

2.1 Incompatibility Between Socialist Infrastructure and Market Economy Requirements

The infrastructure that had been developed during socialist times turned out to be incompatible with the requirements of emerging market economies in the center of Europe, both in quantitative and in qualitative terms. It was shown in the previous chapter that the principles of infrastructure development in socialist Eastern Europe were incompatible with the service function that infrastructure has in the (ideal-typical) market economy, where it mainly has to conform to the conditions of supply and demand. Parallel to the systemic break between socialism and the introduction of market economies, there was a break between socialist and market-oriented infrastructure

– on the *supply side*, concerning the fundamental principles of network planning, financing and operation, and

– on the *demand side*, with respect to the structure and the absolute level of the required infrastructure services.

On the *supply side*, the monopoly of the socialist party to control *network planning* disappeared. In the transformation period, several organizations entered the competition for network planning, among them the central government, the regional governments, large industry, lobbying groups and international financial organizations. Economic arguments played a more and more important role. The options to *finance* infrastructure diversified: transformation countries disposed theoretically of the broad set of private infrastructure investment options that had been developed world-wide, including leasing models, concession (build-operate-transfer (BOT) and other forms), project financing and full-scale privatization (see EBRD, 1996, chapter 4). State financing of infrastructure became subject to economic analysis, too (at least to a certain extent). With respect to *operation*, too, a broad range of organizational options existed to replace the monolithic supply of socialist infrastructure by the state.

The structural break on the *demand side* is also evident. Under socialism, the use of infrastructure was almost free of charge; by contrast in the transformation period, private households and enterprises had to pay real

---

[56] Thanks to Achim I. Czerny for discussions on the models that are presented in this chapter.

money for the use of infrastructure services and thus, had to ration their consumption. The demand for infrastructure from the *corporate sector* was significantly constrained by the collapse of production networks and the drop in industrial output. *Private households'* demand for infrastructure also underwent a structural change: the demand for low-quality basic infrastructure services was reduced (for example, public transport), whereas a new demand developed for formerly unavailable services (such as private telecommunication, diversified higher education, private motorized transport).

2.2 Examples

2.2.1 Transport
At the end of socialism, the transport system that existed in these countries was outdated and unprofitable.[57] Socialism had left behind a time-worn transport system that required modernization and extension. The findings of Gumpel (1999, 5, 13)[58] and EBRD (1996, chapter 3) converge on the fact that both the transport infrastructure and the rolling stock had been neglected in the last years of socialism in such a manner that they were unable to fulfil the requirements of a modern industrial market economy.

Railroad traffic, a central pillar of the socialist transport system, suffered heavily from the systemic break. Most former socialist countries possessed a relatively dense railroad infrastructure.[59] However, the technical quality was rather low, and the extensive use of the infrastructure and neglected investments in replacement and maintenance led to outdated equipment and a low real capacity.[60] Thus, the East European socialist railway system had to undergo substantial change. Inputs such as primary energy, electricity, steel, mechanical engineering, became expensive. The interregional transport coordination within the former CMEA fell apart; in the former Soviet Union, each republic had to develop its own national railway system and also had to *finance* it. Continued lack of investment for repair and maintenance led to a

---

[57] Gumpel, Werner und Peter Hampe (eds) (1993, *Barrieren im Bereich der Verkehrs-, Energie- und Agrarwirtschaft in Ost- und Südosteuropa*. München, Südosteuropa-Gesellschaft, Südosteuropa Aktuell, 15).

[58] Gumpel, Werner (ed.) (1993, *Integration des bulgarischen Verkehrs in das europäische System*. München, Südosteuropa-Gesellschaft, Südosteuropa Aktuell, 16).

[59] The network density (km per capita or per km²) was on average similar to the density in the European Union; the European part of the Soviet Union, Czechoslovakia, Hungary and Bulgaria had particularly high network densities (EBRD, 1996, 44, based on statistics from the International Road Transport Union).

[60] In 1990, over 25 percent of the railway network was in bad technical condition, and the bad state of more than 20 percent of the Russian network led to forced speed reductions (EBRD, 1996, 44 sq.). In Ukraine, the average speed of passenger trains was limited to 30 km/h due to the bad condition of the network.

further degradation of the network. On the *demand* side, the reduction of industrial production led to a reduction of railroad cargo. The changing structure of foreign trade contributed further to the slump in demand: trade of heavy industrial goods within the CMEA (East-East) was replaced by less transport-intensive trade with Western countries.[61] Consequently, railroad cargo was reduced in all transformation countries, by more than 50 percent (EBRD, 1996, 45, see Figure 4.1).[62] Passenger traffic was affected less and recovered relatively quickly after the initial years of transformation. However, passenger transport accounted for only a small share of revenue (and in most cases it was lossmaking).

The *road and highway infrastructure* in Eastern Europe was quite underdeveloped in international comparison; for example, it was far below the EU-average density (EBRD, 1996, 44; and see Table 5.1). According to EBRD, 38 percent of Russian roads required maintenance work or reconstruction, and *another* 25 percent a complete re-surfacing (EBRD, 1996, 45). The highway system for interregional traffic was particularly underdeveloped, at an average 1.8 m/km^2 (EU average, 14.2 m/km^2); it was also significantly below international standards in qualitative terms.[63]

In the course of transformation, the *modal split* between different modes of transport also changed. Public railway transport was replaced by individual motorized road transport, both for cargo and for passenger traffic. The changing trends of logistic supply-chain management also affected the modal split: companies required more flexible, multimodal transport services; individual transport started to dominate traditional mass transport. Value-added services such as planning, real-time product control, and intermodal connection played an increasing role in the newly emerging market for transport services.

---

[61] An example of this tendency is Bulgaria, which had carried out over 80 percent of its foreign trade with CMEA countries in socialist times. In the course of transformation, trade channels were re-oriented: in 1998, over 50 percent of the exports went to EU countries.

[62] The slump was particularly sharp in the heavily industrialized republics of the former Soviet Union. In Ukraine, railroad cargo fell from 474 bn. t-km (1990) to 162 bn. t-km (1996), over two-thirds!

[63] Those who have driven on a highway in socialist Eastern Europe can confirm this. Gumpel and Hampe (1993, 20) report that the section of road designated as a highway in Romania, from Bucharest to Pitesti, required full-fledged renewal; this 'highway' was also used by combines and bicyclists, and herds of sheep regularly crossed it.

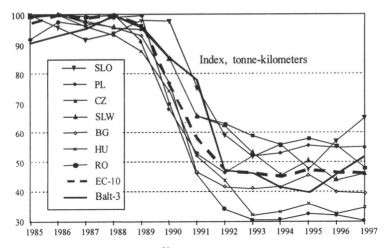

Source: Wissenschaftlicher Beirat (2001),[64] based on national statistics

Figure 4.1 Reduction of railroad cargo in the transformation period (1990–97)

2.2.2 Telecommunication

A structural break could also be observed in telecommunications. Under socialism, telecommunication was not a profit-oriented activity, but it was used by the socialist parties as a means of restraining and controlling information flows. Telecommunication networks used analogue equipment only, with an average rate of misconnections per line of 50–100 per year (EU average, 13). The teledensity (mainlines per 100 inhabitants) had been around 15 on average (EU average, 45; and see Table 5.1). The average waiting period for private telephone lines was more than 10 years (EBRD, 1996, 35), and the granting of telephone services was subject to political discretion.

The opening of the market for telecommunication services and equipment to international competition made the socialist technologies obsolete. The high willingness to pay for telecom services made it possible to switch to new technologies. The digitalization of information flows implied a new standard for switching stations and final consumer equipment, and a large part of the network had to be rebuilt. To a certain extent, the outdated socialist equipment was conducive to establishing new technical standards, as the

---

[64] Wissenschaftlicher Beirat beim Bundesministerium für Verkehr (2001, 'Verkehrspolitische Handlungserfordernisse für den Verkehr mit den Beitrittsländern'. *Internationales Verkehrswesen*, Vol. 53).

network effects in the former system were small, and thus the welfare losses from the installed base were low, too. The growth rates for mobile telephony and Internet in the transformation countries were higher than those in developed market economies (see discussion in EBRD, 1996, 35 sq.; see also Müller, 2000 and Table 5.1).[65]

2.2.3 Other sectors

The break between the socialist infrastructure and the transformation process can also be traced in other infrastructure sectors:

– In the *water* industry, real prices were first introduced during the transformation period, and the negative external effects of wastewater were beginning to be taken seriously for the first time. Under socialism, the use of water had been free for most of the population, but the reliability of supply had also been low, and the quality of water hardly ever corresponded to international standards (EBRD, 1996, 41 sq.; Somlyody, 1994). Wastewater treatment had been neglected, equipment was outdated and metering and communication equipment was insufficient (EBRD, 1996, 43).[66] The necessary investment into water and wastewater equipment were estimated above 1 percent of annual GDP, a reference that the industrial countries of Western Europe had spent between 1980–90 for the modernization of their respective water systems (EBRD, 1996, 44; Somlyody, 1994, 3);

– in the field of *public health*, the free (though rationed) minimum supply from socialist times was replaced by a more differentiated system (Davis, 2001). In most transformation countries, in particular the CIS countries, the health system was de facto monetized, and the entitlement to reasonably priced basic health services was undermined. Just as in telecommunication, the willingness to pay diverged largely between the high-income group and the low-income group. Reforms have not necessarily improved the efficiency of the health system, in particular in the CIS countries such as Russia, where 'health has remained a state sector with low-priority status' (Davis, 2001, 517);[67]

---

[65] On the other hand, the modernization of the telecommunication sector led to a deterioration of welfare of the lowest income groups that had benefited from a low-quality, but costless telecom service. The free services were abandoned, such as free public phones for local calls. The diversification of telecommunication services thus confirms the increasing segmentation of the population into transformation winners and losers.

[66] The connection rate to the waste water system was only 60 percent in Russia (85 percent in urban areas, EBRD, 1996, 43).

[67] Davis (2001, 517) contends that health had been a 'low priority sector' in the Soviet shortage economy, and that it has remained a neglected sector in the transformation period: 'Russian leaders in the transition have resembled Soviet predecessors in their general neglect of the health sector, ignorance of the inter-relationships between health institutions and tolerance of departmentalism. The government has not been effective either in co-ordinating economic and health reform policies or in developing consistent and feasible reforms for the

– in the *energy* sector, a break can be observed in the slump of primary energy production, the reduction of energy consumption, changing relative and absolute prices, and also in the industry-regulator relations (see Table 5.1 and in detail Part II);
– a structural break also occurred with regard to the *environment*, which had been used extensively as a free factor of production in socialist times. In the early years of transformation, most East European countries decided to adhere to international environmental standards (at least formally). Thus the environment also became a rare economic good, the consumption of which had to be taken into account in business and economic analyses.

3. SPECIFIC ECONOMIC AND INSTITUTIONAL CONDITIONS FOR INFRASTRUCTURE POLICIES

3.1 Macroeconomic Crisis and Obstacles to Economic Growth

The most obvious specific characteristic of the transformation process was the unprecedented – and unpredicted – macroeconomic crisis (see Chapter 3). The collapse of GDP in phase I of transformation, resulting from the downturn of all macroeconomic aggregates (mainly industrial production, aggregate investment, government expenditure), was unique in economic history. In all transformation countries, official GDP fell by at least 15 percent, and many countries had to cope with a reduction of over 50 percent (such as in Russia, Ukraine, Lithuania; see Annex). The economic upheaval in the transformation countries was much more severe and lasted much longer than the Great Depression of 1929–33, which also had major political and societal consequences.[68]

In addition, other macroeconomic indicators also behaved erratically: during the early years of transformation, all East European countries (except Hungary) featured extremely high levels of *inflation*, and inflation remained two-digit through all of phase I of transformation. Even in the advanced

---

health sector.' For a case study of the restructuring of the health system in a Russian region see Henke (1999).

[68] During the Great Depression, GDP declined by 'only' 30 percent in the USA, yet this crisis left its mark on the nations' consciousness for half a century (Gregory, 1999, 3 sq.). The Great Depression even brought about a new line of economic thought, Keynesianism. Socio-demographic data confirm the singularity of the transformation period. Thus, the birth rate in the CIS fell significantly between 1985 and 1995 (for example, in Russia from 17/1000 to 9/1000), whereas the death rate increased (in Russia from 11/1000 to 15/1000). Gregory (1999, 4) reports that such drastic changes are in general limited to periods of war and famine. See Davis (2001) for a detailed treatment of Russia and comparative statistics for Eastern Europe.

reforming countries, inflation remained high (5–10 percent) in phase II of transformation as well, and in the less reform-oriented countries, inflation remained unstable even in this second phase. The *exchange rates* were similarly unstable (see EBRD, 1994–2001). After macro-stabilization, economic growth remained weak in most transformation countries ('transformation crisis'). Though some Central and East European countries featured stable growth after 1994, none of them attained rates sufficient to reach the EU average in the medium term. Many CIS economies lacked sustained growth even in phase II of transformation.

3.2 High Investment Requirements

The collapse of socialist infrastructure in the early phase of transformation led to high investment requirements in Eastern Europe, including the extension or the reconstruction of entire networks (such as telecommunication, highways, airports and air security). Investment requirements were determined by objective changes in the demand for infrastructure services, but also by subjective political constraints: East European governments were eager to reach infrastructure equipment levels 'normal' for European countries. The integration into the European and world economy, too, required certain urgent investments, such as for attaining international quality and security standards (for example, in water, energy, telecommunication, and the environment).

The quantification of the investment needs depends crucially upon the point of reference chosen. If one agrees with the political objective that the transformation countries should attain an average EU infrastructure equipment level, the investment needs for the standard sectors of material infrastructure alone amount to about 6 percent of annual GDP (Table 4.1).[69] As the requirements for institutional and social infrastructure are not included in this figure, the true total investment sum is still higher.[70]

---

[69] If the reference is instead defined by the countries with similar *per capita* income levels (middle-income countries according to the World Bank classification (i.e. USD-PPP (1994) between 875-8500 *per capita*, the same level as Ecuador, Panama, Namibia, Botswana), the investment needs would only be about half that level.

[70] Milbrandt (2001, 120 sq.) estimates the financial requirements for European-wide public goods in the existing EU-15 in the field of *institutional* infrastructure at EUR 11.6 bn. per year, which should be distributed among all EU countries on a *per capita* basis. No estimates exist on the requirements of institutional and social infrastructure in the EU-accession countries, but it is fair to consider that they may be as high as for the material infrastructure.

Table 4.1 Investment requirements of transformation countries in selected sectors of material infrastructure (1995–2010)

Sector	Reference	Investment requirements (USD bn.)	Share of annual GDP (for 15 years)
Roads[71]	Modernization/construction of the road network to EU average density	200	1.1%
Railways[72]	Modernization/construction of the railway network to EU average density	85	0.4%
Tele-communication[73]	Teledensity of 35 mainlines/100 inhabitants	170	0.9%
Wastewater[74]	European standards for collection and treatment	290	1.5%
Energy[75]	Network development, oil-, gas- and coal sector reform	270	1.4%
Environment[76]	Compliance with the EU directives on air pollution and waste treatment	71	0.3%
Sum of material infrastructure		*ca. 1,100*	*ca. 6%*

[71] Source: On the basis of European Commission (1997, *Transport Infrastructure Financing in Central and Eastern Europe*. Brussels, European Commission (DG VII)), converted for the CIS countries with one third of the Central and Eastern European network density (21,000 km/107 mn.).

[72] Source: On the basis of European Commission (1997, *Transport Infrastructure Financing in Central and Eastern Europe*. Brussels, European Commission (DG VII)), converted for the CIS countries with one-third of the Central and Eastern European network density (19,000 km/107 mn.).

[73] Source: Müller (2000, 203), does not include the non-European CIS states.

[74] Sources: EBRD (1996, chapter 3), Somlyody (1994); the European Commission (cited in EBRD, 2000, 57) estimates the investment needs for 'water' at EUR 51 bn. for 10 years).

[75] Source: European Commission. Includes network development, updating of the oil, gas and coal sectors (including refining) to international environmental standards; does *not* include expenses for nuclear safety and treatment of radioactive waste. Assumption: gradual reduction of investment needs in EU accession countries from USD 40 bn. (1996–2000) to EUR 35 bn. (2001–05) and EUR 30 bn. (2006–10); *per capita* investment requirements in the European CIS countries are estimated at two-thirds of the EU-accession countries, non-European CIS countries are not taken into account; exchange rate USD:EUR = 1. Brendow (1995, 'Unternehmensstrategien der europäischen Energiewirtschaft in Mittel- und Osteuropa'. *Energiewirtschaftliche Tagesfragen*, October, 647 sq.) quotes a much higher figure of USD 60–70 bn. per year over 30 years, about USD 2,000 bn. for energy alone, which seems to be very high.

[76] Source: European Commission, cited in EBRD (2000, 57); calculated only for the EU-accession countries (composed of EUR 48 bn. for air and EUR 16 bn. for waste treatment; EUR 51 bn. for water is integrated in the above category 'wastewater'); no information available for the CIS countries.

3.3 Limited Access to Finance

During the transformation period, access to infrastructure financing was limited in the public *and* in the private sector. *Public* infrastructure financing was limited by the necessary consolidation of the state budget and the parallel decrease of tax revenues. Besides the reduction of GDP, all East European countries had to cope with a decrease of state revenues over GDP (EBRD, 1996, 52 sq.).[77] With few exceptions, most transformation countries featured substantial budget deficits (5–20 percent of GDP), the reduction of which was a priority in the stabilization programs. In addition, given low flexibility of expenditures for personnel, state investments had to carry most of the burden on the expenditure side: between 1989 and 1995, the share of public investments over GDP fell from 5–10 percent to 2–3 percent (EBRD, 1996, 53).

Private infrastructure finance was constrained by underdeveloped capital markets and high uncertainty and risk. The domestic financial organizations were unable or unwilling to provide financing for long-term infrastructure projects. Real interest rates were high. For foreign private investors, infrastructure investments included a high political, macroeconomic and microeconomic risk, which only risk-taking agents were likely to accept. Public Private Partnerships (PPP) involving several private investors and domestic and foreign public organizations had high transaction costs. The third group of possible investors, *international financial organizations*, therefore played a certain role as a catalyst for infrastructure financing in the early years of transformation (EBRD, 1996, 59). However, the available investment volume was relatively low and could not meet the requirements of the transformation countries (see Chapter 5).

3.4 Extensive Risk and Uncertainty

Infrastructure policies in the transformation period were also affected by the particularly high degree of risk and uncertainty. This implied a conservative approach by private investors and reduced the possibility to implement innovative infrastructure policies with private participation. The ratio of uncertainty to risk[78] was particularly high: little information existed to assess the risks of political or economic developments. In phase I of transformation, there was also a lack of any external reference models that might have

---

[77] The share of budget revenues of GDP fell in the reform-oriented transformation countries from about 50 percent (1989) to 40 percent (1995), in the other countries from 40–45 percent to approximately 25 percent (EBRD, 1996, 52).

[78] For *risk*, objective or subjective information on the probability distribution exists, *uncertainty* is characterized by the absence of such information.

provided some guidance.[79] Thus, uncertainty was omnipresent not only at the level of the choice within rules, but also at the very level of constitutional decisions; in many cases, even the survival of the new nations themselves, emerging from the Soviet empire, was uncertain.

More precisely, three categories of risk and uncertainty can be distinguished:

– *Political* (or systemic) uncertainty resulted from the absence of fundamental constitutional decisions in the early transformation period and the resulting lack of orientation at the working level. For example, in phase I of transformation, many countries had not made an explicit decision to orient their infrastructure policies towards market economic principles. Empirical analyses have shown that political risk is negatively correlated to GDP growth of investment (World Bank, 1997, 5). In the Central and East European countries, political uncertainty was reduced significantly in the course of transformation, in other transformation countries it remained high but was converted to a subjective risk over time;[80]

– *macro* (economic) uncertainty and risk refer to the development of macroeconomic indicators and the reform process in the areas of macroeconomic and fiscal stabilization, foreign trade, etc. Macro risk has a direct impact on the discount rate and thus has a negative effect on investment. In phase I of the transformation process, macro risk was high in all transformation countries, but it levelled out quickly in the Central and East European countries. In phase II of transformation, macro uncertainty did not differ significantly from that in other emerging markets;

– *micro* uncertainty includes the factors determining the investment conditions in a concrete location and a concrete industrial branch. This includes the qualification and the flexibility of the workers and employees, the material and institutional infrastructure, the quality and availability of services, the support from the administration, and so on (Thimann and Thum, 1998, 14).

---

[79] Such as the experience from the Greek accession to the EU in 1981 which was valuable in the 1986 accession of Spain and Portugal. The idea that the integration of the 'new Länder' of East Germany into the Federal Republic could serve as a reference model for the transformation countries turned out to be false (Mummert and Wohlgemuth, 1998).

[80] An indicator for political risk is the reliability indicator of the World Bank which is composed of five institutional factors: predictability of economic policy, political stability, protection of property rights, reliability of the legal system, and corruption (World Bank, 1997, 40 sq.). In a world-wide survey, the CIS countries obtained the lowest reliability index (0.6, in relation to a standardized 1.0 given to high-income OECD countries); the Central and East European countries found themselves somewhere in the middle (0.75, behind South and South-East Asia and the Middle East and North Africa (0.8, respectively), and in front of Latin America (0.7) and Sub-Saharan Africa (0.65).

3.5 Monopolistic and Heterogeneous Market Structures

The post-socialist transformation countries were characterized by regionally monopolistic market structures, and a high cost heterogeneity between producing enterprises across regions or countries.[81] With the transformation process, both market and enterprise structures were transformed significantly. Former monopolistic positions were lost, because i) existing enterprises expanded their product range, ii) vertical unbundling of industrial combines led to competition between intermediate enterprises that had formerly supplied only their own combine, iii) new enterprise start-ups were created by local entrepreneurs or by foreign companies, iv) the opening of foreign trade led to intensified international competition.

According to the evidence available, the homogenization of market structures in transformation countries proceeded only gradually; even into phase II of transformation, the market structures of Central and East European and CIS countries remained heterogeneous when compared with gradually emerging industrial countries:

– Although the dominance of large state-owned enterprises was reduced in the first years of transformation, it did not abide in phase I. The first large enterprise survey carried out by EBRD showed that the state-owned enterprises dominated other forms of ownership even two to three years into reforms, and that they employed more people on average (EBRD, 1995, 128 sq.). Even if one assumes a lower productivity of state-owned enterprises, this still implies a high market share and thus a relatively high concentration ratio;

– the distribution of enterprises by size changed gradually towards a higher share of medium-sized enterprises, but only at a slow pace. In most transformation countries, the average enterprise density (enterprises per 1,000 inhabitants) remained lower than in the EU with 43/1,000 (exceptions, Czech Republic and Hungary). One reason for the slow structural change was the nature of the privatization, which was mainly geared towards selling entire former combines as such (instead of prior unbundling into smaller units);[82]

– an indicator for the slow structural change is the share of employees *not* active in large industry, but in small- or medium-sized enterprises. Although this share had risen from insignificant levels in socialist times to 24 percent in

---

[81] Under socialism, political decisions had favored monopolistic production structures, where one product was produced by only one enterprise (or few enterprises) in one region. Thus, socialist enterprises ('combines') were large in relation to the average enterprise in a market economy, and they featured a high degree of vertical integration. Small and medium enterprises (SMEs) had been largely abolished under socialism (Kornai, 1992, 399 sq.).

[82] A prominent example: within the first wave of privatization in Russia, only 12 percent of the 10,663 enterprises slated for privatization had been partially unbundled beforehand (Joskow, 1994, 34).

1994, it remained below the levels attained in the EU (65 percent) and the USA (53 percent) (EBRD, 1995, 140).

3.6 Formal and Informal Institutional Constraints

In phase I of transformation, the institutional environment within which infrastructure policies had to take place was unstable and not conducive to a coherent competition policy. The *formal* framework for a market-oriented infrastructure policy was underdeveloped in *all* transformation countries. The formal legal and political institutions of socialist infrastructure policies had lost their normative power and since no new ones immediately replaced them, a formal institutional void emerged. General competition laws were developed quite rapidly, but they were insufficient for specific decisions concerning privatization and liberalization. Sectoral legislation, however, lagged far behind due to political struggles and long formal administrative processes. In many cases, sectoral laws were only voted in and applied in phase II of transformation.[83]

In the area of *administration*, the lack of competent and independent regulatory agencies further complicated the implementation of new infrastructure policies. The branch ministries or other 'regulators' of socialist times were in many cases abolished. The resources of highly qualified personnel to design and carry out market-oriented infrastructure policies were limited; this lack could not be filled in the short term by training programs or financial incentives. The most qualified personnel were siphoned off by the newly emerging private corporate sector.

The *low degree of monetization* posed severe problems to infrastructure policy implementation, mainly in the post-Soviet mixed economies. It was indeed difficult if not impossible to design welfare-optimizing marginal cost-oriented tariffs if these marginal costs had to be calculated on the basis of a multitude of barter transactions instead of publicly available input prices. The calculation of marginal cost prices is difficult even in market economies, and in post-Soviet transformation countries it was practically impossible.[84]

As regards *informal* institutions, a fundamental difficulty of applying competition-oriented infrastructure policies stemmed from the lack of consensus on basic legal terms. In developed market economies, legal

---

[83] Waelde and Gunderson (1996) argue that the lack of a strict formal framework in transformation countries should not be overcome by copying foreign law, but by domestically-dominated 'transaction-driven legislation', creating interim law around individual real-time transactions. Quantitative indicators for the development of formal institutions are published in the annual EBRD Transition Report, London.

[84] Take the example of the power sector in Russia or Ukraine, where labor was paid with potatoes from the power plant-owned agriculture, and where the coal was obtained by selling power to a trader, who in turn received some steel that he used to pay the coal mine.

concepts acquire normative power through their regular application in the legal process; however, this routine was unavailable in the transformation context.[85] A further informal constraint was the socialist understanding of infrastructure services as a 'free good' (or 'human right'). This led to substantial opposition against welfare-efficient infrastructure pricing and resulted in pressure on the government to carry out large-scale investment programs themselves. The lacking culture of critical and well-informed public debate increased the danger of misuse of discretionary political power. On the other hand, the demand for a strong regulator, which in Western economies is today accepted, was opposed in Eastern Europe, where the very idea of 'independent regulation' was sometimes considered inimical and harmful (Stern, 1994, 393).

3.7 Expensive Supply of and Low Demand for Competition-Oriented Regulation

The specific conditions prevailing in the early transformation period also affected the 'market' for competition-oriented regulation. As modeled by the new political economy and public choice approaches (for example, Stigler, 1971) and applied concretely to the East European power sector by Stern (1994), regulation emerges from a multi-player game: politicians supply regulation to industry and other interest groups, that have a certain 'willingness to pay' for regulation. In the transformation context, one can consider competition-oriented regulation to be *supplied* by individuals or interest groups within the bureaucracy (government). The structure of supply depends upon economic costs (capital, labor, equipment, etc.) and political costs; the latter are the (opportunity) costs of the bureaucracy of not having pursued other activities to obtain bureaucratic power, votes and the like. Among the determinants of the costs of supply in transformation countries were the *low number of qualified staff, low institutional stability, public resistance* against the notion of 'independent, sectoral regulation', and the *absence of a critical, well informed public* which increased the risk of discretionary decisions by the regulator and thus the political costs.

Demand for competition-oriented reregulation of infrastructure is expressed mainly by the following interest groups (based on Stern, 1994, presented according to their estimated 'willingness to pay'):

– The incumbent *state-owned enterprises* in each infrastructure sector (naturally) had the lowest, that is, a highly negative, demand for deregulation

---

[85] Concrete examples are: a 'fair rate of return', given two- to three-digit inflation rates and open debate on the true growth rate of GDP; 'used and useful' as the basis of capital costs in cost-based regulation designs; 'state of technology' in the conditionality for concession contracts.

and privatization. This applied particularly to vertically integrated monopolies;
– *consumers'* willingness to pay was positive for those who stood to win from efficient pricing, and negative for the rest. It can be assumed that the latter dominated, given the fact that almost no consumer paid the long-run marginal costs of infrastructure services in *any* transformation country. Price rebalancing was slow, too, so that households continued to benefit from lower prices;
– other *governmental agencies* that had benefited from the former system also had a low to negative demand for competition-oriented regulation. For this group, deregulation implied the loss of political levers of infrastructure policy (for example, structural policy), social policy (low prices for low income groups) or even macroeconomic policy (for example, containing inflation by keeping prices low);[86]
– *investors* in infrastructure sectors may have had different demands for competition-oriented regulation, depending on whether they planned to take over a former monopolist (negative demand) or to act as an independent operator (positive demand).
– finally, *international financial organizations* (IFOs) such as the International Monetary Fund, the World Bank and regional development banks, can be considered as an independent actor in the reform process. These organizations had a high interest in deregulation, as this corresponded to their political mission. The IFOs' willingness to pay was expressed in preferential project loans and grants.

Regulation being a collective, or public good, the aggregate demand can theoretically be obtained by aggregation of the individual demands. The demand for competition-oriented regulation is negative for the state-owned infrastructure companies and some of the consumers; other governmental departments and investors may have a positive willingness to pay for some deregulation, but beyond a certain level their aggregate willingness becomes negative. The only interest group to have a positive willingness to pay for all states of deregulation are the international financial organizations. The supply of competition-oriented regulation is quite costly, as shown above. Under the conditions of system transformation, the hypothetical market equilibrium will come about at a rather low degree of deregulation.[87]

---

[86] Usually, it was only the Treasury (Ministry of Finance) that had a strong vested interest in privatization. An advantage of having a distinct regulator for the government was that it was in a position to delegate nasty tasks, such as unpopular price increases, the closure of generation capacity and the like to the regulator.

[87] Minor increases of the costs of supply (such as increased political resistance implying higher political costs) or decreases of demand (for example, the retreat of potential investors and international financial organizations) can lead to an even lower degree of deregulation.

4. ARGUMENTS IN FAVOR OF A TRANSFORMATION-SPECIFIC INFRASTRUCTURE POLICY

The collapse of socialist infrastructure and the specific institutional and economic conditions of the early years of transformation have led many a politician and economist to call for some sort of transformation-specific infrastructure policy. In this section, we discuss different theoretical arguments that support the conduct of such a transformation-specific infrastructure policy, that is, a policy that differs from the market reference model described above.

4.1 Infrastructure Policy for Growth?

4.1.1 Mixed evidence in developing and growth theories

Given the drastic slump of production and the subsequent weakness of economic growth in most transformation countries, calls for a growth-enhancing infrastructure policy were voiced very early on. With reference to American support for economic recovery in post-World War II Western Europe, different proposals for a 'second Marshall Plan' for Eastern Europe were discussed. Additional infrastructure investments, state and private, were supposed to reverse the downslide of economic development and to support sustained growth.[88]

The evidence for a link between infrastructure investments and economic development and growth is weak. Theoretical arguments for a special role of public infrastructure policy were first advanced by Rostow (1960) in his theory of 'Stages of Economic Growth', according to which infrastructure (then called social overhead capital) could be the catalyst in the jump from one development stage to the next.[89] Post-Keynesian growth theory (developed by Harrod and Domar) suggested that public investment could maintain an economy's path towards balanced growth, when private investments were insufficient to balance the assumed exogenous growth of labor supply and labor productivity. The endogenous growth theory (following authors such as Lucas and Romer), too, implies positive growth

---

[88] See, for example, Dutz and Silberman (1993). The European Commission decided as early as 1993 to reorient its technical assistance to Eastern Europe towards supporting infrastructure projects; it was argued that EUR 1 of public support from Brussels would induce about EUR 6 in infrastructure investments (according to Alan Mayhew, General Director of DG I, Handelsblatt, June 11, 1993). EBRD (1996, chapters 3–5) summarizes the early discussion of infrastructure policy options in the transformation context.

[89] Rostow mainly stressed the role of transport infrastructure in the development from subsistence towards the preconditions for economic take-off; for attaining the last stage of development, mass production, communication infrastructure was considered particularly important.

effects from infrastructure investment: infrastructure capital, mainly human capital and R&D, produces positive spillover effects and thus leads to constant or even increasing returns to scale.

The arguments *against* intensive state engagement in infrastructure development are manifold as well. The inefficient use of public funds may lead to crowding out of private investment and thus create obstacles rather than support economic growth. Hirschman (1958) argued early on that development and growth might be spurred by infrastructure *shortage* rather than by an oversupply of public infrastructure: according to him, only once a certain infrastructure service is identified as a definite limiting factor to private sector development should growth-enhancing (private) investment take place. Hirschman also argued that the real obstacle to development was not material infrastructure, but the *personal* and *institutional* infrastructure required to make the most efficient use of the physical infrastructure.[90] Thus, an oversupply of material infrastructure would *not* be conducive to developing the soft skills required for sustainable development.

None of the theories mentioned has been proven empirically. Notwithstanding a large number of studies on the subject, it has been difficult to establish a robust, unidirectional and statistically clear relationship between infrastructure investments and productivity or economic growth.[91] The most intensively applied approach has been to extend aggregate production functions with an infrastructure component. For example, the 'public capital hypothesis' en vogue in the early 1990s, arguing that a lack of infrastructure was responsible for the slowdown of productivity growth in Western countries in the 1970s and 1980s, was based upon such an aggregate approach (Aschauer, 1989). Other approaches estimate the relationship between sectoral or regional infrastructure stocks and productivity gaps between these sectors or regions.[92] However, the results of these studies have

---

[90] 'But the circle to which our analysis has led us ... places the difficulties of development back where all difficulties of human action begin and belong: in the mind. ... Our principal assumption throughout this essay is that the real scarcity in underdeveloped countries is not the resources themselves but the ability to bring them into play.' (Hirschman, 1958, 11, 57). Hulten (1996) has empirically shown what economic logic would suggest in the first place, that 'how well infrastructure capital is used may be more important than how much you have.'

[91] See the surveys by Gramlich (1994), Pfähler et al. (1996), and Schlag, Carsten-Henning (1997, 'Die Kausalitätsbeziehung zwischen der öffentlichen Infrastrukturausstattung und dem Wirtschaftswachsum in Deutschland'. *Konjunkturpolitik*, 43. Jg., Heft 1, 82-106).

[92] For example, Seitz, Helmut (1995, *Public Infrastructure, Employment and Private Capital Formation*. OECD-Jobs Study, Paris, OECD), and Seitz, Helmut, and Gerhard Licht (1993, *The Impact of the Provision of Public Infrastructures on Regional Economic Development in Germany*. *Regional Studies*). Other studies have tempted to isolate individual infrastructure sectors and measure their impact on economic growth (such as telecommunication, education, highways): See for example, Röller, Lars-Hendrik, and Len Waverman (2001, 'Telecommunications Infrastructure and Economic Development: A

been challenged on the grounds of conceptual data problems, the uncertainty of lag structures and other technical details, lack of plausibility and the unresolved issue of causality (from infrastructure to growth, or from growth to infrastructure) make it difficult to put these results to practical use (Gramlich, 1994, 1193 sq.).[93]

4.1.2 Are transformation countries different?

The above discussion implies that in stable, developed industrialized countries, particular efforts to promote infrastructure investments will not necessarily have a significant impact on economic development. The question is whether this also applies to the specific situation of systemic change. Four arguments for a special role of infrastructure investments in a transformation context have been advanced:

– In phase I of transformation, all economies were working far below their potential production possibility frontier, due to the breakdown of socialist production networks and socialist infrastructure. The development of new infrastructure might help to revitalize ailing production capacities and thus provide the economy with an impetus to reach its production potential. The marginal returns to infrastructure investments in transformation countries might thus be significantly *higher* than in developed economies;

– given the economic depression in the first several post-socialist years, a state infrastructure can be considered the least dangerous form of a proactive macroeconomic policy;[94]

– given the institutional void in the early years of reform, investments in the formal institutional infrastructure can be considered potentially very productive (for example, the development of the formal legal system, the

---

Simultaneous Approach'. *American Economic Review*, Vol. 91, No. 4 (September), 909–923.), Koman, Reinhard, and Dalia Marin (1997, *Human Capital and Macroeconomic Growth: Austria and Germany 1960–1992*. Berlin, WZB-Discussion Paper FS IV 97-5), Stephan, Andreas (1997, *The Impact of Road Infrastructure on Productivity and Growth: Some Preliminary Results for the German Manufacturing Sector*. Berlin, WZB-Discussion Paper FS IV 97-47).

[93] Pfähler, Hofmann and Bönte (1996, 103) conclude their *tour de force* of over 70 quantitative studies on the subject with soberness: 'The discussion of empirical findings and the estimation methods applied has shown that answering the question "Does extra public infrastructure matter" is by no means a trivial task and the findings of some 70 empirical studies reviewed above are also not very encouraging for, and not particularly helpful to policy makers. ... Since the literature reviewed is concerned only with the role of extra public infrastructure in developed countries, the empirical findings also provide no guidance for the "start-up" problem of infrastructure in developing or transforming economies.'

[94] Parallels were drawn to the infrastructure programs in the USA during and after the Great Depression (1929–33). A more recent example comes from China, where a contagion of the Asian crisis (1997–99) was avoided by, amongst other things, massively increasing public infrastructure investments.

creation of administrative infrastructure, or the alignment of technical norms to the international level);

– finally, in addition to the marginal effects, it was also argued that in a development context, infrastructure investments could have an *inframarginal* effect, for example, by initiating a certain economic development.

The existing evidence on the impact of infrastructure investments in the transformation period is weak. A very rough qualitative look at the macro-data does *not* reveal a direct relationship between infrastructure investment programs and economic development in transformation countries. State capital investments (measured in percent of GDP, an indicator for infrastructure expenditures) and rates of economic growth seem to be unrelated. Some countries with high state capital investments featured particularly low growth rates in phase I of transformation (Czech Republic and Hungary; see Table 4.2); however, in contrast, some countries with relatively low state investment have achieved high growth rates early on (Poland and Slovenia, see Hirschhausen, 1999, 419).[95]

A positive relation between infrastructure and growth has been identified for the *institutional endowment* of certain transformation countries. Piazolo (1999) has shown that countries achieve higher growth rates if they succeed in achieving institutional change towards a market economy; further institutional change, mainly inspired by accession to the European Union, will spur growth even more.[96] However, none of the crucial institutional parameters can be concretely shaped in the short term by an infrastructure policy, nor can they be bought with money (such as foreign assistance).

We conclude that, lacking a coherent quantitative analysis on the issue, the empirical test should consist of *case study* evidence on the micro-effects of public investments programs; this is done in Chapter 6.

---

[95] A simple back-of-the-envelope pool regression using the above data of GDP (lagged by one year) on state capital expenditure (as a proxy for infrastructure investment) reveals a positive correlation (coefficient: 0.1326), but is statistically insignificant (t-statistic: 0.408, R^2 of only 0.36 percent, Durbin-Watson statistics of 1.430); omitting the last year of data (1999) which was distorted by the Russian financial crisis, improves the statistical results only marginally (coefficient: 0.1434, t-statistic: 0.422, R^2: 0.4 percent, DW: 1.654). Dodonov et al. (2002) present initial evidence on a positive link between market-oreinted infrastructure regulation in the transformation countries, and *per capita* GDP growth. More research in this area should produce more complex models and more significant results.

[96] Havrylyshyn et al. (1999) have also shown econometrically that the factors of growth in transformation countries are mainly a combination of reducing government size (through institutional reform), and accelerating progress on structural reforms.

Table 4.2 State capital investments and economic growth in transformation countries (1993–99)

		1993	1994	1995	1996	1997	1998	1999
Czech	state capital investment							
Republic	(growth in %)	6.8	7.1	7.7	4.1	5.5	5.2	5.7
	real GDP growth (%)	0.1	2.2	5.9	4.8	-1.0	-2.2	-0.2
Estonia	state capital investment							
	(growth in %)	2.0	4.1	4.6	5.0	4.4	4.4	4.5
	real GDP growth (%)	-9.0	-2.0	4.3	3.9	10.6	4.7	-1.1
Hungary	state capital investment							
	(growth in %)	4.8	5.0	4.4	3.9	6.0	5.9	5.6
	real GDP growth (%)	-0.6	2.9	1.5	1.3	4.6	4.9	4.5
Latvia	state capital investment							
	(growth in %)	1.1	1.1	0.9	1.7	2.5	3.9	4.7
	real GDP growth (%)	-14.9	0.6	-0.8	3.3	8.6	3.9	0.1
Lithuania	state capital investment							
	(growth in %)	3.2	3.0	3.0	2.2	3.1	4.0	..
	real GDP growth (%)	-16.2	-9.8	3.3	4.7	7.3	5.1	-4.2
Poland	state capital investment							
	(growth in %)	3.3	3.2	2.9	2.8	3.6	3.7	..
	real GDP growth (%)	3.8	5.2	7.0	6.1	6.9	4.8	-4.1
Slovak	state capital investment							
Republic	(growth in %)	5.7	4.5	5.0	4.0	7.0	6.2	..
	real GDP growth (%)	-3.7	4.9	6.7	6.2	6.2	4.1	1.9
Slovenia	state capital investment							
	(growth in %)	2.3	3.1	3.0	3.5	4.8	5.3	..
	real GDP growth (%)	2.8	5.3	4.1	3.5	4.6	3.8	4.9

Source: National statistics, World Bank, UN-ECE Economic Survey of Europe; author's own
calculation

4.2 Infrastructure Policy to Accelerate Structural Change?

The industrial economic argument for a specific infrastructure policy in transformation countries stresses the potential positive impacts on structural change and the intensity of competition. The development of infrastructure, in this case mainly transport and communication, can contribute to the reduction of local monopolies and thus favor the market entry of new, low-cost enterprises. Infrastructure thus results in a direct effect, the reduction of production costs, and an indirect effect, the increase of competition and thus welfare. Traditional cost-benefit-analysis does not capture these dynamic effects appropriately and thus underestimates the effects of infrastructure investments.

The industrial economic argument picks up the idea of the agrarian and regional economist Johann Heinrich Thünen (1842) of the 'isolated state'. In the extreme case of *no* transport infrastructure, a local supplier is a monopolist and will supply his or her goods at the Cournot-price (no price discrimination). If one assumes that infrastructure is built so that a multitude of suppliers from other regions can enter the market at negligible transport costs, the good will be supplied under the conditions of a perfect market (price = marginal costs, see Figure 4.2). The infrastructure investment thus creates welfare (shadowed area) that may be far beyond the required investment sum.

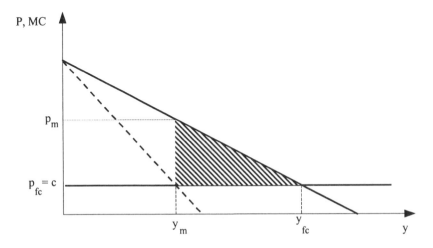

Figure 4.2 The potential gross welfare effects of an infrastructure investment

Along similar lines, Milbrandt (2001, 83 sq.) argued that preference should be given to infrastructure development in less developed regions of Eastern Europe, because the marginal revenue of such investments was likely to be higher than in developed regions of Western Europe. Under the conditions of historically-determined very heterogeneous equipment levels across Europe, horizontal tax sharing and temporary financial support to poorer countries may be justified to increase the allocative efficiency of investment. By contrast, this support should not be a permanent one in order not to distort the natural convergence process of infrastructure equipment, and to take into account different degrees of other locational factors of production.

By developing Thünen's idea further and applying it to the specific conditions of transformation countries, Aghion and Schankerman (1999) were the first to model the micro-foundations of the relation between infrastructure investments and economic growth. Aghion and Schankerman make a distinction between established industrial countries and transformation countries. Contrary to gradually developing industrial countries with homogenous cost structures where the indirect effect of additional infrastructure is small, the 'transformation impact' of infrastructure investments in Eastern Europe is particularly high. The argument is based upon the particularly strong cost asymmetry between old, post-socialist firms (*high cost*) and new, potentially more efficient firms (*low cost*, for example, unbundled parts of former combines, start-up firms). The model analyzes Nash-equilibria in markets with horizontal product differentiation, where all firms with average costs c_i choose the same price p_i ($i \in \{H,L\}$); *low cost* enterprises (c_L) sell at a lower price than *high cost* enterprises (c_H).[97] In the inception of transformation, high cost state-owned enterprises dominate the regional markets. An infrastructure investment induces the following effects (Aghion and Schankerman, 1999, 91 sq.):

– An *expansion effect* results from an intensification of competition, independent of any cost heterogeneity. This leads to an increase in aggregate output and thus in aggregate consumption; this in turn leads to higher welfare;

– the *selection effect* results from a more competitive environment (higher α) which raises the market share of low-cost firms relative to high-cost firms. Thus, total consumption for a given amount of money rises. In a physical sense, the selection effect can be thought of as a result of lower transport costs that challenges the dominant market share of regional high-cost monopolists;

– in addition, a *market entry effect* is induced by the fact that 'infrastructure investment enhances the incentives for relatively low-cost firms to enter the market and thus improves the efficiency of the entry process' (Aghion and Schankerman, 1999, 79). The probability of high-cost firm entry in the market is lower than the probability of low-cost firm market entry, because the latter get a larger market share in equilibrium and thus larger profits than high-cost firms.[98]

According to the Thünen or the Aghion and Schankerman approach, the dynamic effects of infrastructure investments increase with increasing cost asymmetry between the firms, with the initial market share of firms with high costs, with the effort required for restructuring, and with low costs of market entry for new firms. These conditions are precisely fulfilled in the transformation context, so that state infrastructure investments in these countries should induce particularly high indirect effects.

---

[97] $p_i = c_i/\alpha$, with α = substitution elasticity between different goods.

[98] If the initial cost asymmetry is high, as is assumed for transformation countries, then the market entry effect dominates the 'Schumpeter-effect', which *dis*courages market entry with increasing product market competition.

The empirical evidence on the strength of the effects is scarce. However, the effects themselves can be identified here and there. There is only one econometric study on the relationship between infrastructure and the competitiveness of Central and Eastern European transformation countries, and it is limited to the availability of *road* infrastructure: Meißner (1999) claims to have identified a relationship between the network density of roads (expressed in km of roads/km^2) in Central and Eastern Europe and the inflow of net foreign direct investment (which is taken as an indicator for competitiveness). This lends some support to the hypothesis of a selection effect.[99] Dutz and Vagliasindi (1999) find a robust relation between the institutional infrastructure for the competition policy (measured by the capacity to implement laws, the competition orientation of competition policy and the political independence of the anti-monopoly offices) and the structural change towards efficient private enterprises. This, too, supports the hypothesis of a positive relation between (institutional) infrastructure investments and induced structural change.

Other studies of a more qualitative character also lend some credibility to the argument. A large enterprise survey conducted by EBRD (1995, 133 sq.) shows that high-cost state enterprises have indeed undertaken less restructuring than low-cost firms. This result is consistent with the assumption that low-cost enterprises have higher incentives to restructure, as this increases their market share over-proportionally. Some additional anecdotal evidence on the structural effects of early infrastructure investment comes from Hungary, where the privatization of infrastructure proceeded particularly quickly, for example, in banking, telecommunication and the energy sectors.[100] One helpful factor here was the loose liberalization policy pursued by the Hungarian government: most private investors were granted temporary monopoly status. This infrastructure plus the additional reputation acquired by Hungary may have spurred the market entry effect by attracting significant amounts of foreign direct investment.[101]

---

[99] However, it would be far-fetched to draw any policy conclusions from this; for example, in the sense of extending the road network to enhance foreign direct investments. In particular, no concrete infrastructure policy can be designed as long as no information is available on the qualitative parameters (such as surface quality, bottlenecks, geographic orientation of the network, delays at national borders, etc.), on the willingness to pay of potential users, on the possibility to raise private finance, and so on.

[100] See EBRD (various issues); OECD (1995, *Telecommunication Infrastructure: The Benefits of Competition*. Paris; ICCP, No. 35); OECD (1996, *Review of Telecommunications Policy. Hungary*. Paris); International Energy Agency (1999).

[101] This approach may help to explain the fact that by 1995 Hungary had accumulated USD 8 bn. of FDI, out of a total of USD 18 bn. for Central and Eastern Europe, thus almost as much as all other countries combined. As of 2000, some other countries were keeping up with Hungary in foreign direct investment, mainly Poland and the Czech Republic; yet in terms of *per capita* FDI, Hungary remained by far the most successful country (USD 1,764

On the other hand, as described above, the dominance of large (state-owned) enterprises was *not* significantly reduced in the early years of transformation (EBRD, 1995, 128 sq.); the shift towards small- and medium-sized enterprises proceeded only gradually. Thus, although there are indications supporting the hypothesis of infrastructure as an accelerator of structural change, nothing can be said about the concrete effects. Hence the industrial economic argument provides little in terms of concrete guidelines for the design of infrastructure policy; whether more infrastructure investments would have accelerated industrial development significantly remains an open issue.

4.3 Investment Support for Early Investors?

A third line of reasoning in favor of transformation-specific infrastructure policies stresses the role of the state in triggering investments in a context of high uncertainty. Thimann and Thum (1999) have applied the theory of investment under uncertainty to the specific conditions of transformation countries. In the latter, potential investors had little information about the general conditions surrounding their investment, and also on the input quality of the countries, such as the quality of infrastructure, the quality of the institutional environment, the local investment conditions, the quality of the labor force, etc. It is assumed that private or public agents in the region are unable to provide a reliable signal about the quality of the region (problem of adverse selection). Given the large political, macro- and micro-uncertainties, and the lack of information available from other investment projects, 'waiting and learning' about other investors' experience was the dominant strategy for all potential investors. In such a situation, positive information externalities stemming from investment projects may be foregone, and a sustainable investment blockade may develop, which is harmful to welfare and growth. Thimann and Thum argue that in such a situation, a time-limited subsidization of early investors may be justified, in order to reduce the uncertainty about the investment conditions of the recipient country. What Thimann and Thum do not mention explicitly, but what the model suggests, is that supporting *infrastructure* projects in this early transformation phase may have a particular impact, as these play a particular role in directly triggering productive investments. Besides a direct subsidization of early investment projects, the state can also decrease the uncertainty of other investors by more subtle means, such as strengthening the legal and institutional infrastructure, facilitating access to information on quality, or building up their reputation by pursuing particularly coherent policies (such as equal treatment of all

---

vs. USD 1,447 for the Czech Republic, and USD 518 for Poland).

investors, highest possible degree of transparency). One may also think of investment as a road that facilitates access to a certain region, and thus lowers the risks of an investment that relies on the region's accessibility.

Technically, the argument is developed as follows (see Thimann and Thum, 1998, 9 sq. for the complete model): investors in transformation countries with uncertain quality can be classified according to the minimum input quality q_i they require in order to ensure their project's success. The true quality of a country, g^*, is a random variable which is either higher than q_i, in which case the return of the project is positive ($R > 0$), or it is lower, in which case the project fails (see Figure 4.3). In a *one period* setting, the expected benefit can be written as:

$$(1-q_i)\frac{R}{r}+q_i 0$$

where r denotes the interest rate and $(1 - q_i)$ and q_i the probabilities for a high and low productivity region; with a probability of $(1 - q_i)$ the true quality of the regional input g^* lies above the minimum requirement of investor q_i. The private investment decision (*laissez-faire*) of a risk-neutral investor results from a comparison of the return from the uncertain investment with an alternative riskless financial asset, which yields a return of rK per period. The maximal minimum quality requirement, that is, the requirement of the marginal investor is $q_i = q_m = 1 - K_r/R$, whereas q_m denotes the 'Marshallian trigger' solution: all investors with input requirement below q_m will undertake the uncertain investment, all others will leave their capital in riskless financial assets.

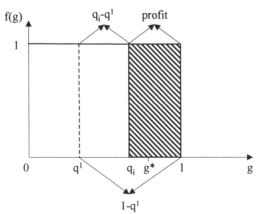

Source: Thimann and Thum (1999, 9)

Figure 4.3 Distribution of the unknown 'quality' of a region

In a *two period* model, a potential investor who has the option to wait one period, must weigh the advantage of additional information he gets as a result of the early investment decisions by other investors against the possible disadvantage of foregone expected profits. In the second period the expected value of the investment is (Thimann and Thum, 1999, 11):

$$V_2 = \underbrace{q^1 K}_{\substack{option\ value}} + \underbrace{(1-q^1)}_{\substack{probability \\ of\ success\ in\ t}} \left[\underbrace{\frac{q_i - q^1}{1-q^1} 0}_{\substack{failure\ in \\ t_2}} + \underbrace{\frac{1-q_i}{1-q^1} \frac{R}{r}}_{\substack{success\ in \\ t_2}} \right] = q^1 K + (1-q_i)\frac{R}{r}$$

Assuming the waiting investor gets no information about the failure after the first period, which occurs with a probability of $(1 - q_i)$, he knows that the true quality in the country lies between $q_1 \leq g^* \leq 1$. The strategy of waiting is worthwhile as long as

$$\underbrace{\overbrace{(1-q_p^1)R - rK}^{\substack{increases\ with\ falling \\ input\ requirements}}}_{\substack{benefit\ due\ to\ an \\ early\ investment}} \geq \underbrace{q_p^1 K}_{\substack{disadvantage \\ of\ an\ early\ investment}}$$

The interesting point about the model is that the state ('social planner') explicitly takes into account the positive information externality generated by the first period projects. He can therefore improve welfare by initiating more first period projects than in the private solution. The social value comprises the benefits of the first period projects and the benefits of the second period projects, the latter being a function of the number of first period projects. To maximize the investment value, the social planner has to initiate the socially optimal amount of investments in the first period. Thimann and Thum (1999, 15) derive that the socially optimal first period investment q_1^s is implicitly given by:

$$(1-q_s^1)R - rK + \underbrace{K[q^2(q_s^1) - q_s^1]}_{\substack{learning\ effect}} = q_s^1 K$$

Figure 4.4 compares the Marshallian trigger solution (q_m, no waiting possible), the private solution under laissez-faire (q_p^1), and the socially optimal solution (q_s^1). It can be seen that by initiating a larger amount of first period projects than in the private solution, the state can improve welfare (the shaded area).

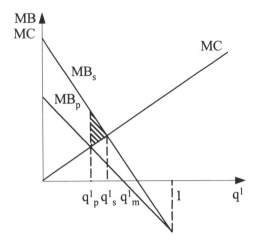

Source: Thimann and Thum (1999, 16)

Figure 4.4 The socially optimal choice of first period projects

The idea that the state can overcome the retention of investors (the so-called 'waiting-and-learning' effect) critically hinges on two assumptions: first, the social planner has to be well informed in *which* region the investment subsidies may trigger the largest positive externalities; second, the *limited time horizon* of the subsidy to private investors must be credible. Both assumptions are not necessarily fulfilled in the policy process in the transformation context: it is more likely political pressure than objective economic analysis that determines the regions to be subsidized; and the feasibility of stopping a running subsidy scheme is always low, whether the program is successful (in which case it may be argued that future success hinges upon continued subsidies) or unsuccessful (in which case pressure to continue subsidies may be even higher). In the latter context, international financial organizations may be particularly useful, as their participation relieves the pressure from the national governments and transfers responsibility (and political damage) to an external scapegoat, the supranational agencies outside of the domestic policy-making process, such as the IMF, the World Bank or the European Union. Thimann and Thum (1998, 20) therefore conclude that 'the international linkage creates an opportunity of establishing an effective, long-run oriented and credible economic policy in these [transformation] countries that helps to overcome the informational problems described above in the first place.'[102]

---

[102] Actually, one can think of the Sectoral Adjustment Loans given by the World Bank as an

The empirical evidence of the beneficial role of public support and of attempts to spur early infrastructure investments is, once again, weak. A 'bandwagon' effect of early investment may be identified in Hungary, where the privatization of some key infrastructure sectors proceeded particularly quickly (telecommunication, energy, banking, see above). However, public investment was not significantly higher in Hungary than in other countries, and thus, it may be that the institutional support was not particularly costly, and could have been carried out by any other transformation country as well. On the other hand, the particularly strong support to infrastructure investments in Russia (see Chapter 5) does not seem to have had any bandwagon effect on private investment. One argument for rejecting the demand for a particular infrastructure policy to spur investments in Eastern Europe is that sufficient information about the quality of each country's and region's infrastructure *was* already available in the early years of transformation, mainly through private sector activities, in which case the potential information externalities of additional policies were small.

4.4 Timing of Liberalization and Privatization

4.4.1 Arguments in favor of delayed privatization and liberalization

The last argument refers to the timing of deregulation in the transformation context. In the ideal-typical reference model of a market-oriented infrastructure policy (see Chapter 2), there is no reason to delay the restructuring process, that is, a far-reaching vertical disintegration of former monopolistic enterprises, the creation of competition at all possible levels, and the regulation of the remaining 'natural' monopolies. All newly created enterprises should be privatized, put under hard budget constraints, and thus spurred to increase their productive efficiency. The result of efficient regulation should be allocative and productive efficiency.

One argument for carrying out liberalization and privatization *particularly* rapidly in transformation countries is the short *window of opportunity*, that is, the time span within which fundamental reforms are possible. This argument was also applied to support radical economy-wide reforms, the so-called *big bang* strategy (for example, Lipton and Sachs, 1990). As the danger of a coalition *against* competition-oriented reforms was particularly high in the traditional infrastructure sectors, and the danger of a roll-back of reform efforts was in general high in the early phase of reform, it was argued that

---

instrument to overcome the investment blockade in transformation or emerging countries. These loans are usually given to lead sectors for economic development (such as telecommunication and transport). It is hoped that these adjustment loans will trigger an investment-bandwagon. However, evidence on this latter effect is scarce and difficult to verify.

substantial reform was possible only in the very early phase of reform. Another argument in favor of an immediate reform was the positive external effects of a successful implementation of reforms in one sector for the reform process as a whole. Self-binding reforms in a politically sensitive infrastructure sector decrease the regulatory risk across the economy (see the above discussion on Hungary). This argument would also imply that regulation should be carried out by one central agency rather than sector-specific regulatory agencies in order to strengthen the reputation of and to reduce regulatory risk in a given country.

Arguments in *favor* of a delayed deregulation and privatization usually rely on assumptions of incomplete information and institutional instability. It is argued that given high uncertainty in the early transformation period, both on the side of the regulator and on that of the enterprises, delaying the reform process may be welfare-enhancing: the option value of delaying reforms is higher than the expected loss of welfare from not having reformed immediately. In the following, we shall briefly touch upon the issue of privatization, and go into more detail on the sequencing of liberalization.

Information asymmetries may justify the delay of *privatization* of an infrastructure enterprise in the early transformation period: as more (subjective and objective) information becomes available to the private investor, the evaluation of the enterprise value may increase. The risk to sell to a 'wrong' investor decreases with decreasing information asymmetry between potential buyers, which is another reason for delaying privatization. In general, it is also preferable to wait with privatization until the major price adaptations have been carried out. In the opposite case, when the first action of the new private owner is to raise prices substantially, the entire privatization process may be discredited. On the other hand, extending state ownership increases the risk of productive inefficiency, the welfare losses of which have to be weighed against the welfare gains of delaying privatization.

One general argument for delaying *liberalization*, in other words, market opening for potentially competitive segments and regulation of the remaining natural monopoly, is the high uncertainty on what the optimal sequencing might be for a transformation country. Given the large political, macro- and micro-uncertainty, a reasonable argument can be made that the direct transfer of established Western regulatory models to the Eastern European transformation countries was not possible.[103] As more information about the state of the industry, potential investors, the reform options, etc. unfolds, the risk of embarking on the wrong reform path is reduced. Just as for private investors, governments can also learn from the positive or negative experiences of other countries' deregulation processes in order to improve the

---

[103] For a legal interpretation see, for example, Waelde and Gunderson (1996).

chances for successful reforms in their own countries. In this context, too, 'waiting' can be a dominant strategy, and it may require some incentive from the outside (for example, international financial organizations) for a country to be the first reformer.

A transformation-specific argument for delayed *liberalization* is the objective need for large investments in an institutionally unstable environment, that is, a high regulatory risk. It was shown above that the investment requirements to replace the obsolete socialist infrastructure were high, in particular in the Central and East European countries headed for EU accession. In addition, political constraints increased the investment requirements beyond the immediate economic ones; an example was the obligation to fulfil EU norms in the case of accession (environmental standards, quality and reliability of technical standards, and so on). Armstrong and Vickers (1996) have developed a model that accepts urgent investment requirements as a (politically) given external constraint, and then asks what this implies for the speed of liberalization. In that model, the optimal timing of liberalization is a function of the two risks that an investor faces in the transformation context:

– The *expropriation risk* is the danger of losing the quasi-rent once the investment is sunk; this can occur through ex-post modifications of the regulated price structure, or, in the extreme case, by physical expropriation of the investor by the regulator. The share of the total revenue of the investment that the investor can expect to keep decreases with the hazard rate of expropriation (h_x);

– the *liberalization risk* consists of the fact that the formerly monopolistic market can be opened without prior notice, and that thus the expected monopolistic profits do not materialize. It is assumed that after liberalization, free market entry reduces any supernormal profit to zero. The share of the expected revenue which an enterprise receives on a liberalized market increases with increasing liberalization risk (h_l).[104]

In the real world, the two risks can be thought of as being embodied by different organizations with different objectives. One can imagine a regulatory agency responsible for price regulation, embodying the risk of expropriation, and a branch ministry or a general anti-monopoly office embodying the liberalization risk. The model is then specified as follows (Armstrong and Vickers, 1996, 309 sq., appendix): investment costs of $C(Q)$ (in annual terms) are needed to build a capacity of Q (in this example: telephone lines, the marginal costs of operation are assumed to be zero); then

---

[104] Armstrong and Vickers (1996) distinguish two cases: a) with no comittment to a date of liberalization (T), there are two parallel risks: expropriation *and* liberalization; b) with a credible comittment to liberalization (T), the risk of expropriation is prevalent until t = T (it is assumed that after liberalization, the expropriation risk disappears).

the profit function can be written as $\pi(Q) = R(Q) - C(Q)$, whereas $R(Q) = Qp(Q)$. The *regulatory risk* is specified by parameter α which describes a proportion of the net present value of the revenue $R(Q)$ the firm expects to keep for itself; α is determined by the 'hazard rate' of being expropriated (h_x): $\alpha = r/(r + h_x)$; in the break-even situation, $\alpha R(Q) = C(Q)$.

To analyse interactions between liberalization policy and regulatory risk in the case of delayed liberalization, Armstrong and Vickers (1996) assume a proportion β of the expected net present value of revenue, which the incumbent firms receive from a liberalized regime. If liberalization takes place randomly, the policy risk h consists of the two components: $h = h_X + h_L$, whereas h_L denotes the 'hazard rate' for liberalization (that is, deregulatory risk). The expected profit of the investor is then composed of the revenues in case of a monopolistic market, discounted with the regulatory risk (αR), and the revenues from a liberalized market ($R_L \beta = R_L h_L / (r + h)$), and the revenues in case of expropriation (which are 0) minus the costs of investment (Armstrong and Vickers, 1996, 315):

$$\pi(Q) = \frac{1}{r}\left[\underbrace{\frac{r}{r+h}R(Q)}_{\substack{\text{revenues in a monopolistic} \\ \text{market}}} + \underbrace{\frac{h_L}{r+h}R_L(Q)}_{\substack{\text{revenues in a} \\ \text{liberalized market}}} + \underbrace{\frac{h_X}{r+h}R_X(Q)}_{\substack{\text{revenues=0} \\ \text{in case of} \\ \text{expropriation}}} \right] - C(Q)$$

Consideration of the two risks yields that
– profits (and thus investments) are always decreasing in h_x, that is, a higher expropriation risk reduces investments; however, the relevant point with respect to liberalization is that
– raising the hazard rate h_L has a *positive* effect on infrastructure capacity Q if and only if revenue with liberalization exceeds regulated monopoly revenue adjusted for regulatory expropriation risk, that is (Armstrong and Vickers, 1996, 310)

$$R_L(Q) > \frac{r\,R(Q)}{r + h_x}$$

This holds (only) if the expropriation risk is high in relation to the liberalization risk; on the other hand, a low expropriation risk would suggest that a later date of liberalization is conducive to increasing investments.

In the case of a significant expropriation risk one may ask why liberalization should not be carried out immediately, that is, on day 1 of transformation. The argument is that immediate liberalization may imply duplication of investments, which is welfare reducing when compared to a maintained regulated monopoly. Bolton and Farrell (1990, summarized by Armstrong and Vickers, 1996) weight the two options available to the regulator that wants rapid investment *and* competition, but has no reliable information about the cost type of the enterprises (high-cost or low-cost, $c_{H,L}$): i) under *laissez-faire* market conditions, several enterprises can enter the market. This leads to the danger of welfare-reducing duplication of supply (if both enterprises are low-cost) or the delay of investments (if both enterprises are high-cost, and thus are not committed to market entry in the first round). Only in the case of an uneven cost structure ($1 \times c_H$, $1 \times c_L$) will the result be socially efficient; ii) on the other hand, if the regulator chooses *one* monopolistic supplier, it runs the risk of not choosing the most efficient one.[105] Bolton and Farrell conclude that a temporary monopoly (with open tender and specified investment obligations) may be the better solution if the investment requirements are high and the information asymmetry between state and investor is low (thus limiting the danger of the wrong selection). On the other hand, immediate liberalization should be carried out as long as investment requirements are not so urgent, and/or if the information asymmetry between the private enterprise and the state is large. This concurs with the conclusions of Armstrong and Vickers (1996, 313) that 'a reasonable case can be made ... for phased instead of immediate liberalization in basic fixed-link telephony, provided that there is *ex ante* competition for any time-limited monopoly concession, that its duration is short, that explicit investment requirements are agreed in return for the concession, and that there are effective safeguards against monopolistic abuse in the interim.'

In order to test the Armstrong and Vickers argument in favor of delayed liberalization, one would need to find indicators for the relative strength of the *expropriation risk* and the *liberalization risk*. There is some evidence that the expropriation risk was high in the first several years of transformation: in the telecommunication sector, for example, foreign investors faced classical hold-up situations in Russia and Ukraine (where some re-nationalization took place) and in Latvia (where agreed price increases were withheld by the government).[106] Given a relatively high expropriation risk, *early* liberalization might have been the appropriate answer. However, one observes that liberalization was *delayed* in most transformation countries, with respect to the initial reform projects.

---

[105] Given incomplete information there is a danger of choosing the wrong supplier, that is, the high-cost enterprise; the costs of this choice would be ($c_H - c_L$) with a probability of 25% (corresponding to a 50 percent chance of choosing the wrong supplier within a combination of c_H/c_L, which itself occurs in 50 percent of the cases ($c_{H,L}$ = high-cost, low-cost type enterprise, see Armstrong and Vickers, 1996, 307).

[106] Public Network Europe (various issues, *Yearbook*. London, The Economist Group).

One intriguing model of immediate privatization but only gradual liberalization comes from the Hungarian power sector, where the early privatization of large shares of power generation and power distribution companies brought foreign investment and technical knowledge to the sector, while the *gradual* liberalization reduced the regulatory risk (see Chapter 9). The compromise thus struck between early investment, productive efficiency and the gradual phasing in of competition turned out to be viable, preparing Hungary's power sector for EU accession better than that of any other transformation country. Armstrong and Vickers (1996) observe a similar gradual strategy in the Hungarian telecommunication sector, where phased liberalization assured a fast extension of the outdated system and thus favored network externalities and economic development. The subsequent empirical studies in Part II reveal further evidence of this, although universally valid answers cannot be given.

4.4.2 An unconventional solution: the unregulated monopoly

A radical solution to unstable institutional environments in a transformation or developing context has been proposed by Cowen and Cowen (1998): it is to *abandon* price or structural deregulation, in other words, to provide the enterprise with an unregulated (natural) monopoly. In this model, vertical integration is maintained, and the entire industry is auctioned off to a private company. The private monopolist then is allowed to price discriminate among different consumers, while at the same time having an incentive to produce efficiently and to serve as many clients as possible (as long as their willingness to pay is above the marginal costs).

According to Cowen and Cowen (1998, 30), and peculiar as it may sound, the unregulated monopoly simultaneously solves three central issues: i) *allocative efficiency* is assured through marginal cost pricing for the last client, thus socially inefficient exclusion does not occur;[107] ii) *productive efficiency* results from the incentives of the producer to engage in cost reductions, which are fully translated into profits; iii) a perfectly price discriminating monopolist has incentives to choose the adequate product *quality*, as the monopolist will choose the quality that maximizes gross consumer surplus (and thus profit, net of the production costs).

Five arguments have been raised against the simple solution of unregulated private monopoly (Cowen and Cowen, 1998, 31 sq.): first, price discrimination must be *possible* to a large degree; while this may be socially unwanted, technically it is not very complicated, and it has in fact already

---

[107] Note, however, that allocative efficiency is only assured in the *partial* model, limited to the sector under consideration. In the *general* equilibrium model, the price distortion in one sector leads to inefficiencies in the subsequent donwnstream sectors.

been practiced.[108] Second, *equity* and *distribution* problems may not be appropriately addressed, for example, the fact that the entire rent goes to the producer; however, it is questionable whether infrastructure policy could be a very efficient means of achieving distribution objectives anyway. Also, distribution of shares to the poor can relieve the equity issue to some extent. Third, *rent-seeking* costs for obtaining the monopoly position may consume real resources and thus be socially inefficient; however, these rent-seeking costs do occur in other regulatory regimes as well, and some money is economized due to the low expenses for regulation. Fourth, a limited ability of the government to *commit* to the unregulated regime may lead it to expropriate the private company just after the investment is sunk. However, the regulatory risk in an unregulated regime is not any higher than in a regulated one. Fifth, a *political economy* argument is that once the unregulated monopoly is installed, there will be no possibility to switch to a more competition-oriented regime later on, as the monopolist has obtained such a strong position that will prevent further reform.[109]

In sum, there are valid arguments against unregulated monopoly, however, most of them also apply to more competition-oriented regulatory models, and may even be worse in the latter. Cowen and Cowen (1998, 40) conclude that 'unregulated natural monopoly will bring problems of partial exclusion, bargaining costs, rent-seeking costs, and imperfect government credibility, but in comparative terms we do not see a knock-down argument against unregulated private provision in this context. Unregulated privatization should join the roster of plausible policy alternatives ... ' Clear evidence as to whether the delay of privatization and liberalization observed in many transformation countries had beneficial effects is not available. Some of the arguments mentioned will be checked concretely in the subsequent empirical chapters.

5. CONCLUSIONS

In this chapter, we have discussed arguments in favor of a specific infrastructure policy in Eastern Europe in the early phase of transformation.

---

[108] Cowen and Cowen (1998, 32) cite the water department of Los Angeles which has sufficient information about the determinants of demand of its clients (household size, size of yard, temparature zone, and so on) to perform some form of price discrimination; in reality, price discrimination may proceed by blocks (different blocks of a city are likely to have different price elasticities).

[109] While this effect could indeed be observed in transformation countries (such as the Russian gas monopolist Gazprom), it can also be argued that the institutional capabilities of the regulator, too, increase over time, so that alternative regulatory outcomes become feasible that are unavailable in the early transformation period.

The economic and institutional conditions for infrastructure policy were indeed specific: the 'socialist' infrastructure that had been underinvested in was insufficient to meet the requirements of a modern market economy; this structural change was accompanied by an economic depression more severe than the Great Depression of 1929–33. The subjective necessity to develop an infrastructure appropriate for European countries, and objective investment requirements (for example, to attain quality standards required for EU accession) lead to high short-term investment needs (estimated above USD 1,000 bn., about 6 percent of transformation countries' GDP for 15 years). A lack of state and private finance, high transaction costs, a particularly high level of risk and uncertainty, and a weak institutional environment furthermore constrained the implementation of traditional competition-oriented infrastructure policies.

One can identify four broad theoretical strands of reasoning in favor of a transformation-specific infrastructure policy:

– The *macroeconomic* argument suggests that additional infrastructure investments can help to overcome the depression, and that long-run economic growth is positively related to infrastructure investments due to the latter's positive spillover effects. As for Eastern Europe, there is little evidence either to support or to contradict this hypothesis for the first years of transformation;

– the *industrial economic* argument is based on the dynamic effects that infrastructure may have on the intensity of competition, on sectoral restructuring and on market entry. Phase I of transformation was indeed characterized by a high degree of market concentration and heterogeneous cost structures, so that infrastructure investments (both material and institutional) could be expected to have a particularly strong impact. Though it is impossible to quantify any of the proposed dynamic effects, some qualitative evidence can be identified to support this hypothesis;

– the theory of *investment under uncertainty* stresses the danger that in an uncertain context, 'waiting' may be the dominant strategy for all investors, leading to underinvestment and the absence of positive information spillovers concerning the investment conditions in a given country or region. Some authors argue that under these conditions, temporary state investment subsidies are justified to set the investment bandwagon in motion. However, it is unclear how an optimal institutional infrastructure policy to overcome the investment blockade should be conceived, which sectors should receive priority, and whether the dangers of state failure (such as continued subsidies) can be overcome;

– finally, the theory of *regulation* under uncertainty provides arguments in favor of only *gradual* liberalization and privatization, as long as the regulatory risk is high and investment and modernization are politically considered to be urgent.

Part II
Empirical Analysis

5. Survey and Methodology

Briefly, there is a lack of empirical work on the subject [institutional economics]; it is not sexy, and it is drudgery and hard work.
Douglas North (1999): Presidential Lecture at the Annual Conference of the International Society for New Institutional Economics.[110]

1. INTRODUCTION

This chapter links the theoretical discussion of Part I to the empirical analyses of Part II. Section 2 presents quantitative and qualitative evidence on infrastructure sector developments in Eastern Europe over the last decade, including evaluations made by international organizations such as EBRD and the European Commission. Section 3 then derives the methodology for empirical tests that is applied throughout the rest of this book. We employ a *comparative institutional approach* to assess the reforms and results of infrastructure polices in transformation countries over the past decade. Furthermore, we discuss the degree to which the empirical evidence can be regarded as representative for East European infrastructure policies in general.

2. QUANTITATIVE AND QUALITATIVE SURVEY

2.1 Some Key Indicators

Infrastructure in East European transformation countries has undergone substantial change during the last decade. The underlying theoretical reasons for this were discussed in Chapter 4. In essence, infrastructure from the socialist past did not correspond to the requirements of modern market economies. Table 5.1 provides some indicators of material infrastructure development over the last decade (1990 vs. end of 1990s). These indicators are not meant to provide bibliographic statistical coverage, but to highlight some aspects of infrastructure capacities and use:

---

[110] Reprinted in Ménard (2000, 7 sq.).

– *Telephone density* has risen sharply in all East European countries. The density of fixed lines has risen from an average of 15 percent in 1990 to about 30 percent in 1999. While this is still far from OECD teledensity levels, some countries are approaching them, for example, Slovenia and Hungary;

– even more spectacular is the rise of *cellular mobile subscriptions* which have risen from nil to an average of 25 per 100 inhabitants. In 2000, Slovenia featured the same number of subscriptions per capita than the USA, whereas the Czech Republic and Estonia have reached OECD levels;

– on the other hand, traditionally strong sectors such as *passenger transport* and *railway cargo* declined drastically during the 1990s (as indicated in Chapter 4), whereas both increased in Western Europe;

– the length of motorways increased at very modest rates (exceptions are Hungary and Slovenia). Motorway development remained behind the ambitious developments plans set out in the early 1990s (see for details Chapter 8);

– the development of *energy intensity* (in relation to GDP) shows two characteristics: first, energy intensity in Eastern Europe has been significantly higher than in Western industrialized countries, by a factor of up to 10 (Bulgaria, Romania, Russia) and even 15 (Kazakhstan, Ukraine) when compared to the average of OECD countries. Second, energy intensity dropped sharply in most East European countries (most drastically in Poland, Estonia, the Slovak Republic).[111]

---

[111] The absolute drop in energy consumption is moderated by the drop in GDP. It can be expected that even as GDP growth picks up again, energy intensity will decrease further, due to sectoral change and increased energy prices.

Table 5.1 Infrastructure development in the 1990s: selected indicators

	Main telephone fixed lines per 100 inhabitants		Subscriptions to cellular mobile services per 100 inhabitants		Passenger kilometers, index 1988=100		Ton kilometers, index 1988=100		Length of motorways in kilometers		Primary energy consumption per GDP (tons of oil equivalent per thousand 95 US-dollar)	
	1990	1999	1990	2000	1988	1999	1988	1999	1995	2000	1992	1999
Bulgaria	24.2	34.2	:	9.1	100	47	100	30	314	324	1.7	1.6
Czech Republic	15.8	37.1	:	42.3	100	51	100	38	414	499	0.9	0.7
Estonia	20.3	35.3	:	40.8	100	16	100	97	64	93	1.2	0.8
Hungary	9.6	40.2	:	30.7	100	59	100	32	293	448	0.6	0.5
Latvia	23.2	30.0	:	17.0	100	25	100	61	0	0	1.0	0.7
Lithuania	21.0	31.4	:	13.8	100	25	100	35	394	417	1.3	1.1
Poland	8.6	26.0	:	17.5	100	50	100	46	246	358	0.9	0.6
Romania	10.5	16.7	:	9.0	100	36	100	23	:	113	1.7	1.3
Slovak Republic	13.5	30.8	:	20.5	100	51	100	38	198	296	1.1	0.8
Slovenia	22.0	42.7	:	57.2	100	40	100	64	218	427	0.3	0.3
Ukraine	13.6	19.1	:	:	100	65	100	31	:	:	2.6	3.6
Russia	14.2	19.7	:	:	100	52	100	46	:	:	1.8	1.9
Belarus	15.4	26.1	:	:	100	106	100	37	:	:	1.4	0.8
Kazakhstan	8.0	10.8	:	:	100	49	100	22	:	:	2.9	1.7
Germany	51.0	42.0	0.90	63.5	100	177	100	121	11,000	11,515	0.1	0.1
USA	55.0	64.0	0.30	58.7	100	94	100	142	654,000	701,363	0.3	0.3
OECD Europe	40.0	46.0	2.10	40.0	:	:	:	:	:	:	0.2	0.2

Sources: National statistical yearbooks, IEA, EBRD, ECMT

2.2 Infrastructure Investments

Infrastructure investments have lagged behind official requirements, and were also lower than hoped for at the inception of reforms. As data on national infrastructure investment is scattered and highly diffuse, we take the investment activities of the three largest international financial organizations in this field as a proxy.[112] Between 1992 and 1999, some USD 25 bn. were invested directly in infrastructure projects in Eastern Europe in which the World Bank,[113] the EBRD,[114] and the European Investment Bank (EIB) took part (see Table 5.2). After a smooth start in the early 1990s, investments accelerated somewhat in the second half of the decade, but they did not come even close to reaching the investment requirements necessary for catching up estimated at over USD 1,000 bn.[115]

Figure 5.1 shows the distribution of the international financial organizations' infrastructure investments in Eastern Europe by country. In general, the early reforming transformation countries have received more investments than the late reforming countries in Eastern Europe.[116] Figure 5.2 presents the distribution of infrastructure projects among the main sectors of material infrastructure; investments into the transport and energy sectors are the most important ones, followed by telecommunication.

---

[112] One can assume that this data is proportional to the (unknown) domestic infrastructure finance. Foreign direct investment in infrastructure *without* the participation of large international financial organizations was rare in the first decade of reforms, and thus its omission does not alter the results substantially, with the possible exception of telecommunication.

[113] The data does not include sector adjustment programs.

[114] Only project finance.

[115] Until 1995, 12 percent of the financing by international financial organizations for emerging and developing countries was given to Eastern Europe and the CIS (EBRD, 1996, 59). Credits of *all* international financial organizations to private infrastructure projects world-wide amounted to USD 30 bn. during 1990–95; of this, about 10 percent (USD 3.2 bn.) went to transformation countries (EBRD, 1996, 59).

[116] The high figure for Russia has to be considered as a political contribution rather than the result of a particular comparative advantage of Russia in infrastructure.

Table 5.2 Infrastructure investments of international financial organizations in Eastern Europe and the CIS (1991–99)

USD mn.	1991	1992	1993	1994	1995	1996	1997	1998	1999	1991 –1999
World Bank	460	336	1063	1476	1296	1742	1627	1073	844	9917
EBRD	n.a.	506	808	623	732	823	968	690	816	5966
EIB	n.a.	219	528	350	690	1116	1533	2375	2737	9548
Total	460	1061	2399	2449	2718	3681	4128	4138	4397	25431

Source: Bank publications (by year of credit approval; EUR converted to USD at 1:1)

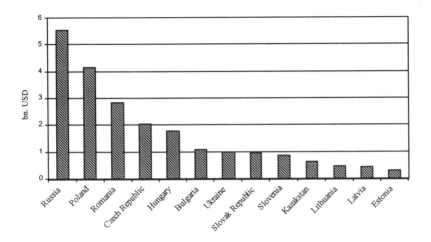

Source: Bank publications

Figure 5.1 Infrastructure investments of international financial organizations by country (1991–99)

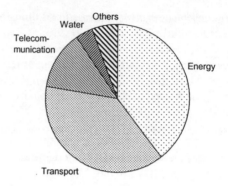

Figure 5.2 Infrastructure investments of international financial organizations by sector (1991–99)

2.3 Infrastructure Reform Indicators of EBRD

The evaluation of structural and regulatory sectoral reform also provides a yardstick for comparing the real results of a decade of reform with the initial expectations. Qualitative evaluations are carried out regularly by EBRD from a regulatory perspective, and from the European Commission from the political perspective of surveying the process of EU accession. The point of reference is, in both cases, the state of Western European infrastructure policies, and thus *not* an ideal-typical market competition-oriented model.

The *infrastructure indicators* have been developed and assessed systematically by EBRD since 1998 as a part of the overall evaluation of economic and political progress of transformation countries (see Carbajo and Fries, 1997 for an initial analysis). The indicators cover the most important material infrastructure sectors: telecommunication, railways, power, roads, water and sewage (the two latter categories were introduced in 1999 only, see EBRD, 1998, 44 sq., 1999, 50 sq., 2000, 41 sq., 2001a, 14 sq.). For each sector, an indicator assesses to what degree reforms were introduced. The evaluation is based on three criteria:

– *tariff reform*, that is, the introduction of cost-covering and allocative efficient price structures;

– *commercialization*, that is, the transformation of corporate governance structures, the introduction of hard budget constraints and, eventually, privatization;

– *regulatory and institutional reform*, that is,the setting-up of independent regulatory agencies with appropriate checks and balances, the definition of the formal institutional framework and the like.

Table 5.3 shows the aggregated infrastructure reform indicators for the five sectors from 1998–2002. The scale ranges from 1 (no market economy-oriented reforms at all) to 4.3 (full implementation of the sectoral regulation of Western European market economies). According to the EBRD indicators, three countries have come close to the Western European standards: Estonia (4.0), Hungary (3.7) and Poland (3.7); most other countries of Eastern Europe and all CIS countries are still not meeting the reference model; some countries have carried out virtually no reforms at all (Belarus, Tajikistan, Turkmenistan). On average, the reform-orientation of infrastructure policies has not progressed much in the late 1990s (average from 2.3 in 1998 to 2.5 in 2001). Whereas some market-oriented reforms can be observed in telecommunication (from 2.4 to 2.7) and power (from 2.1 to 2.6), reforms in railways, roads and water progressed more slowly.

The reforms of the infrastructure policies lag behind their point of reference, and they are judged inferior to the overall reform process of the transformation countries. Figure 5.3 compares the EBRD indicator for overall economic and political reform with the infrastructure indicator for each country. It turns out that in most countries, the infrastructure indicator falls short of the general reform indicator (an exception being Hungary).

The EBRD infrastructure indicator also confirms the emergence of three distinct groups of countries towards the end of transformation (Figure 5.4): in general, the *Central and Eastern European market economies* feature the most progress in infrastructure reform; in the *post-Soviet countries* (Russia, Ukraine, Belarus), reforms do occur, but at a low level; and the *Caspian state economies* are almost fully reform-resistant.

Table 5.3 EBRD infrastructure reform indicators

	Telecommunication				Railways				Roads			Power				Water and sewage		
	1998	1999	2000	2001	1998	1999	2000	2001	1999	2000	2001	1998	1999	2000	2001	1999	2000	2001
Albania	1.3	1.3	3.3	3.3	2.0	2.0	2.0	2.0	2.0	2.0	2.0	2.0	2.0	2.3	2.3	1.3	1.3	1.0
Armenia	2.3	2.3	2.3	2.3	2.0	2.0	2.0	2.0	2.3	2.3	2.3	2.0	3.0	3.3	3.3	2.0	2.0	2.0
Azerbaijan	1.3	1.3	1.3	1.0	2.0	2.0	2.3	2.3	1.3	1.3	1.0	2.0	2.0	2.0	2.0	2.0	2.0	2.0
Belarus	1.3	2.0	2.0	2.0	1.0	1.0	1.0	1.0	2.0	2.0	2.0	1.0	1.0	1.0	1.0	1.0	1.0	1.0
Bosnia-Herz.	1.3	1.3	3.3	3.3	2.0	2.0	2.0	2.3	1.7	2.0	2.0	2.0	2.0	2.0	2.0	1.0	1.0	1.0
Bulgaria	3.0	3.0	3.0	3.0	3.0	3.0	3.0	3.0	2.3	2.3	2.3	2.0	3.0	3.3	3.3	2.0	3.0	3.0
Croatia	2.3	2.3	3.3	3.3	2.3	2.3	2.3	2.3	2.3	2.3	2.3	2.3	2.3	2.3	3.3	3.3	3.3	3.0
Czech Republic	4.0	4.0	4.0	4.0	2.3	2.3	2.3	2.3	3.3	4.0	4.0	2.0	2.0	2.0	3.0	4.0	4.0	4.0
Estonia	4.0	4.0	4.0	4.0	4.0	4.0	4.0	4.0	2.0	2.0	2.0	2.0	3.0	4.0	4.0	4.0	4.0	4.0
Georgia	2.0	2.0	2.3	2.3	3.0	3.0	3.0	3.0	3.3	3.3	3.3	2.3	3.0	3.3	3.3	2.0	2.7	2.0
Hungary	4.0	4.0	4.0	4.0	3.3	3.3	3.3	3.3	3.3	3.0	2.0	4.0	4.0	4.0	4.0	4.0	4.0	4.0
Kazakhstan	2.0	2.3	2.3	2.3	2.0	2.0	2.3	3.0	2.0	2.0	2.0	3.3	3.3	3.0	3.0	1.3	1.3	1.0
Kyrgistan	2.0	2.0	2.3	2.3	1.3	1.3	1.3	1.0	1.0	1.0	1.0	2.3	2.3	2.3	2.3	1.0	1.0	1.0
Latvia	3.0	3.0	3.0	3.0	3.3	3.3	3.3	3.3	2.3	2.3	2.3	2.3	3.0	3.0	3.0	3.0	3.0	3.3
Lithuania	3.3	3.3	3.3	3.3	2.3	2.3	2.3	2.3	2.3	2.3	2.3	2.3	2.3	3.0	3.0	3.0	3.3	3.3
Macedonia	2.0	2.0	2.0	2.0	2.3	2.0	2.0	2.0	2.0	2.0	2.0	2.3	2.3	2.3	2.3	1.3	1.3	2.0
Moldova	2.3	2.3	2.3	2.3	3.0	2.0	2.0	2.0	2.0	2.0	2.0	2.3	3.0	3.3	3.3	2.0	2.0	2.0
Poland	3.3	3.3	4.0	4.0	3.3	3.3	4.0	4.0	3.3	3.3	3.3	3.0	3.0	3.0	3.0	4.0	4.0	4.0
Romania	3.0	3.0	3.0	3.0	4.0	4.0	4.0	4.0	2.3	3.0	3.0	2.3	3.0	3.0	3.0	3.0	3.0	3.0
Russia	3.0	3.0	3.0	3.0	2.3	2.3	2.3	2.3	2.0	2.0	2.0	2.0	2.0	2.0	2.0	2.3	2.3	2.3
Slovak Republic	2.3	2.3	2.3	2.3	2.0	2.0	2.3	2.3	2.3	2.3	2.3	2.0	2.0	2.0	2.0	2.7	2.0	2.3
Slovenia	2.3	2.3	2.3	3.0	3.3	3.3	3.3	3.3	3.0	3.0	3.0	2.3	2.3	3.0	3.0	4.0	4.0	4.0
Tajikistan	1.3	1.3	1.3	2.3	1.0	1.0	1.0	1.0	1.0	1.0	1.0	1.0	1.0	1.0	1.0	1.0	1.0	1.0
Turkmenistan	1.0	1.0	1.0	1.0	1.3	1.3	1.0	1.0	1.0	1.0	1.0	1.0	1.0	1.0	1.0	1.0	1.0	1.0
Ukraine	2.3	2.3	2.3	2.3	1.3	1.3	2.0	2.0	1.3	2.0	2.0	2.3	2.3	3.0	3.3	1.3	1.3	1.0
Uzbekistan	2.0	2.0	2.0	2.0	2.0	2.0	2.3	2.0	1.0	1.0	3.0	1.0	1.0	1.0	1.0	1.0	1.0	1.0
AVERAGE	2.4	2.4	2.7	2.7	2.4	2.3	2.4	2.4	2.1	2.2	2.2	2.1	2.4	2.5	2.6	2.3	2.3	2.3

Table 5.3 EBRD infrastructure reform indicators (continued)

	SUM 1998	AVERAGE 1998	SUM 1999	AVERAGE 1999	SUM 2000	AVERAGE 2000	SUM 2001	AVERAGE 2001
Albania	5.3	1.8	8.6	1.7	10.9	2.2	10.6	2.1
Armenia	6.3	2.1	11.6	2.3	11.9	2.4	11.9	2.4
Azerbaijan	5.3	1.8	8.6	1.7	8.9	1.8	8.3	1.7
Belarus	3.3	1.1	7.0	1.4	7.0	1.4	7.0	1.4
Bosnia-Herz.	5.3	1.8	8.0	1.6	10.3	2.1	10.6	2.1
Bulgaria	8.0	2.7	13.3	2.7	14.6	2.9	14.6	2.9
Croatia	6.9	2.3	12.5	2.5	13.5	2.7	14.2	2.8
Czech Republic	8.3	2.8	14.6	2.9	14.6	2.9	15.6	3.1
Estonia	10.0	3.3	18.3	3.7	20.0	4.0	20.0	4.0
Georgia	7.3	2.4	12.0	2.4	13.3	2.7	12.6	2.5
Hungary	11.3	3.8	18.6	3.7	18.6	3.7	18.6	3.7
Kazakhstan	7.3	2.4	10.9	2.2	10.9	2.2	11.3	2.3
Kyrgistan	5.6	1.9	7.6	1.5	7.9	1.6	7.6	1.5
Latvia	8.6	2.9	14.6	2.9	14.6	2.9	14.9	3.0
Lithuania	7.9	2.6	13.2	2.6	14.2	2.8	14.2	2.8
Macedonia	6.6	2.2	9.6	1.9	9.6	1.9	10.6	2.1
Moldova	7.6	2.5	11.3	2.3	11.6	2.3	11.6	2.3
Poland	9.6	3.2	16.9	3.4	18.3	3.7	18.3	3.7
Romania	9.3	3.1	15.3	3.1	16.0	3.2	16.0	3.2
Russia	7.3	2.4	11.6	2.3	11.6	2.3	11.6	2.3
Slovak Republic	6.3	2.1	11.3	2.3	10.9	2.2	12.2	2.4
Slovenia	7.9	2.6	14.9	3.0	15.6	3.1	16.3	3.3
Tajikistan	3.3	1.1	5.3	1.1	5.3	1.1	6.3	1.3
Turkmenistan	3.3	1.1	5.3	1.1	5.3	1.1	5.0	1.0
Ukraine	5.9	2.0	8.5	1.7	10.6	2.1	10.6	2.1
Uzbekistan	5.0	1.7	7.0	1.4	7.3	1.5	9.0	1.8
AVERAGE		2.3		2.3		2.4		2.5

Sources: EBRD, 1998, 44 sq., 1999, 50 sq., 2000, 41 sq., 2001a, 14 sq., some data estimated

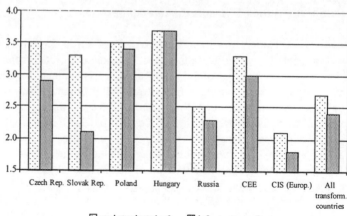

□ market-oriented reform ▒ infrastructure reform

Figure 5.3 Comparison between overall reform indicator and infrastructure reform indicator (2000)

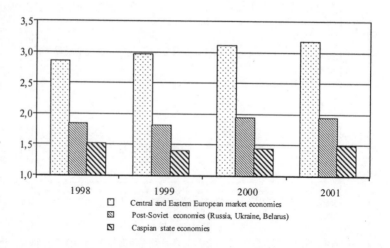

□   Central and Eastern European market economies
▨   Post-Soviet economies (Russia, Ukraine, Belarus)
◪   Caspian state economies

Sources: EBRD, 1998, 44 sq., 1999, 50 sq., 2000, 41 sq.

Figure 5.4 EBRD infrastructure reform indicators, by group of countries

2.4 Fulfilment of the EU *Acquis Communautaire*

The *political* evaluation of infrastructure sector reform in Eastern Europe is carried out regularly by the EU. In this case, the reference model is the degree to which the *legal framework* of the European Union is attained in each sector (*acquis communautaire*, which is not always purely market-oriented). The criteria have been fixed in the White Book of the European Commission 'Preparation of associated countries of Central and Eastern Europe to the integration in the internal market'.[117]

Table 5.4 shows the number of chapters in the White Book that each transformation country complied with as of 1997, that is, in the middle of phase II of transformation.[118] The compliance with EU legal standards was uneven, the average compliance rate being 44 percent. Two countries that were generally considered to have only a weak orientation towards reform featured the highest compliance rates (Romania, Slovak Republic), while reforming countries such as Estonia or the Czech Republic had advanced less in the adaptation of their legal systems. Among the sectors, environment and energy lagged behind with compliance rates of only 40 percent.

The development of the legal framework continued to be uneven after 1997 as well. The EU Accession Report 1999 reported that *Hungary, Latvia* and *Bulgaria* had made some progress in compliance with EU legal norms, while Poland and the Czech Republic still lagged seriously behind.[119]

---

[117] Document COM (95)163 final, Luxembourg, Office of Official Publications of the European Communities. The 'White Book' is part of the association strategy for the Central and East European countries decided by the European Council meeting in December 1994 (Essen). The White Book is supposed to guide the associated countries on the way to participation in the EU internal market. For each sector, the White Book specifies the central measures to be taken, the sequencing of reform, and the required adaptation of legal norms.

[118] More recently, analyses of compliance with the White Book are published by the European Commission in the annual 'Progress Reports on Accession'.

[119] 'The slow speed with which these countries [Poland and the Czech Republic] pursue the harmonization, and the policy of piecemeal steps are incompatible with the potential will of these countries to an early EU-accession.' (European Commission, 1999, Annex 2/99, 21, translated from the German original).

Table 5.4 Compliance rates with the EU White Book 'Association' in different infrastructure sectors

	Transport (no. of measures: 55)		Environment (no. of measures: 45)		Telecom-munications (no. of measures: 16)		Energy (no. of measures: 15)		Aver-age %
	ful-filled	compl. rate (%)	ful-filled	compl. rate (%)	ful-filled	compl. rate (%)	ful-filled	compl. rate (%)	
Bulgaria	1	2	2	4	1	6	2	13	6
Czech Republic	27	49	13	29	3	19	2	13	28
Estonia	9	16	7	16	0	0	7	47	20
Hungary	22	40	25	56	13	81	6	40	54
Latvia	24	44	6	13	6	38	4	27	30
Lithuania	37	67	20	44	10	63	10	67	60
Poland	33	60	15	33	9	56	7	47	49
Romania	40	73	38	84	11	69	9	60	71
Slovak Republic	52	95	29	64	11	69	8	53	70
Slovenia	43	78	24	53	3	19	5	33	46
Average (%)		52		40		42		40	44

Source: Bulletin of the European Union, Annexes 6-15/97

2.5 Difficulties with Pilot Projects

The assessment of infrastructure policy reform in transformation countries is also based on the difficulties of pilot projects attempting institutional innovation. In the early days of reform, governments, international financial organizations, industry and consultants competed with innovative proposals for how to realize a particularly rapid catching-up process of the Eastern European infrastructure. These innovative approaches have not led to the results hoped for:

– No major *private project financing* has been completed successfully in the 1990s.[120] The pilot project of private highway financing in Hungary (M1) was abandoned after only two years of operation; other projects of this type in Poland and Romania were modified at a later stage;[121]

---

[120] Hainz (2001) suggests in a theoretical model the opposite, implying that project financing is an important instrument for capital-starved infrastructure projects in transformation countries.

[121] Similar developments were observed in private infrastructure finance in other sectors (for example, independent power production in Poland, private concession for a communal water supply in Albania, concession financing of an airport extension in Ukraine).

– *private-public partnership* (PPP) models that boomed in Western Europe in the early 1990s faced difficult institutional conditions in post-socialist Eastern Europe and did not develop as dynamically as expected;[122]

– attempts to *unbundle* formerly vertically integrated infrastructure monopolists and to implement market-oriented regulatory models did not immediately work out (for example, power sector reform in Poland, Ukraine, Kazakhstan; railroads in Estonia), though gradual progress was achieved (for example, in Hungary and Kazakhstan);

– rapid price reform, which was often agreed upon in structural adjustment programs was delayed. Almost ten years into transformation, significant structural and absolute price distortions persist in power and gas (International Energy Agency, 2001: Energy Prices and Taxes; Stern and Davis, 1998), water (EBRD, 1999, 50), housing and, to some extent, also in telecommunication;

– instead of using the privatization proceeds to reduce the structural debt, these receipts were sometimes used to fill running budget deficits, a policy explicitly criticized by the EU.[123]

Positive surprises in the form of new, hitherto untested infrastructure policies, did *not* emerge in the transformation countries. In light of this fact, Schrader's (1999) criticism of the overall transformation process also applies for *infrastructure*: the transformation countries have not oriented their reforms towards a market- and competition-oriented infrastructure policy; instead their 'reforms' tended to emulate the reference system of the EU, which is only partially market-oriented.[124]

3. METHODOLOGY FOR EMPIRICAL TESTS

3.1 Comparative Institutional Approach

In this section, we describe the general approach to test the hypotheses developed in Part I empirically. *Quantitative* analysis cannot be used due to

---

[122] See EBRD (*Annual Report*, various issues) for some positive evidence. Breithaupt, et al. (1998) contend that private-public partnership *may* become a key instrument for infrastructure finance in transformation countries.

[123] 'The use of privatization proceeds to finance current expenditures gives rise to concern, in particular with respect to the considerable infrastructure investment requirements in all candidate countries, and the necessity of a sustainable financial equilibrium in the public budget ... ' (European Commission (1999, translated from the German original).

[124] Schrader (1999, 221) finds that the opportunity to introduce innovative, market-oriented solutions has not been used by the transformation countries; instead, the latter have followed traditional, conservative pathways. The infrastructure sectors are unlikely to provide an impetus towards institutional development in the transformation countries.

the insufficient data on institutional parameters; besides, the use of a quantitative, econometric approach to explain institutional dynamics within a relatively brief time span may not be adequate at all, given the unstable context. In view of the particular role of institutional factors in the transformation process and the instability therein, a traditional welfare economic analysis is also difficult to apply. In a situation of 'shooting at moving targets', the *comparative institutional approach* seems to be suited to providing guidelines for analysis and policy-making.

The comparative institutional approach is a method of analysis developed by institutional theory that is geared towards real-world problems, and rejects the idea of 'first-best' institutional settings.[125] In essence, the comparative institutional approach rejects the idea of a precise notion of 'efficiency' in a world full of indivisibilities, information asymmetries and other kinds of market failure (Demsetz, 1969, 19). If these market failures, called the facts of life 'can not be erased from life at zero cost, then truly efficient institutions will yield *different* long-run equilibrium conditions than those now used to describe the ideal norm.' (Demsetz, 1969, 19, emphasis added).[126] Whereas the comparative institutional approach does not lead to general policy conclusions, it is useful for comparing *specific* situations and thus for deriving *specific* policy recommendations (Demsetz, 1969).

In practice, the comparative institutional approach seeks to compare the real institutional arrangements with alternative ones, with regard to their capacity to attain certain pre-defined goals (for example, reduction of market and state failure, attaining certain prices, achievement of certain political objectives).[127] The comparative institutional approach can be pursued with different hypotheses and different methodologies, that is, quantitative measures, comparisons across countries and regions and stand-alone case studies (Alston, 1996, 29 sq.). Our choice of the *case study approach* is based

---

[125] '... Users of the comparative institution approach attempt to assess which alternative real institutional arrangement seems best able to cope with the economic problem; practitioners of this approach may use an ideal norm to provide standards from which divergences are assessed for all practical alternatives of interest and select as efficient that alternative which seems most likely to minimize the divergence.' (Demsetz, 1969, 1).

[126] The mere observation of suboptimal functioning of the market system does not automatically justify state intervention, as the efficiency of the latter to combat the inefficiencies of the former is in general not proven, nor is the very feasibility of state economic policy always clearly established. Fritsch et al. (1999, 357) consider the comparative institutional approach an indispensable policy tool that enables one to determine whether state economic policy is likely or unlikely to lead to an improvement in social welfare.

[127] By its very philosophy, the comparative institutional approach is geared towards *positive* results, though these can serve as a basis for normative policy conclusions (such as the definition of alternative arrangements to combat market failure). The comparison may cover the institutional arrangements in a given sector in different countries (cross-section) or over a certain period of time (longitudinal analysis).

on the fact that quantitative measures of institutional change and its impact on infrastructure policy are not available for the transformation countries.

In the following chapters, the comparative institutional approach is used to focus on the development of *sectoral regulation* from a dynamic perspective, including the process of information gathering, decision making, conduct and correction of regulatory measures; all this we shall call the *regulatory process*. The regulatory process results from interaction between regulatory agencies on the one hand and enterprises and other parties (for example, consumer interest groups, public administration) on the other: an interaction that is governed by explicit and/or implicit contracts. The regulatory process can be thought of as being determined by three sets of factors (Figure 5.5):

– Technical and economic *sector specifics* (such as capital intensity, cost structure, network effects, technical progress) determine the market structure and thus the potential role of regulation within a given sector. The assessment of sector specifics depends to a certain degree upon the exogenous point of reference (for example, when evaluating the state of technology, the point of reference can be socialist technology or the international state of the art). The analysis of sector specifics also includes the assessment of investment needs (for example, resulting from technical backwardness, or the objective necessity to fulfil certain technical standards);

– *actors*, *interest groups* and *organizations* should be considered in every institutional analysis (Wink, 1995). Schematically speaking, the outcome of the regulatory process can be interpreted as resulting from the supply of and demand for regulation on the 'market for regulation' (Stern, 1994). However, the structure of the actors and the distribution of interests may vary between countries and sectors. Therefore, the stylized presentation of organizations and interest groups set out above needs to be adapted to the sector and country specifics of the respective cases;

– in addition to these traditional building blocks of comparative institutional analysis, the regulatory process in Eastern Europe also depends upon the specific aspects of *systemic transformation* in these countries during the 1990s. Some transformation specifics are applicable to *all* transformation countries, such as the collapse of socialist infrastructure, whereas others differ according to the country or sector in question (for example, the urgency of investments, political, macro- and micro-risks, or the dependence upon Russian energy resources and technology).

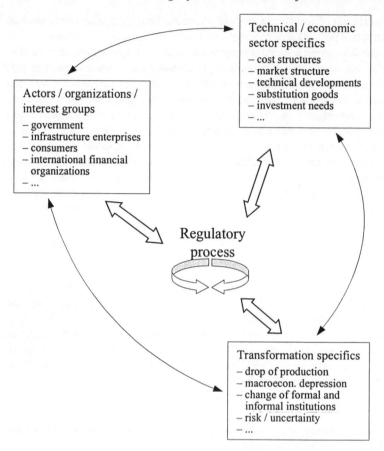

Figure 5.5 Stylized approach to infrastructure policy analysis in Eastern Europe

3.2 Selection and Conduct of Empirical Tests

In the remainder of Part II the comparative institutional approach is applied to analyze infrastructure policies in Eastern Europe. In each case we analyze the point of inception, the conduct and the results of reform with special reference to the specific sectoral, organizational and transformation aspects. The empirical studies are mostly longitudinal analyses, covering the transformation period from 1991–2001; in some cases, cross-section analyses covering several East European countries were added (Chapters 6, 7, 9, 10, 11). The empirical studies represent a broad range of infrastructure policies in

Eastern Europe. Most of the criteria set out in Chapter 2 in the definition of infrastructure policies are covered:

– The three aspects of infrastructure are dealt with: *material* infrastructure (highways, power, gas, Chapters 8, 9, 10), *institutional* infrastructure (options for private infrastructure finance, design of public infrastructure investment), different approaches to sectoral reform such as a big bang as opposed to gradual restructuring (Chapters 6, 8, 9) and *personal* infrastructure (innovation systems, Chapter 7);

– all four theories upon which arguments for a specific infrastructure policy were based are discussed: public investment, structural policy, investment triggering and transformation-specific sequencing and speed of deregulation (Chapters 6, 9, 10);

– the two main categories of transformation outcomes are described: the Central and East European market economies (Chapters 6–9), and the post-Soviet mixed economies (Chapters 7, 9, 10, 11);

– the need for infrastructure investment is determined as ranging from urgent (Chapters 8, 9, 10, highways, power, and gas sector) to not so urgent (chapters 7, 11, innovation systems and estimation of gas reserves).[128]

The empirical analysis was carried out between 1996–2001 within the framework of diverse research projects. Most of the data were obtained through *on-site* visits, thus, insights could be gained and the authenticity of information assured, which is difficult in ordinary desk research.[129]

4. CONCLUSIONS

Infrastructure development in Eastern Europe has been difficult, and it has not met the expectations, both in quantitative and in qualitative terms, in particular in phase I of transformation. The absolute figures on infrastructure investments provide evidence of this, as does the assessment of infrastructure sector reform made by some international organizations, such as EBRD and the EU. Innovative infrastructure policy instruments (such as private infrastructure project finance, big bang price and structural deregulation) have not delivered the expected results. One hypothesis to be tested is to what

---

[128] We have to acknowledge that the analysis does not cover all sectors, among those not treated in detail are telecommunication, water and transport infrastructure other than highways.
[129] Within the framework of this research program, about 30 infrastructure enterprises in several East European countries were visited; in addition, numerous meetings were held with regulatory agencies, other enterprises, national and international financial organizations and other participants of the regulatory process. The information thus gathered was enhanced and developed in further discussions with Western enterprises, banks, and governmental bodies.

extent the specific institutional and technical conditions prevailing in Eastern Europe at the time of systemic transformation may explain these findings.

The comparative institutional approach seems most appropriate when analyzing different approaches to and results of infrastructure reform policies in transformation countries. In addition, it provides applicable, real-world policy conclusions. Hence, the subsequent analysis focuses on the interpretation of the *regulatory process*. The latter is shaped by three factors: technical and economic sectors specifics, organizational structures and interest groups, and the specifics of system transformation themselves. The approach is applied to concrete infrastructure policies observed throughout the first decade of systemic transformation (1991–2001) in Eastern Europe.

6. Lessons from Public Investment Programs

For Russia, it would not be easy to refuse outright the offer of 60–80 billion US dollars. Europe, which should shoulder the lion's share, would not be paying too much. These funds are not grants. If successful, all this money will be paid back and Russia will avoid the abyss.
Alfred Steinherr (1999, 174): *Russia After the Downfall: Should Europe Watch or Act?*

1. INTRODUCTION

This chapter assesses some empirical evidence on the effects of large public investment programs (PIP) on infrastructure development in Eastern Europe. These programs were used by several governments as a strategic policy instrument, for example, in Poland, Romania, Lithuania, Latvia, Estonia, Hungary and Georgia. Later on, even post-Soviet countries (Russia, Ukraine) tried to institutionalize PIP. We test the hypothesis that governments and international financial organizations should provide massive financial support to infrastructure development in order to enhance economic development. Section 2 describes the philosophy of public investment programs as a policy instrument. Section 3 analyzes the sectoral priorities and sources of financing of PIP in the Baltic countries between 1994 and 1999. Section 4 presents macro-evidence on the problems of 'plan fulfilment', followed by Section 5, which presents evidence from project case studies. Section 6 concludes.[130]

2. PUBLIC INVESTMENT PROGRAMS: A CUMBERSOME PROCEDURE

What do infrastructure policies look like in the real world? This section provides an overview of PIP using the three Baltic countries as a case study:

---

[130] This chapter reproduces and updates parts of Hirschhausen (1999); thanks to Rasa Morkunaite, Gediminas Rainys, Raita Karnite, Peteris Gulans, Olev Lugus, Kaarel Kilvits and Jürgen Bitzer for critical discussions and background information.

Lithuania, Latvia and Estonia.[131] The very concept of public investment programs (PIP) can be regarded as a mixture between Soviet-style state planning and a Western-style medium-term investment program in the public sector. Officially, the objectives of PIP, as defined by the respective governments, are (i) to streamline public expenditure policies, (ii) to compensate for the lack of private investment and (iii) to create conditions conducive to private sector development by providing needed infrastructure, accelerating deregulation and creating market competition. As the number of domestic and foreign administrations participating in a PIP is large, complex coordinating mechanism have to be set up. Although these mechanisms vary from country to country, the *Estonian* scheme described here can be regarded as representative:[132]

In 1994, upon the recommendation of the World Bank, the foundations were laid for a state investment program that was to appear explicitly in the budget. Under the tutelage of the Ministry of Finance, a first round of projections took place in which each administrative level and budgetary organization set its investment requirements (for 1995: EEK 22 bn., ca. EUR 1.5 bn., were required). These 'plans' were then reduced in a second round to reflect the financial means available, (in that case: EEK 4.8 bn., not even one-fourth of the initial requirements).[133] The projects were supposed to be funded by a variety of sources: the central government budget, local budgets, foreign credits, foreign loans and foreign technical assistance, domestic financial markets and enterprises (self-financing). The projects are rolled over on an annual basis, that is, modified and updated yearly.

Within the Baltic economies, PIP play an important role. Table 6.1 relates the investment expenditures as projected in the national PIP to each country's

---

[131] There are several reasons for conducting a comparative analysis of these countries: due to their similar situations at the start of economic reform, infrastructure policies can be compared and evaluated directly. In addition, because of the post-Soviet nature of the Baltics, they share specific problems in their infrastructure policies, but reap benefits in terms of foreign support because of their upcoming integration into the EU. The diverging transformation paths that the Baltic countries have followed may also open up another interesting perspective: while Estonia is generally considered to be among the most successful transformation countries in Central and Eastern Europe, Latvia and Lithuania are still struggling with the implementation of structural reforms.

[132] Based on Kilvits (1998); the major difference from the other countries is that in the latter, PIP were mostly in the responsibility of the respective Ministries of Economics.

[133] A sub-department within the Ministry of Finance, with approx. 5-10 employees, was in charge of managing the process, whereas each line Ministry is responsible for its sector program. 'Intra-sectoral guidelines are established to screen project proposals according to a number of economic and social criteria. These criteria include strategic considerations (links to government objectives, the rationale for and appropriate form of government intervention, the overall policy context); economic viability; project design and costing; financing (sources of financing; recurrent cost-implications); and the project's impact on the poor.' (Kilvits, 1998, 4).

GDP: the result is usually in the order of 3–5 percent and in some cases is as high as 7 percent (Lithuania in 1997). In all Baltic countries, an increase in the projected ratio of investment to GDP could be observed between 1995 and 1996, with some reductions thereafter.

Foreign assistance is provided by long-term experts who usually are associated with the Ministry of Finance and paid by the EU's Phare program or World Bank projects. The main impetus that foreign institutions provide, however, is that they condition financial support for concrete investment projects upon the existence of a medium-term PIP. In other words, the very existence of a PIP is likely to improve the chances of financing infrastructure projects in a given country. All in all, the process of drawing up and coordinating PIP seems to be rather bureaucratic; in particular, the decision-making process is complex, and political considerations easily dominate economic arguments.

Table 6.1 Projected expenditures of PIP in percent of GDP (1995–99)

	Lithuania	Latvia	Estonia
1995	5.8	3.2	4.0
1996	6.1	4.6	4.9
1997	7.0	4.4	4.1
1998	5.5	4.0	4.1
1999	3.8	3.4	n.a.
2000	n.a.	2.1	n.a.

Source: National public investment programs[134]

3. SECTORAL PRIORITIES AND FINANCING IN THE BALTIC COUNTRIES

At first glance, the PIP of all three Baltic countries look very traditional and also seem to be similar in nature to one another; the two dominant areas are *transport* and *energy* (see Table 6.2). However, at a second glance, some peculiarities can be observed:

---

[134] Estonian Ministry of Finance/Assistance Coordination UNIT (PHARE/G-24) (1997, Public Investment Program 1995–97 (unofficial English translation). Tallinn); Ministry of Economic of the Republic of Lithuania (1995, Public Investment Program 1995–97, Main Report. Vilnius); Ministry of Economy, Republic of Latvia (1995, Public Investment Program 1995–97. Riga).

– *Agriculture* is a PIP title in its own right in all three countries. Projects include the modernization of production structures, organization of agricultural administration and privatization and training programs. The share of agriculture within the PIP was particularly large in the first years of reform;

– *health and welfare* increased their share in total PIP programs between 1995 and 1998, but at a relatively modest level (3–7 percent). This is in line with other post-socialist countries where public welfare has been placed at the lower end of their priority scale;

– *environment* plays an important role, and in Estonia, it comes second only to transport;[135]

– the low score of *education and science* in all three countries contrasts with the importance placed on environmental programs. In Lithuania and Latvia, education and science obtain particularly low (and decreasing) scores in PIP (1–3 percent).

As concerns *financing*, it has become evident that PIP depend heavily upon *foreign* contributions, be they in the form of bank loans, grants or other types of assistance (see Table 6.3). Foreign financing is clearly dominant in Lithuania and Latvia, and in Estonia it contributes almost half of total resources. Within the state financing, the *central* budget dominates, with local financing intervening in minor sectors only. This phenomenon presents a contrast to Western countries, where infrastructure is mainly financed at the local level. In only one country, Lithuania, are enterprise funds taken explicitly into account; these represent mainly self-financing from public infrastructure enterprises.

---

[135] Estonia may have a particularly strong incentive to bring its environmental policy up to EU norms, since it is strongly supported by neighboring Baltic Sea countries (Finland, Sweden).

Table 6.2 Sectoral priorities of PIP in the Baltic countries (1995–98)

in percent	Lithuania				Latvia				Estonia			
	1995	1996	1997	1998	1995	1996	1997	1998	1995	1996	1997	1998
Transport and communication	32.9	33.5	22.8	25.9	22.1	40.1	41.0	43.6	27.5	28.8	26.6	24.3
Energy	33.9	41.7	29.6	34.1	29.0	33.1	32.7	12.1	6.1	7.8	5.9	4.1
Environment	19.5	16.7	9.5	9.6	16.8	8.0	10.6	21.3*	25.4	22.4	21.1	24.1
Municipal services	0.0	0.0	5.1	4.4	-	-	-	-	5.2	5.3	5.0	7.9
Education & Sciences	1.7	2.6	1.0	1.5	3.2	3.6	4.7	2.1	3.7	5.0	5.0	4.5
Health & Welfare	1.9	3.8	2.7	2.6	5.3	5.7	5.6	7.3	1.9	3.0	4.2	5.9
Agriculture	3.9	0.5	2.6	0.4	7.2	1.5	1.4	0.6	3.9	3.8	3.8	3.9
Industry and Construction	2.8	0.8	15.2	5.6	-	-	-	-	-	-	-	-
Ministerial projects (unspecified)	-	-	-	-	3.2	1.7	1.8	10.5	-	-	-	-
Culture	-	-	-	-	5.2	3.2	1.2	0.8	-	-	-	-
Others	3.4	0.4	11.5	15.9	8.0	3.1	1.0	1.7	26.3	23.9	28.4	26.1
Sum	100	100	100	100	100	100	100	100	100	100	100	100

* including regional development

Source: National public investment programs

Table 6.3 Financing of PIP in the Baltic countries (1995–98)

in percent	Lithuania					Latvia						Estonia			
	1995	1996	1997	1998	1999	1995	1996	1997	1998	1999	2000	1995	1996	1997	1998
Central State Budget	17.5	26.3	22.1	31.1	38.9	36.2	18.8	16.3	26.9	38.5	43.9	45.2	46.8	54.8	55.9
Local State Budgets						29.0	33.1	32.7	12.1			2.3	3.0	3.1	2.6
Foreign loans, grants, assistance	53.1	49.8	59.2	55.4	47.3	42.5	49.3	48.6	60.1	37.3	35.1	44.9	41.3	32.1	36.1
Enterprise funds (self-financing)	29.2	23.1	18.1	13.5	13.6										
Other (special funds, state enterprises, unmentioned)						21.4	32.1	35.1	12.8	24.2	21.6	7.6	8.9	10.0	6.4
Sum	100	100	100	100	100	100	100	100	100	100	100	100	100	100	100

Sums do not always equal 100.00 due to rounding

Source: National public investment programs

4. DIFFICULTIES OF FULFILMENT AND CONTROL

Just as in the old socialist days, it is easy to draw up investment 'plans'. The real question, however, is whether PIP bear any relation to *real-world* infrastructure investments or whether, by contrast, they have remained the Potemkin villages of the past. A country-by-country analysis shows that in their early years, PIP could *not* be considered serious measures for stabilizing investment plans: in their first two or three years of implementation, the rate of fulfilment was unexpectedly low. On the other hand, some improvement in plan fulfilment over time may eventually suggest that the measure is being employed more earnestly:

– In *Lithuania*, the first year of implementation of the 1995–97 PIP have to be considered a failure when judged in quantitative terms: only 29 percent of the 1995 PIP were realized, with energy (36.2 percent) and social welfare (36.1 percent) scoring best. According to Morkunaite (1998, 16), the insufficient fulfilment of the 1995 PIP was caused by the lack of up-front analysis of projects and badly anticipated financing schemes. Whereas the projects financed out of the state budget were realized most successfully, extra-budgetary financial resources could seldom be obtained.[136] The most acute problem of PIP realization is a *lack of control* and coherence, stemming mostly from the bureaucratic struggle between the Ministry of Finance, the Ministry of Economy, other ministerial levels and the Department of Statistics;

– in *Latvia*, the first PIP (1995–97) was carried out almost as badly as in Lithuania (Karnite, 1998). Due to badly anticipated reductions in the state budget deficit and inefficient internal coordination, not even half of the original PIP was executed in 1995 (48.8 percent) and only 24.1 percent of the foreign loans were used.[137] Though the budget expenditures were more stable in 1996, the fulfillment of the PIP-plan remained low in 1996, at 40.9 percent for state funds and as low as 20.1 percent for foreign loans;[138]

---

[136] The same tendency continued through 1996, although an improvement in the overall rate of realization was observed: 49.9 percent of the PIP-planned investment volume was executed (state-budget financing: 61.8 percent, foreign loans: 51 percent, enterprise funds: 34 percent). The discrepancy between state budget resources and other sources of finance seems to remain structural, however, and in particular, the fulfilment ratio of industrial enterprises is deceiving, indicating rent-seeking behaviour (that is, promising intensive use of their own resources but ultimately relying upon state budgets).

[137] Due to the lack of appropriate execution of large projects in energy, transport, and environment, the two major ongoing projects of the 1995 PIP, amounting to 42 percent of total financing, were in the cultural sector only: the reconstruction of the National Opera House and of Riga Castle.

[138] According to Karnite (1998, 43), the discrepancy between the plan and the real outcome can be explained by delays in contracting of investment projects. Administrative delays are a further obstacle to execution, the 1996 PIP having been fixed in July 1996 only, that is, at a

– *Estonia* seems to be an exception to the rule, with a fulfilment ratio of the 1995–97 PIP of 99.5 percent (Kilvits, 1998). However, this data does not seem to be very reliable: not less than 13 of 19 executing bodies (ministries, local governments) are quoted as having fulfilled the PIP 100 percent or more, a fact that strangely recalls Soviet-type plan fulfilment ratios. Thus, a serious analysis of PIP fulfillment in Estonia is not possible.

5. EVIDENCE FROM PROJECT CASE STUDIES

The success or failure of PIP in Eastern Europe depends ultimately upon the way in which concrete projects are set up, financed and carried out. Case studies of two of the largest individual projects within the Baltic PIP may shed some further light on the functioning of infrastructure policies in these countries.

5.1 The Lithuania–Poland Electricity Project

The case of the Lithuania–Poland electricity interconnection is an example of a well-defined project that obtained early priority in the PIP, but which – for commercial, political, technical and institutional reasons – has not advanced much since. As early as the mid-1990s, a memorandum was signed between the Lithuanian and Polish governments to connect the two neighboring countries' electricity grids and thus to link the power systems of Central Europe (CENTREL) and the former Soviet Union (UPS). Beyond having a highly political and symbolic character (that is, linking the Baltic countries with Central Europe and closing the 'Baltic Electricity Ring'), the project also had a very concrete commercial rationale: it would allow Lithuania to sell cheap peak-load power from the Ignalina Nuclear Power Plant to Poland (about 3,300 GWh per year at a price of 3.5 US cents/kWh, produced at costs of 1.5 US cents/kWh only). The project was included in the Lithuanian Energy Strategy in 1994 and was given the highest priority in the preparation of the first PIP; indeed it was the largest project to be financed by 100 percent out of the PIP (USD 81 mn.).

However, notwithstanding the high priority, as of late 2001 negotiations between Lithuania and Poland have still not advanced, not even since the beginning of the first stage of construction (i.e. the extension of the Kruonis pump station). The inclusion into the PIP has not helped the project to

point in time where most investment decisions for the fiscal year have already been taken. Karnite (1998, 43) concludes that in Latvia 'these results evidence that PIP is not a serious planning instrument yet.'

advance at all, nor has it succeeded in attracting international investors. The project is facing difficulties for a variety of reasons (not all of them directly linked to the PIP):

– *Commercially*, it is not certain whether the investment costs (USD 81 mn., which seems to be a conservative estimate), will be covered by the price differential between Lithuania and Poland;

– *politically*, the export of peak-power to Poland is facing resistance from the Polish side, where – just as in Lithuania – the power sector remains largely state-controlled. The import of 3,300 GWh, it is argued by Poland, might result in the loss of about 12,000–15,000 jobs in Poland (including coal mining and indirect job loss);

– the *technical* complexity of the project seems to have been underestimated, in particular the quality criteria under which the CENTREL-grid, now synchronized with the Western European UCTE-grid, has to operate (frequency regulation, security standards, reliability of supply). The quality aspects have not been properly accounted for in the USD 81 mn. investment plan;

– last but not least, the *institutional infrastructure* of commercial projects of this type is not in place in the Lithuanian power sector, which is by and large run as a state ministry. The state company Lietuvos Energia has been formally commercialized but does not operate under hard capitalist budget constraints; the Ignalina nuclear power plant belongs to the unit for nuclear energy within the Ministry of Economy. The privatization of Lietuvos Energia, which could potentially spur massive capital inflow into the company, is not yet being pursued.

Under these unfavorable conditions, the 'priority project' within the PIP will not advance until the institutional conditions of the project are improved. Prerequisites include a substantial restructuring of the national power company, liberalization of the subsidized electricity prices, and the definition of a legal framework upon which domestic and foreign companies can rely in their medium-term development plans.[139]

5.2 The Estonian Railway Transit Expansion Project

The Estonian Railway (Eesti Raudtee) infrastructure program for the extension of transit freight between Russia and Estonia shows how a PIP-project considered to be commercially viable has been delayed because of the lack of structural reform in the sector; it also reveals that infrastructure projects, whether public or not, cannot be judged outside of the institutional

---

[139] Should Lithunia join the EU, there will be additional resistance to the project, as the Ignalina nuclear power plant is strongly opposed by the anti-nuclear movement in Europe.

and regulatory framework in which they take place. The railway connection between the St. Petersburg area and Tallinn has played a major role in transport for a long time, connecting the industrial centers along the Baltic coast (Petersburg, Narva, Köhtla–Järve) with the closest ice-free port in Tallinn (Muuga). In socialist times, this was an intra-Soviet Union connection, for which only physical capacity limitations (and no economic ones) existed: oil and oil products were transported from east to west, while oil shale and grain were the major products shipped in the opposite direction. With Estonian independence, Eesti Raudtee became the monopoly railway operator in Estonia and owner of the infrastructure. Russian traders continue to use the route for exporting oil and oil products, to the benefit of Eesti Raudtee: in 1996, the Narva–Tallinn track contributed about 80 percent of Eesti Raudtee's revenue (Kilvits, 1998, 24).[140] Considered strategic by the Estonian government in 1994, the modernization of the Narva-Tallinn track (in particular, the Tapa–Narva trunk) was integrated in the 1995–97 PIP and international support was gained from EBRD for the preparation of the 'Tallinn–Narva Line Capacity Study'.[141]

However, just as in the Lithuanian power plant case, the project has not advanced thus far: besides overall acceptance of the Tallinn–Narva Capacity Study, no concrete action has been taken to carry out the investment project, neither by Eesti Raudtee nor by the government or an international financier, and least of all by the Estonian Ministry of Finance, manager of the PIP. This can be explained by the fact that the potential of the project seems to have been overestimated and that the objective of increasing transit capacity could be attained by different, less costly means:

– The demand projections upon which the project was built seem to be unrealistic, given the drastic reduction of freight turnover (1990: ca. 7 bn. t-km railway freight turnover, 1996: about 4 bn. t-km only);[142]

– the plan is based on subsidized freight rates which – should Eesti Raudtee try to become a profitable enterprise – need to be significantly increased. This fact is left unmentioned in the feasibility study, though it is a critical assumption for forecasts;

---

[140] Estonian clients mainly use the route to transport oil shale from the quarries to the two power stations in the east of Estonia and to oil shale chemistry enterprises.

[141] A three-tier investment project was conceived, consisting mainly of the purchase of locomotives (to operate 6 kiloton trains), the upgrading of tracks and passing loops, and the installation and improvement of freight handling facilities in Tapa and Narva (Estonian–Russian border). Total investment volume is about USD 200 mn. (USD 41.6 mn. of which in the first priority and USD 93.7 mn. in the second priority round).

[142] The estimated increases of Russian oil export capacities through Tallinn from 7.5 mn. t (1995) to 21.1 mn. t (2000) and even 31.3 mn. t in 2006 (cf. Kilvits, 1998, table 5) seem to be unrealistic, too.

– there seems to be no immediate need for an increase of capacity, given the fact the 'there was no evidence that traffic was lost due to capacity constraints' (Kilvits, 1998, op cit, 25);

– finally, the institutional conditions for foreign investment are unfavorable in this case. Estonia has agreed to implement EEC Directive 91/440 (requiring the commercialization and accounting unbundling of the former railway monopoly), but has not fully implemented it until 2001.[143]

What is needed in order to advance the Tallinn–Narva modernization is not so much a PIP but a policy of deregulation of the railway system, including price liberalization. The east–west transit route under study is the cash-cow of the Estonian railways system. The sustainable modernization of the Estonian railway, including the Tallinn–Narva track, could be achieved by the following policy measures:

– Increase prices to levels where full cost recovery is achieved. The Tallinn–Narva track has to make a substantial marginal profit in order to cover a large part of Eesti Raudtee's fixed costs;[144]

– commercialize Eesti Raudtee fully;

– eventually separate infrastructure from operation, thus introducing competition in the (potentially profitable) operation business. Once competition in operation has been introduced, the remaining problem for the Estonian state would be to secure non-discriminatory access to the grid.[145]

6. CONCLUSIONS

What can be said on the usefulness of PIP in Eastern Europe? Empirical evidence suggests that efficient infrastructure investment policies are more easily 'planned' than actually carried out. This point is highlighted by the case studies of PIP in the Baltic countries (Lithuania, Latvia, Estonia), both at the macro-level and at the level of the projects themselves. Though the idea of streamlining public expenditure plans and improving internal and external coordination is attractive, it is difficult to demonstrate that these programs actually achieve the intended results. As is the case in most bureaucracies,

---

[143] The formal privatization of Eesti Raudtee, scheduled for 1997 had not been carried out by early 2002; even if one of the three private bidders is selected, it will not obtain full ownership of the railway, but rather obtain a management contract, including some investment obligations (Deutsche Verkehrszeitung (DVZ), 22.02.2001).

[144] If not even this route can be run profitably, then one is tempted to ask whether the Estonian Railway system should not be closed down altogether.

[145] At least three operators are potentially interested in managing the superstructure: the operation division of Eesti Raudtee, the operation division of the Russian October Railways, and the railway division of Muuga port; eventually, the large oil groups (such as Lukoil) would also want to compete with their own railway operation units.

problems of coordination, access to information and power struggles between administrations seem to dominate the real issue at stake, that is, the allocation of scarce (public) resources to their most efficient use.

Most PIP in Eastern Europe have targeted the classical infrastructure sectors such as transport, energy and the environment, where financing is relatively easy to obtain once the institutional conditions for investment and cost-oriented prices are put in place. Other infrastructure – for example, social, health and welfare, educational, scientific, and cultural infrastructure – was underrepresented. While PIP were already highly complex in their set-up procedure, this was even more so when it came to the procedures of *verification* and *sanctioning*. Plan fulfilment rates have been low in the early years of operation, and there does not seem to be an appropriate control structure in place. The skepticism towards PIP is confirmed by case studies at the level of individual projects. The analysis of two large, representative projects reveals that the decision to finance a project does not seem to depend upon the project being integrated into some kind of superior 'plan'.

The lessons for infrastructure policies in Eastern Europe seem to include the following: do not waste time or resources drawing up 'plans' as long as they can be only marginally executed and are not conducive to the success of individual projects anyway. Given the institutional instability in the region in the 1990s, large public infrastructure programs were not an indispensable policy instrument to streamline long-term investment, nor were they automatically conducive to economic growth. At the *micro-level*, an appropriate infrastructure policy seems to consist of creating the conditions conducive to private investment; for example, phased deregulation of former protected monopolies, gradual privatization of firms or parts of firms, and price liberalization. For non-commercial infrastructure (such as basic education), the principles of fiscal federalism should be implemented as extensively as possible, in order to allow regions and communes to react to local demand. A large Marshall Plan for infrastructure development is unlikely to be beneficial to East European countries.

7. Innovation Policies towards a Market Economy?

Departments and entire institutes have to end their work once their research subjects are outdated or are no longer carried out with the necessary scientific quality.

Dagmar Schipanski (1997): President of the German Science Evaluation Committee (Wissenschaftsrat).

1. INTRODUCTION

This chapter analyzes an infrastructure sector that is in general considered particularly important in the 'new economies' of Eastern and Western Europe: R&D and innovation. National innovation policies are often considered a catalyst for sustainable growth. For this reason, national innovation policies and the modernization of domestic science and technology systems (S&T systems) have been seen as necessities for the East European countries. Many hopes for a successful restructuring process were pinned on the presumption of an abundance of *immaterial* or *personal* assets in the Eastern European countries, such as solid S&T systems, a highly qualified labor force, sound technical education and therefore a breadth of innovative skills. Even today policy programs continue to be based on this assumption (for example, Cleaver, 2002). Thus the sector, though differing from the material infrastructure sectors that are analyzed in the subsequent chapters, fits into the analysis of infrastructure developments in East European reform process.

We propose a *qualitative, comparative approach*. Section 2 recalls the institutional specifics of innovation systems in the East European countries. Section 3 summarizes the existing literature on the reforms of the innovation systems at the sectoral level; it argues that innovation was mainly driven by the integration of East European enterprises into *international* innovation, production and distribution networks. Section 4 asks what the role of national innovation policies could have been under these conditions; we observe structural change may be blocked rather than accelerated by too much state engagement. Section 5 concludes in favor of demand-oriented innovation policies.[146]

2. INSTITUTIONAL CONDITIONS FOR THE REFORMS OF EAST EUROPEAN INNOVATION SYSTEMS

2.1 Different Approaches to Innovation Policy[147]

Before analyzing innovation policies in the context of transformation, it is useful to recall the fundamental difference between the ideal-typical functioning of an innovation system in socialism and in a market economy:

– In *socialism*, the structures and objectives of the innovation system were determined by the state. Competition within the innovation system could take place only within the political decision-making process;

– by contrast, in a *market economy*, innovation is but one factor amongst many others that determine the dynamic competitiveness of corporate enterprises. Innovation is not an objective or a value in itself, but rather is one parameter of enterprise strategies, or one axis of competition. Competition within the innovation system is governed by the willingness of the private (and to a certain extent, the public) sector to pay for the services offered.

The different approaches to innovation policies can be characterized as *supply-oriented* and *demand-oriented* (see Bitzer, 2000, 21 sq.): in a supply-oriented approach, the state tries to improve the conditions of the innovation process by means of input subsidies, preferably to so-called 'strategic branches', in the hope that the subsidies to the input side will improve performance on the output side. This approach corresponds perfectly to what Hayek had called the 'fallacy of knowledge' (*'Anmaßung von Wissen'*). In a context of systemic transformation characterized by structural breaks, supply-oriented innovation policy seems to be a particularly risky allocation of scarce resources. By contrast, a demand-oriented innovation policy is based on

---

[146] This chapter is based on the results of a research program at DIW Berlin within the framework of the TSER Project 'Restructuring and Reintegration of Science and Technology Systems in Countries in Transition', financed by the European Commission (GD XII), 1996–99. See Hirschhausen and Bitzer (2000) and the survey article Bitzer and Hirschhausen (2000).

[147] This section does not aim at providing a general discussion of the theory of innovation, but rather to point out the differences between the socialist and the market-oriented concepts. For a broader survey of innovation economics, see Dosi, Giovanni (1988, 'Sources, Procedures, and Microeconomic Effects of Innovation'. *Journal of Economic Literature*, Vol. 16, No. 5 (September), 1120–1171), Teubal et al. (1996), and Grupp, Hariulf (1998, *Foundations of the Economics of Innovation: Theory, Measurement and Practice*. Cheltenham, UK, Edward Elgar).

monetary demand as the dominant criterion for allocating funds. Only once a bottleneck in an innovation system has been clearly identified, and the private sector has shown an interest in filling that gap by *demanding* innovation services (and paying for them) might the government eventually intervene to support these innovation activities with funding. The demand-oriented approach assumes that the private corporate sector has an information advantage over the state in assessing the existing innovation potential.

2.2 Structure of the Socialist Innovation System

In socialism, 'innovation' was considered as an individual industrial activity in its own right. The socialist 'innovation sector' was organized, just as other sectors of production, according to short-, medium- and long-term *plans*. This reflected the fact that 'innovation' was considered not to be a service, benefiting other sectors, but an objective in itself. The planification process was oriented towards quantitative indicators and targeted mainly *input* factors.[148] Figure 7.1 presents the structure of the planification process of the socialist S&T system. In particular, it depicts the nature of that system's linear, input-oriented policy. The national and international socialist innovation systems were characterized by deep organizational hierarchies. Priorities were politically set, in particular the strengthening of the military-industrial complex.

The organizational structure of the socialist innovation system can be stylized as follows (Bitzer, 2000; Meske, 1998; Couderc, 1996):

– The institutes of the *Academies of Sciences* were the dominant actors in the field of basic research; in addition, they supplied some services to other R&D organizations (for example, database management, design, information gathering). These institutes were integrated into the hierarchy of the Ministry for Research, which implied an important organizational separation from the second pillar, the Branch Institutes;

– *Branch Institutes* for research and design were responsible for the development of technologies and new products up to the prototype level. Each branch institute carried out research on its respective industry. The branch institutes were subordinated to the branch ministries. However, there were few contacts with the sites of production – that is, with the real users of industrial R&D. The exchange of information and services between research

---

[148] According to the socialist theoreticians Kinze, et al. (1983, 406), the planification process of the R&D potential included the following quantitative indicators: a) the definition of the quantity of staff in research and development, including the differentiation of staff in universities and in polytechnic schools; b) the total expenses for science and technology, classified by the source of finance; c) the investments for research and development organizations.

and production was defined by the plan, which gave both sides ample margin for opportunistic behavior;[149]

– the *Science and Production Associations in the Military Sector* (NPO) were an attempt to overcome the discrepancy between research and production in this strategic sector (Couderc, 1996, 7). The NPOs were conglomerate networks that were coordinated *directly*, not through the planning hierarchy. They included research and design institutes, prototype testing, as well as production facilities;

– finally, the *Universities* also engaged in some research, although their main task was education.

Figure 7.2 shows the structure of the socialist innovation system that resulted from the socialist ethic of sharing work (see Bitzer, 2000, 15 sq.). The arrows indicate relations coordinated by the plan (an exception being the military NPOs). The strictly hierarchical, centrally coordinated innovation systems led to the following adverse effects that limited the productivity of the system (Berliner, 1976; Bitzer, 2000; Couderc, 1996):

– Concentration on scientific fundamental research, and less weight placed on the development of prototypes, testing and mass production of new products;

– low absorptive capacities, that is, the ability to convert externally available knowledge and research into the production process;

– few spillover effects within an industrial branch or between industrial branches;

– high share of S&T in total expenditure;

– tendency towards decentralized, autarchic developments, isolation from international R&D developments;

– dominance of *imitation* research in all areas where international technology was available.

---

[149] Research institutes could pretend to have fulfilled their planned objective by simply delivering a design, without having proven its usefulness in production; on the other hand, the production units could always argue that the research output they received was inappropriate and that subsequently they were unable to fulfil their plans. Also, the production units could argue that they were unable to change the product range, due to lacking innovation from the institutes. The results of this organizational design were products and production processes that remained unchanged for years or even for decades (such as the East German car 'Trabant'). This organization may be seen as the major reason for the low innovative capacity of the civil sector.

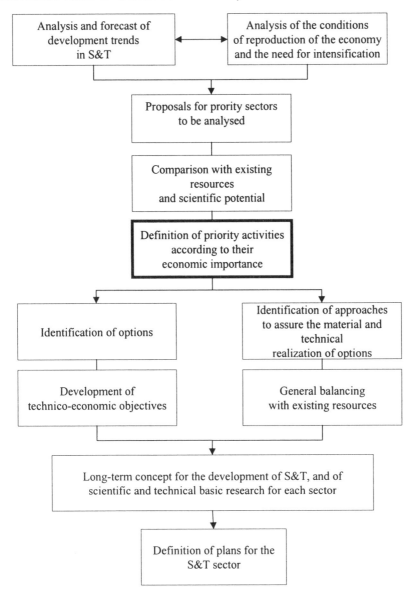

Source: Kinze et al. (1983, 406, translation by the author).

Figure 7.1 Long-term development planning of the socialist S&T system

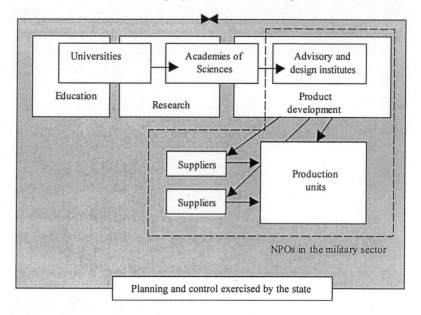

Source: Bitzer (2000, 16)

Figure 7.2 Stylized structure of the socialist innovation system

2.3 Disintegration of Socialist Innovation Systems

The breakdown of socialism left the East European countries with disintegrated innovation systems: the dissolution of the state power that had organized the innovation process led to the demise of the innovation systems (Bitzer, 2000, 23). In particular, *applied* research, which under socialism was performed separately from production, found itself without a function within an innovation system organized on market principles. The process of restructuring proved difficult. Although different paths of transformation can be identified between different countries, all reforming countries faced similar initial conditions (Bitzer, 2000, 23 sq.; Meske, 1998):

– The main challenge consisted in adapting the innovation system to *market economy* requirements. In a market economy, innovation and R&D are above all a matter for private enterprises, unless some substantial market failure can be proven (such as large positive external effects in basic research). The degree of outsourcing of R&D ('make-or-buy') is also a decision that *private* companies should make, and it depends largely upon the transaction costs of internal or external supply. The existence of private R&D

institutes should depend upon the willingness to pay that the market expresses for its services;[150]

– the breaking-up of the former socialist sharing of work between CMEA countries reduced the potential of individual institutes significantly. The patterns of national and international cooperation had been defined on political terms; the disintegration of these relations implied an individualization of the R&D institutes and a loss of both supply and demand networks;[151]

– the abrupt end of socialist technological trajectories reinforced the slump of demand for the socialist innovation capacities (Bitzer, 2000, 27). The technological systems that had been developed in socialist times were in most cases neither compatible with the international state of technology, nor competitive as stand-alone technologies. Examples of the break in technological trajectories are the computer and software industries and telecommunication, but also more traditional branches such as shipbuilding and the food industry (see below);

– given the modified structure of demand for innovation services, the socialist innovation 'potential' was significantly reduced. The devaluation of the innovation potential was particularly heavy in applied research and in design. But even in basic research, the necessary adaptation to international standards (for example, publications, quality standards, participation in international research projects) led to a devaluation of the human capital accumulated in socialist times;

– with the opening of the transformation countries to foreign trade, the R&D organizations, too, were forced into international competition. East European enterprises could choose between domestic and foreign supply of R&D services. This option was used extensively by the corporate sector. The integration into the global market of innovation services also forced the transformation countries into a specialization of R&D activities;

– the major macroeconomic determinant of restructuring was the slump of GDP and the reduction of public financing of the innovation system.

Given the specific conditions of systemic transformation, the disintegration of the socialist innovation system and the subsequent fragmentation could not have been avoided even by the most voluntaristic state innovation policy. Figure 7.3 sketches out the structural break within the innovation system that led to the fragmentation of the former system and the diversification of

---

[150] The fact that these principles are not always applied in market economies either does not change the theoretical foundation of the argument.

[151] A striking example are the R&D institutes in the Baltic Soviet Republics that had been created in socialist times to supply the production of military and civil electronic devices for 271 mn. people. In the transformation period, the supply chains of production disappeared, and the markets were reduced to small national or at best intra-regional (Baltic) markets of about 10 mn. people.

enterprise structures (see Bitzer, 2000, 24 sq.). The former links between the universities, the academies of sciences and product development were cut. The former branch institutes were transformed into business research enterprises (or disappeared altogether). The planned links between the design institutes and the production enterprises were also largely abolished, the latter having to establish new networks for R&D and innovation services.

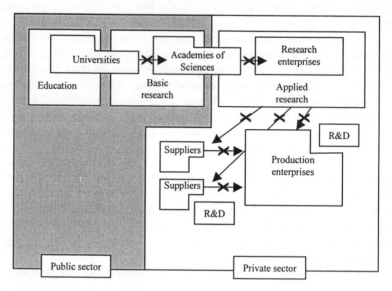

Source: Bitzer (2000, 25)

Figure 7.3 Structural breaks in the innovation systems in transformation

The sharpness of the transformation of socialist towards market-oriented innovation systems can also be indicated by some aggregate figures such as employment and R&D expenditures:

– In all East European transformation countries, employment in the innovation system was sharply reduced, by around 45 percent in the Central and East European countries and by almost 50 percent in the post-Soviet countries (Meske, 1998, 36 sq.). Country studies show that the reduction of employment was particularly marked in *industrial* R&D: whereas in socialist times industrial R&D had featured the highest employment figures, the figures dropped in the early 1990s to levels similar to those of the academies and universities;

– the R&D intensity of GDP was reduced in the first years of reform, *parallel* to the drop of GDP itself (Table 7.1). This drop was particularly marked in countries with an initial high R&D intensity, such as the Czech

Republic and Slovakia. A stabilization can be observed in phase II of transformation, in some countries the R&D/GDP ratio even increased slightly.

From a macro-perspective, the drastic quantitative and qualitative changes in the innovation system should not be regarded as negative, but rather as the starting point of an alignment to 'normal' levels. Given the change of the entire innovation system, a reduction of quantitative inputs (employment, financing) seems to have been unavoidable. The productivity of the socialist S&T system had been low and heavily oriented towards basic research and, in internationally comparative terms, it had been excessively large with respect to *per capita* income. In spite of the scaling down that had already occurred, R&D intensity in the East European transformation countries was not lower than in EU countries with a comparable *per capita* income, or in comparable emerging countries.[152]

The following two sections draw a more differentiated picture of the development from a *bottom-up* perspective, in particular the growing duality between rapid adaptation at the enterprise level and structurally conservative innovation policies conducted by the East European CIS governments at the national level.

---

[152] Thus, the R&D intensity in Slovenia and in the Czech Republic was twice that of Portugal and Greece in the second half of the 1990s; research intensity in the Slovak Republic was about as high as that in Italy, although Italy's per capita income was more than twice as high (Bitzer and Hirschhausen, 2000, 185). An extensive statistical analysis by Radosevic and Auriol (1999) confirms that Eastern European R&D expenditures were in fact *not* as low as generally assumed when compared to other countries of similar income and that the contrary might even be the case.

Table 7.1 R&D expenditure by Central and East European countries
(1991–99, percent of GDP)

	1991	1992	1993	1994	1995	1996	1997	1998	1999
Czech Republic	2.12	1.84	1.36	1.26	1.12	1.10	1.16	1.24	1.25
Slovak Republic	2.56	1.88	1.45	1.02	1.04	1.02	1.18	0.82	0.68
Hungary	1.12	1.09	1.01	0.93	0.76	0.68	0.74	0.68	0.69
Poland	1.10	0.85	0.83	0.84	0.75	0.72	0.72	0.72	0.75
Bulgaria	1.53	1.64	1.19	0.88	0.62	0.52	0.52	0.59	0.59
Romania	0.90	0.79	0.88	0.74	0.71	0.71	0.58	0.49	0.41
Slovenia[1]	-	1.49	1.61	1.75	1.69	1.44	1.42	1.48	1.51
Estonia[1]	-	-	0.60	0.73	0.61	0.57	0.57	0.61	0.75
Latvia[1]	-	-	0.49	0.43	0.53	0.48	0.43	0.45	0.40
Lithuania	-	-	0.43	0.51	0.48	0.52	0.57	0.57	0.52
EU accession candidates	1.56	1.37	0.98	0.91	0.84	0.76	0.71	0.76	0.71
EU 15[2]	1.90	1.92	1.94	1.91	1.89	1.88	1.86	1.87	1.92
of which:									
Germany	2.61	2.48	2.42	2.33	2.30	2.29	2.30	2.31	2.44
Italy	1.24	1.20	1.14	1.07	1.01	1.03	0.99	0.99	1.04
Spain	0.85	0.89	0.89	0.82	0.82	0.85	0.86	0.85	0.86
Portugal	-	0.63	0.60	-	0.63	-	0.65	-	0.76
Sweden	2.87	-	3.19	-	3.58	-	3.82	3.75	3.80

[1] In percent of GNP
[2] Excluding Luxembourg

Source: Bitzer and Hirschhausen (2000, 184); Eurostat

3. THE GLOBALIZING INNOVATION NETWORKS OF EAST EUROPEAN ENTERPRISES

3.1 Different Types of International Integration

The literature on industrial development and catching up usually distinguishes three types of international integration: *market* integration is the purely downstream-oriented integration in international markets (for buying and selling products), *production* integration also includes the integration of international production processes and networks, whereas *innovation* integration also covers the upstream innovation process, that is, an enterprise's participation in product or process innovation.

Most development economists consider innovation integration to be more important for a sustainable catching-up process than production integration, which is in turn considered superior to pure market integration.[153] This may be based on the idea that innovation integration favors the development of an indigenous human capital and therefore may have longer-term effects than simple market-integration. On the contrary, a market economic approach implies that the degree of integration should be determined by the marginal costs and the marginal benefits it brings about and that there can be no priority of one particular form of integration over the other. One-sided support of innovation integration is therefore inadequate.[154]

Given the dissolution of former innovation networks in Eastern Europe and the necessary reorientation of production and sales strategies of the enterprises, each element of the socialist innovation system (research units, institutes, production enterprises, etc.), too, was obliged to develop or integrate into *new* innovation networks. In this process, most units have striven to transform themselves into commercial enterprises. The immediate availability of internationally leading technology and products resulted in a low need for an original domestic R&D activity by Eastern European enterprises. Furthermore, the specialization most of them adopted was in labor-intensive, relatively low-tech products. Thus, their reorientation depended less on product or production innovation and more on the adaptation of *existing* knowledge and technology. The most important success factor on the way to competitiveness was not the ability to innovate, but the ability to *imitate*, that is, the ability to identify internationally existing knowledge and adapt it to one's own production and sales activities. This is shown in Figure 7.4, the stylized structure of the innovation system of a transformation country, in the strong links between domestic production enterprises and international networks.

Under the specific conditions of systemic change in Eastern Europe, national innovation or S&T systems were unlikely to have a strong impact on enterprise restructuring, the latter depending mainly on the access to markets, knowledge and technology. This process was largely driven by the integration of enterprises into *existing* or *emerging* global production and sales networks or their development, leaving little space for domestic, sectorally-oriented policies. Thus it is the *globalization of industry and innovation* that contributed to the restructuring of national innovation systems, rather than national innovation policies. By contrast, independent problem-solving

---

[153] This opinion is expressed *inter alia* by Radosevic, in Hutschenreuter, et al. (1999).
[154] One could even argue that in Eastern European, market integration (for example, the purchase of foreign technology) is a *precondition* for product integration (such as the participation in containership production using imported electronic systems), the latter may then lead to true innovation integration (for example, the joint development of radar systems for navigation).

strategies, whether at the national or even at the regional level, were unlikely
to be successful.

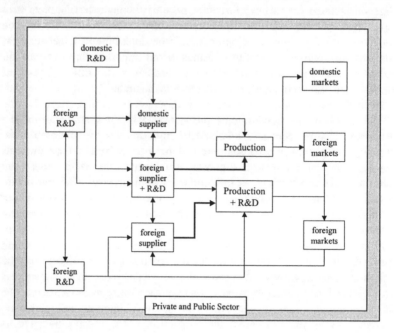

*Figure 7.4 The stylized innovation system in East European countries after
transformation*

3.2 Evidence from Sectoral Case Studies

The importance of the globalization of industry and innovation networks as
the major driver of catching-up of Eastern European enterprises can be shown
by detailed studies of the changing nature of *sectoral* innovation processes.
The following section summarizes evidence from an extensive survey of
industrial restructuring in Eastern Europe, presented in-depth in Hirschhausen
and Bitzer (2000, which also explains the choice of sectors, the methodology
used, and so on).

– The *car industry* in Eastern Europe is a case of both radical restructuring
in the post-socialist context and a very quick integration into *international*
multi-layer R&D, production and sales networks.[155] Today, the leading car
producers in the EU accession countries, such as Skoda (Czech Republic),

---

[155] See Richet, Xavier, and Frederic Bourassa (2000, 'The Reemergence of the Automotive
Industry in Eastern Europe'. In: Hirschhausen and Bitzer, 2000, 59-94).

FSM Fiat (Poland) and Magyar Suzuki (Hungary), all sell their cars on Western European markets. The modernization of Eastern European enterprises relied on a variety of factors: not only the restructuring of existing firms, the liquidation of obsolete assets and the development of new functions, but also the development of new, international networks of subcontracting companies and the reliance on skilled labor, new services and financing. It follows that the automotive industry in Eastern Europe does not need to rely on high technology to remain competitive in its dominant segments.[156]

– The case of the *shipbuilding* industry shows how the restructuring of a supposedly 'heavy' industry in Eastern Europe also depended on the integration of shipyards into international networks characterized by high-tech, information-dominated, logistically intensive processes.[157] In this industry, supplier networks are playing an increasingly crucial role in the development and the production of ships, covering up to 70 percent of the added value. In Eastern Europe, restructuring from highly integrated shipyards towards non-integrated production structures with an efficient supplier network was a basic condition for success. The technological gap turned out not to be a problematic factor for restructuring. Thus, the two most advanced Polish shipyards (Szczecin and Gdynia) have quickly integrated international supplier and downstream networks such as shipping companies and finance, and are now competing successfully on international markets.[158] A specific innovation policy was not needed as there was no evidence for constraints through proprietary technology and financial restructuring is well under way. In general, there was little evidence of market failures which would warrant state support for national shipbuilding.

– The *telecommunication* sector, too, had to be completely restructured in the transformation countries.[159] The creation of equipment enterprises and the transformation of former monopolist service providers have been dominated by *foreign investment*, introducing most of the technical and regulatory know-how. The overall macroeconomic framework on the one hand, and sector-specific conditions such as the regulatory framework and treatment of foreign

---

[156] The situation in Eastern Europe may be compared to the UK, a country which no longer has any domestic car producers and where the appropriation of know-how has generally been facilitated not by setting up specific S&T institutions but by the accumulation of experience gained through the cooperation with foreign car manufacturers.

[157] See Hirschhausen Christian, and Jürgen Bitzer (2000, 'Eastern European Shipbuilding's Cruise Towards World Markets'. In: Hirschhausen and Bitzer, 2000, 129-160).

[158] See for example, the early case study on the Szczecin-yard by Johnson, Simon, David T. Kotchen, and Gary Loveman (1995, 'How One Polish Shipyard Became a Market Competitor'. *Harvard Business Review*, Vol. 6, 53–72). The example of Poland, which emerged as the fifth-largest shipbuilding country world-wide, shows that the potential can be put to work once the external conditions favor restructuring.

[159] See Müller (2000).

direct investment on the other, have had significant consequences for the development of the basic access networks and related services. The East European countries showed different approaches to policy reform, ranging from opening the market to dominant foreign investors (for example, Latvia and Hungary) to a much more state-controlled approach (for example, Russia). The cases in which domestic equipment producers were protected (for example, by local-content obligations) do not seem to have had beneficial results (for example, Poland).

– Computer *software* is another case of profound reorganization of industry and innovation structures.[160] The rapid introduction and absorption of new international hardware technologies after the collapse of socialism required a completely *different* kind of software, not only in terms of the software technology used, but also in terms of the areas of application. With the development of the computer market, the demand for more complex software solutions increased and led to more sophisticated activities on the part of Eastern European software enterprises. The remaining segments were dominated by the well-known international software companies. The software sector was not a specific target of any of the Eastern European governments' innovation policies, and indeed, there seems to be no need for this.

– The restructuring of the Eastern European *computer* industry is to a certain extent a success story: domestic enterprises developed international supply networks from scratch and applied their own ingenuity to emerge among the domestic market leaders.[161] Initially, the new enterprises started to trade in Western computers, computer components and suitable software. After having gained some experience in this business, they started to assemble PCs themselves. The required components were mainly imported from the Far East or the USA, that is, from the S&T systems of their *foreign* suppliers. The fact that only PC assembling is carried out in Eastern European countries (and thus no mainframe or supercomputer production) should not be seen as a negative development, because it is in line with global PC production structures. Given the low barriers to entry and the smoothness of the restructuring process thus far, there seems to be little opportunity for a public policy to support the development and improve the competitiveness of the East European computer industries.

---

160 See Bitzer, Jürgen (2000, 'Software: New Industries and New Enterprises in Eastern Europe'. In: Hirschhausen and Bitzer, 2000, 227-256).
161 See Bitzer, Jürgen (2000, 'The Eastern European Computer Industry: National Champions with a Screwdriver'. In: Hirschhausen and Bitzer, 2000, 257-282); see also the more detailed study by Bitzer, Jürgen (2000, *The Applicant Countries' Ability to Withstand Competitive Pressure upon EU-Accession: The Information and Telecommunication Sector*. Berlin, Brussels, Study carried out for the European Commission, DG Enterprise).

4. OBSTACLES TO MARKET-ORIENTED INNOVATION POLICIES

4.1 Dominance of State Financed R&D and Employment

Whereas many East European enterprises have adapted their needs for innovation services rapidly to the new production and sales networks, many East European *governments* have attempted to maintain the former structures of the socialist innovation system as such, in particular the Institutes of the Academies of Science and some of the Branch Institutes. In many cases inadequate efforts were made to verify whether such institutions would in fact manage to become competitive. In most East European countries, the high research intensity, in relation to per capita incomes, was maintained through *public* spending (Table 7.2).[162] In Poland, Romania, Estonia and Latvia, state-financed R&D accounts for a larger proportion of the national total than the average figure for the EU; in the Czech and Slovak Republics and in Slovenia, the figure was equal to the EU average.[163] Thus Eastern Europe featured an inverse structure of financing, when compared to the EU, in which over 50 percent of R&D is financed by the *private* corporate sector. Few East European counties have achieved a significant increase of private sector R&D financing.

Other indicators for structural conservatism come from country studies of national innovation policies. Thus, Meske (1998, 49 sq.) observes far-reaching restructuring of industrial research in only one East European country, the Czech Republic; all other countries were still trying to restructure the state-financed industrial R&D, with more or less success. The problematic nature of public support for R&D also emerges from the analysis of the distribution of *R&D personnel* between the public and the private sector, if compared with EU averages (Table 7.3). In all East European countries, with the exception of the Czech Republic and Romania, considerably more than half of total R&D employment was in the state sector and higher education. Clearly, structural change in the innovation system has made only sluggish progress, particularly in the Baltic countries.

In spite of the efforts made by government to promote R&D, most of the countries have so far failed to bring about a substantial increase in the role played by *private* companies in R&D, either in the form of in-house R&D efforts or as demanders of R&D services. Two main reasons may be put

---

[162] This analysis refers mainly to phase I of transformation, for which full data is available.

[163] Moreover, it should be noted that these figures are likely to represent the lower limit, as many East European companies are still owned by the state, even if their shares are traded on the stock market, and their R&D expenditure is counted as private sector R&D (examples are Bulgaria and the Slovak Republic).

forward for this: first, the East European transformation economies were characterized by a corporate structure based largely on small- and medium-sized firms,[164] a fact normally associated with limited R&D efforts. Second, enterprises in these countries focus on the production of labor-intensive and low-tech goods, the area in which they enjoy a comparative advantage over EU enterprises.

Table 7.2 Spending on R&D by Central and East European countries, by source of funds (1995)

	Source of funds					Memo item		
	Private sector	Govern- ment	Higher edu- cation	Non- profit organi- zations	Foreign	Relative size of public sector		R&D expen- ditures as a % of GDP
						EU-15 = 100	As a % of GDP	
Czech Republic	63.1	32.3	1.3	-	3.3	83	0.36	1.12
Slovak Republic	60.4	37.8	0.1	-	1.6	97	0.39	1.04
Hungary	36.3	49.3	-	4.0	4.6	127	0.37	0.76
Poland	31.8	64.4	2.1	-	1.7	166	0.48	0.75
Bulgaria	60.5	35.1	3.8	0.4	0.1	90	0.25	0.72
Romania	32.9	63.3	0.5	-	3.2	163	0.45	0.71
Slovenia	45.5	40.9	-	10.3	3.3	105	0.69	1.69
Estonia	12.9	71.3	6.2	-	9.6	183	0.43	0.61
Latvia	20.5	53.0	-	3.7	22.8	136	0.28	0.53
Lithuania	24.7	68.7	-	-	6.6	177	0.33	0.48
EU- accession candidates	37.9	50.6	2.3	4.1	5.2	130	0.41	0.84
EU 15[1]	52.5	38.9	0.6	1.3	6.8	100	0.75	1.93
of which:								
Germany	61.1	36.8	-	0.3	1.8	95	0.85	2.30
Italy	41.7	53.0	-	-	5.3	136	0.54	1.01
Spain	44.5	43.6	4.4	0.8	6.7	112	0.36	0.82
Portugal	19.0	65.2	1.0	3.0	11.9	168	0.41	0.63
Sweden	68.5	21.6	0.9	1.0	8.1	56	0.29	1.34

[1] Excluding Luxembourg

Source: Bitzer and Hirschhausen (2000, 187)

---

[164] European Commission (1998, *Enterprises in Europe*, Fifth Report, SME Project. Luxembourg, Office for Official Publications of the European Community, 488 sq.).

Table 7.3 R&D personnel by sector

| | Year | Sector | | | | |
		Private sector	Government	Higher education	Total public sector	Total
Czech Republic	1995	50.0	33.7	16.3	50.0	100
Slovak Republic	1995	30.0	41.9	28.1	70.0	100
Hungary	1995	34.7	33.1	32.2	65.3	100
Poland	1995	31.7	26.2	42.1	68.3	100
Bulgaria	1996	14.1	59.2	26.6	85.8	100
Romania	1995	78.8	17.0	4.2	21.2	100
Slovenia	1995	41.1	28.3	30.6	58.9	100
Estonia	1994		43.2	56.8	100.0	100
Latvia	1995	15.0	43.6	41.4	85.0	100
Lithuania	1996	2.6	48.2	49.3	997.5	100
EU - accession candidates		32.1	36.1	31.8	67.9	100
EU 15[1]		54.5	18.3	27.2	45.5	100
of which:						
Germany	1995	61.7	16.4	21.9	38.3	100
Italy	1995	42.5	23.3	34.2	57.5	100
Spain	1995	34.5	22.6	42.9	65.5	100
Portugal	1995	31.4	30.5	38.1	68.6	100
Sweden	1992	66.5	5.9	27.6	33.5	100

[1] Excluding Luxembourg

Source: Bitzer and Hirschhausen (2000, 188)

4.2 Institutional Interpretation

One interpretation of the conservative state innovation policies is the following: the respective East European governments *could* have pursued a demand-oriented approach and carried out structural reform including tougher cuts of state-financed R&D, but they did not *want* to. The fact that governments *could* have pursued more market-oriented reforms is evidenced by the successful adaptation of the corporate sector and its integration into global innovation networks at low cost. A competition-oriented infrastructure policy would have required, amongst other activities, the transfer of the former industrial branch research institutes into the private enterprise sector, and the re-orientation of basic research according to international standards.

The fact that most East European governments did not *want* truly market-oriented reforms is shown by efforts to maintain state-financing of the old R&D structures. These attempts made to prop up the research establishments as far as possible were justified by arguing that their potential would be required at a later date, and that it could be brought up to international standards at low cost. Given the specific conditions of transformation, these arguments seem to be invalid: on the one hand, the devaluation of the existing stock of innovation capital that occurred in the transformation from socialism to the market economy proved to be greater than had initially been thought; on the other hand the East European countries had neither the possibility nor the necessity to catch up to the international cutting edge of R&D in so-called 'strategic' sectors.

The driving force behind the conservative innovation policies may have been specific interest groups who opposed more market-oriented reforms. This applies mainly to the organizations of the former innovation system themselves, for example, institutes, academies and universities.[165] One informal reason for maintaining a conservative innovation policy may have been the broad consensus, not only in Eastern Europe but also in Western Europe, on the significant technological and research 'potential' in the former socialist countries (Cleaver, 2002).

5. CONCLUSIONS

This chapter has analyzed policy options to restructure East European innovation systems. Though this sector is not immediately recognized as 'infrastructure' by many, we contend that it is at least as important for sustained development as roads or energy. Hence innovation systems, a 'personal' infrastructure as defined in Chapter 2, need to be analyzed parallel to material infrastructure sectors. We observed that the innovation systems in Eastern Europe had to undergo substantial change. The remaining fractions of the former socialist innovation systems were only loosely connected to the newly emerging production and sales networks; the innovation 'potential' of Eastern Europe was furthermore devalued by the necessary adaptation of enterprises to international technological trajectories and the immediate competition with innovation systems and enterprises around the world. The governments of the transformation countries faced a dilemma in choosing an infrastructure policy: they could either assist the creative destruction of the former system, which might have been economically justified but politically

---

[165] But also the organizations at the fringe of the innovation system tried to withhold structural change, such as the bureaucracy of the S&T system and the state organs to which the organizations belonged. The danger of cutting international co-financing by cutting state financing may also have been put forward as an argument to maintain high domestic expenditures. International co-financing was above 5 percent in 1995, with a rising tendency.

dangerous; or attempt to maintain some of the old structures through substantial state support, which was likely to be inefficient but politically less dangerous. Most transformation countries opted for the second solution.

In contrast to the public sector, the *private* enterprises in Eastern Europe showed little interest in maintaining the existing innovation networks, as was expressed by their low willingness to pay for domestic innovation services. Instead, many enterprises that succeeded in catching up relied upon the integration into *international* innovation, production and sales networks. *Imitation*, rather than their own innovations or R&D, was the preferred strategy. The evidence from sectoral case studies shows that the globalization of industry and innovation in Eastern European transformation countries was not only the more direct approach, but also the less costly one.

In view of the disappointing results achieved by proactive innovation policies in Eastern Europe, the supply-side approach pursued to date should give way to a more *demand*-oriented strategy, one geared to the willingness of enterprises to *pay* for innovation. This would put scarce resources at the disposal of R&D activities whose innovation capacity and demand-orientation has been proven in the new international networks. In sum, innovation is an infrastructure sector for which the hypothesis of a positive link between higher state expenses and sectoral or even macroeconomic development can be rejected for Eastern Europe.

8. Private Project Financing of Highway Development

We see the possibility to successfully apply our concepts [for private infrastructure financing] in Eastern Europe, and thus to get closer to their realization in Germany as well.

Hermann Becher,
President of the German Association of the Construction Industry (1992).

1. INTRODUCTION

This chapter analyzes attempts to introduce innovative financing instruments for infrastructure in Eastern Europe. The concrete example chosen is private project finance of highways, which is analyzed with regard to institutional, transport economic and financial aspects. Section 2 presents a stylized market-economy reference model for private highway financing and discusses the experiences of some Western countries. Section 3 provides an overview of approaches to private financing in Eastern Europe; none of the 20 or so concretely planned projects was carried out successfully in the 1990s. We analyze possible reasons for this, in particular the choice of the wrong financing model ('the wrong model in the right country') and the unfavorable institutional and economic conditions period ('the right model in the wrong country'). Section 4 discusses a concrete case, the project financing of the Hungarian M1 motorway. Section 5 presents some policy conclusions.[166]

---

[166] Thanks to Thorsten Beckers for comments. We acknowledge that other transport infrastructure, for example, inter- and intra-city roads, may be as important for economic development as highways. The selection of highways in this case study is based on the complexity of financing and operation and the multitude of actors involved in this area.

2. REFERENCE MODEL AND INTERNATIONAL EXPERIENCE

2.1 Models of Private Participation in Highway Financing

2.1.1 Organizational models

The private financing of infrastructure projects and user-specific fees are by no means an exception in economic history.[167] Apart from the fiscal objective (relief for the state budget) private finance is considered to be conducive to *productive* and *dynamic* efficiency. As discussed in Chapter 2, one can assume that normative requirements (such as a minimal supply of road infrastructure to every citizen) can be handled at the level of network planning.[168] Competition between private enterprises for the financing, construction and operation of infrastructure will generate information decentrally, which facilitates the choice of the most efficient solution (for example, by providing different estimates of market development and project risk). Private financing also facilitates the introduction of innovative payment mechanisms. Efficient private financing requires some ex-ante competition between potential operators. The task of the state (as the principal) is to limit the information rent of the monopolist private operator (the agent). As long as this is assured, decentralized private allocation of financing and operation of highways is a feasible solution.

A comparison between alternative models suggests that, as more functions and manageable risks are transferred to the private sector, productive and dynamic efficiency are likely to rise (Ewers and Rodi, 1995, 106). The

---

[167] Road pricing is as old as inter-city roads themselves: tolls were charged on the connection between Syria and Babylon in ancient times, while in Europe, road pricing is documented in England as early as the twelfth century (McKay, Charles, 1989, *Möglichkeiten der privatwirtschaftlichen Finanzierung von Verkehrsinfrastruktur-Investitionen in der EG*. Beiträge aus dem Institut für Verkehrswissenschaft an der Universität Münster, Heft 119. Göttingen, Vandenhoeck und Ruprecht, here: p. 32). In the USA, Estache, Romero and Strong (2000, 10) claim that 'in the first half of the nineteenth century, private toll roads outnumbered public roads.' In the late nineteenth and in particular, the first half of the twentieth century, public financing became dominant, partly due to increasing problems with levying tolls on private roads with free public parallel roads. By the 1980s, however, private financing moved back to the top of the policy agenda, both in the USA and in Europe.

[168] Here we do not discuss the question of whether network planning itself can or should be privatized; for a proposal to privatize network planning through a Clarke-Groves mechanism see Tegner, Henning (2000, 'Verhandlung statt Enteignung. Kann das Planungs- und Genehmigungsverfahren für Verkehrsinfrastruktur privatisiert werden?' In: Hartwig, K.-H. (ed.): *Neuere Ansätze zu einer effizienten Infrastrukturpolitik*. Beiträge aus dem Institut für Verkehrswissenschaft an der Universität Münster. Göttingen, Vandenhoeck and Ruprecht, 129-164).

participation of private capital in infrastructure projects can take different forms:
- In *leasing* models, private agents take over responsibility for financing, construction and operation. In fact, the state becomes the customer of a private operating company. The payment of construction costs is assured by the state through leasing rates that are negotiated ex-ante;
- in *concession* models, the concessionaire also carries (a part of) the market risk, as his or her investment is paid for by user fees. All non-sovereign functions can be transferred to the private concession company (financing, construction, maintenance, marketing). The state continues to be responsible for sectoral long-term planning. *Project finance* is a special form of concession model, in which all costs are covered exclusively by project revenues. Based upon a financial analysis of the investment project, the financing is structured in such a way as to exploit the debt potential as far as possible;
- the *club model*, developed for roads by Ewers and Rodi (1995) on the basis of Buchanan's (1965) club theory, is an entirely private solution to infrastructure operation: a private, self-organizing 'club of users' is responsible for financing, construction, operation *and* network planning. The role of the state is limited to some supervisory activities (e.g. assuring quality standards).[169]

2.1.2 Principles of pricing and risk allocation

The welfare-optimizing tariff scheme is largely independent of the organizational model. Highway construction is characterized by substantial sunk costs and strong variations in the intensity of use (daily, weekly, yearly peaks). This requires split three-part tariffs, consisting of a *fixed* fee to cover fixed costs, a *variable* fee to cover marginal costs and a *peak-load* fee to minimize the social costs of congestion (Brenck, 1992; Ewers and Tegner, 2000, 28 sq.);[170] both the fixed and the variable fee can be differentiated by the elasticity of demand (Ramsey prices). In practice, the conflict of interest between a far-reaching price differentiation on the one hand, and exponentially rising transaction costs on the other, calls for an extensive standardization of tariffs. Ewers and Tegner (2000, 29) propose a compromise of three tariffs:

---

[169] Whether the private club model will yield higher productive and dynamic efficiency than the concession models depends mainly on the transaction costs of implementing and operating the private club, and on an efficient solution to the inherent principle-agent problems.

[170] In addition, a fee for external users should be provided. See also on welfare-optimal road pricing Hau, Timothy (1992, *Economic Analysis of Road Pricing – A Diagrammatic Analysis*. Washington, D.C., World Bank, Policy Research Working Paper No. 1071), on the political economy aspects see Lehmann, Carsten (1996, *Die politische Ökonomie des Road Pricing*. Göttingen).

– One split tariff with a high fixed fee and low user fees (which will be chosen by frequent users);

– another split tariff with a low fixed amount but high user fees (designed for irregular users);

– a guest tariff consisting of a high fee, proportional to the driven distance, covering at least average costs.

Besides private participation and socially optimal prices, a third condition of the reference model is the efficient *allocation of risks* among the project participants. Due to the high investment requirements, long life and irregular revenues, infrastructure projects imply particularly high risks. The risk can be separated into technical, economic and political risks; within economic risks, one can distinguish between macro- and micro-risks.[171] The absolute level of risk has an impact on the financial feasibility of an infrastructure project. The success of a project depends crucially on the efficient *allocation*: risks should be allocated to the party that can handle them in the least costly manner, and that has the highest incentive to maximize the difference between benefits and costs of carrying that risk (Ewers and Tegner, 2000, 47). This includes an active participation of the *state* in risk bearing.

Table 8.1 shows an ideal-typical reference model for the allocation of risks in a highway project. It is unavoidable that the state intervenes in the project, at different federal levels: it intervenes directly, for example, by defining or modifying the technical and legal conditions and by setting specific tax rates; the indirect intervention comes from industrial and regional policies that also affect competing projects. In the reference model, the state should bear the risk of discretionary changes of the framework conditions, as well as the general political and regulatory risk. The operator has a comparative (information) advantage concerning the operating risk, the price risk and the demand risk, and should also carry the exchange-rate risk and the *force majeure* risk.[172] Finally, the highway users should carry a share of the demand risk and, eventually, of the *force majeure* risk, in the form of higher tariffs (Beckers, 2002).

---

[171] Among the technical risks are the non-finalization risk, the cost-overrun and process-technical risks; the economic risks include operating risk, demand risk, supplier risk, exchange rate and interest risk; among the political risks are the regulatory risk and the convertibility and transfer risk. Furthermore, in all cases a *force majeure* risk exists; see Backhaus, Klaus, und Heinrich Uekermann (1990, *Projektfinanzierung – Eine Methode zur Finanzierung von Großprojekten*. WiSt, Heft 3, März, 106-112).

[172] See also Estache, Romero and Strong (2000, Section 3.4), and Irwin, et al. (1999) including further references. In practice, the realization of efficient risk distribution between the private sector and the state often does not occur because the state, contrary to theory, is unwilling to accept risks. The state is more likely to offer a fixed contribution to the financing of an infrastructure investment (for example, a fixed subsidy), rather than to take responsibility for political risk in a purely private project.

Table 8.1 Distribution of risks in private infrastructure financing

Risk	Participating Parties		
	Operator	State	User
Technical risks	(x)		
Regulatory risk (change of taxes, laws, environmental standards, etc.)	x	x	
Operation risk	x		
Price and demand risk	x		x
Exchange rate risk	x		
Political risk	(x)	x	
Force majeure risk	x	(x)	(x)

Source: on the basis of Ewers and Tegner (1997); Beckers (2002)

2.2 International Experience

International experience with concession models for toll roads is decidedly mixed: it shows that private financing of toll roads *is* possible, but that it requires significant institutional capabilities that are often not available in emerging or developing countries. In particular, the litigation of ex-post disturbances of contracts proves to be a major obstacle; furthermore, the allocation of risks coming from *different* federal levels makes large road projects a highly risky affair. Estache, Romero and Strong (2000), Estache and Carbajo (1996), Engel, Fischer and Galetovic (1999), Ewers and Tegner (2000) and several other authors have reviewed the international experience of road concessions, the former three in particular in emerging and developing countries. The number of privately financed projects is increasing rapidly.[173] The following case studies highlight some of the factors of success and of failure:

– A successful pilot toll road project is the *Express Lane SR 91* in Los Angeles County (California, USA), the first privately financed toll road in the USA for 50 years.[174] A private investor was in charge of financing and

---

[173] Between the 1950s and the late 1980s, privately financed toll roads were very uncommon in industrialized *and* developing countries; in the few countries that developed toll roads (France, Italy), they were mainly state-managed and carried little economic risk. However, a wave of toll roads was started in the late 1980s: between 1985 and 1998, some 121 projects were started in developed countries, and another 280 public-private partnerships in road construction were recorded in developing and emerging countries between 1990 and 1997 (Estache, Romero and Strong, 2000, 10–11).

[174] Ewers and Tegner (2000, 35), and detailed description by Garnier, Phillipe (1998, 'Le télépéage et la modulation des tarifs: l'exemple des 91 express lanes'. In: Ecole Nationale des Ponts et Chaussées (ed.): *Road Financing*. Paris, Presses de l'Ecole Nationale des Ponts et Chaussées, 445-451).

operating four separate lanes within an already existing highway: these additional lanes are priced, whereas the rest of the highway can be used for free. Following the Ramsey rule, the toll is increased in peak periods. The concession is provided for 35 years; beyond a certain threshold, profits are shared between the state and the concession company. According to the operator, the main factor of success is the high demand on this particular route at peak hours;[175]

– the *tunnel Prado-Carrenage* in the city of Marseille was the first toll-financed construction project in France.[176] In September 1993, after three years of construction, it was opened and broke even financially as early as 1997, although the expected number of users had not been reached (real users: 30,000 per day). One reason for its financial success is seen in the differentiation of tariffs, reflecting the needs of different groups of users (for example, price reduction for frequent users, price reduction for pre-paid tickets, price differentiation for peak and off-peak periods);

– the *Chilean* experience with toll financing is particularly enlightening: the country has not only completed several project negotiations successfully, but it has also developed a new mechanism for auctioning concessions that reduces the demand risk inherent in any long-term road concession. Between 1993–98, not less than 14 roads were tendered to the private sector, totaling investment of over USD 3 bn.[177] The participation of private investors was already actively sought for the first step of operation, project identification. The institutional innovation was the introduction of the *least-present-value-of-revenue* (LPVR) auction (Engel, Fischer and Galetovic, 1997).[178] Under this mechanism, the winner is chosen based on the least present value he requires over the project lifetime, whereas the time span of the concession is *not* fixed in advance. In Chile, the LPVR-auction has proven to be an efficient solution to mitigate demand risk (Engel, Fischer and Galetovic, 1997);[179]

---

[175] In addition, the particular marketing efforts deployed by the concessionaire contributed to the public's acceptance of the project. Garnier (1998, op. cit.) also mentions an informal institution conducive to reform: the positive attitude of the U.S. population towards market-economy solutions

[176] Ewers and Tegner (2000, 34), and detailed description by Abraham, C. (1998, 'Le tunnel Prado-Carrenage'. In: Ecole Nationale des Ponts et Chaussées (ed.): *Road Financing*. Paris, Presses de l'Ecole Nationale des Ponts et Chaussées, 195-201).

[177] These include the Pan-American Highway, several highways connecting the nation's capital Santiago with nearby cities, several highways within Santiago and a number of local roads (see Engel,Fischer and Galetovic, 1999, 16, 41). Indicators of the success of the projects are its high number of (foreign and domestic) bidders (between three and six), the stability of its regulatory framework thus far, the lack of need for significant renegotiations up to the present and the meeting of all financial targets to date (Engel, Fischer and Galetovic, 1999).

[178] See for analysis Beckers (2002).

[179] For example, the present value demanded by the winner of the Santiago-Valparaiso highway concession was *below* construction costs estimated by the government. An additional advantage of the mechanism is that it allows determination of the precise value of the

– by contrast, in *Mexico* a large-scale attempt to increase the efficiency of infrastructure supply through concessions failed (see Ewers and Tegner, 2000, 30 sq.; Engel, Fischer and Galetovic, 1999; Irwin, et al., 1999). In the early 1990s, some 29 concessions were given to private operating companies. But in the mid-1990s, at least 23 of them showed high deficits: costs had by far outstripped the projections, whereas the revenues turned out lower than expected. After an attempt to rescue the operating companies by increasing the concession period from 20 to 30 years, the state bought back the 23 concessions in 1997; the other contracts had to be modified as well. Institutional and organizational factors had contributed to the failure: thus, the first round of tenders was limited to local consortia in an intransparent procedure; the Mexican administration seems to have been unprepared in terms of both personnel and technology to confront the new tasks (Ewers and Tegner, 2000, 34). In addition, the low commitment of the government to stick to the initial rules favored, via an *implicit* guarantee, the development of financially unsound projects and white elephants. (Irwin, et al., 1999, 234).

The available evidence confirms that the success of privately financed toll-road projects hinges not only upon realistic assumptions of costs and revenues, but also on the institutional and organizational conditions, such as a competent, specialized and politically independent administration. The existence of a competent administration is considered a key factor in the success of private-public partnerships in the UK and Chile, whereas its absence is held responsible for the Mexican failure (Ewers and Tegner, 2000, 37). Institutional factors also determine other variables, such as the quality of forecasts and the introduction of differentiated tariffs. Table 8.2 lists general determinants of success and failure of private concession models.

---

franchise at any given point in time and thus facilitates renegotiations between the government and the private sector. The LPVR mechanism also served to detect a white elephant (an inter-urban highway in the capital Santiago, Engel, Fischer and Galetovic, 1999, 17 sq.). As a general conclusion on Chile, Engel, Fischer and Galetovic (1999, 35) find that whereas not all pitfalls have been avoided, 'there are marked improvements over similar concession programs abroad'.

Table 8.2 General determinants of success and failure of private concession models

Factors of success	Factors of failure
Conservative demand projections, explicit recognition of risk and uncertainty in feasibility studies	Overestimation of future demand
Price differentiation	Undifferentiated prices; average cost pricing
Competent administration and regulation	Missing administrative capabilities and contract management
Efficient allocation of risks between the public and the private sector	Transfer of *all* responsibility to the private investor; unpredictable change of the regulatory framework (regulatory risk)
Public acceptance campaigns by operator and/or government	Formal and informal resistance against cost-efficient pricing; lack of public support

Source: on the basis of Ewers and Tegner (2000, 36)

3. PROBLEMS OF APPLYING THE REFERENCE MODEL TO EASTERN EUROPE

3.1 Attempts at Private Highway Financing

At the very beginning of economic reform in Eastern Europe, Western industrial enterprises and banks developed models for the private financing of transport infrastructure in this region. Given the low competitiveness of the railway systems and the underdevelopment of road infrastructure, these models concentrated on the construction of highways and interstate roads, including large construction projects such as bridges and tunnels.[180] The main reason to transfer models of private financing to Eastern Europe was the high investment requirement and the limited availability of budget financing, while the fact that private financing can also lead to higher efficiency was also acknowledged. Table 8.3 and Figure 8.1 present the private highway infrastructure financing projects that were attempted in Eastern Europe in the

---

[180] Besides its direct impact, private infrastructure financing in Eastern Europe also had a pilot function: to prove the feasibility of private financing in this region, even as many *Western* countries were still voicing doubts about its feasibility. Given the small number of success stories of private infrastructure financing in Western Europe, the transformation countries were seen as a test case for the implementation of innovative financing techniques under particularly difficult conditions (Hauptverband der Deutschen Bauindustrie, 1999, 22). The investment requirements for highway construction alone in the the 10 Central and Eastern European countries were estimated between EUR 44–64 bn. (Gaspard, 1996, Task Force Transport Infrastructure Needs Assessment, TINA, 1999).

early transformation period (1990–97). These projects can be roughly divided into two groups:
– Fully private financing through user charges, without major state guarantees, turnover guarantees, shadow tolls, and so on. This more ambitious approach was taken, for example, in Hungary and Poland;
– private financing with a significant state contribution (for example, in Romania and Ukraine).

Ex post, the attempts to introduce private highway finance in Eastern Europe have to be assessed *critically*. Among the 20 projects conceived by the transformation countries for private highway financing, only one has in fact been realized in the 1990s (the Hungarian M1) and even this project did not work out as expected. The other projects have either been dominantly financed by the state in a traditional way, or have been put on hold altogether.[181]

---

[181] This result applies to other transport projects as well (such as ports, railways). EBRD (2001b, 22) concludes that 'in spite of high hopes of attracting private finance for transport infrastructure in the Bank's countries of operations, up to the end of 1996 only four privately financed, Bank-supported transport infrastructure projects had reached financial closing: the M1-M15 and M5 Toll Motorways in Hungary, the Yuzhny Fertiliser Terminal in Ukraine, and the Giurgiulesti Oil Terminal in Moldova, with total investment of ECU 754 million equivalent.' In 2002, the two exceptions are the M5 highway in Hungary and the A4 highway in Poland (Kattowice-Cracow), where individual tolls are levied. Project financing of the A2 (Warsaw-Frankfurt/Oder) is under negotiation.

Table 8.3 Projects of private highway financing in Eastern Europe in the early phase of transformation

Country	Project	Status (as of 2001)
Hungary	- M1 Györ-Hegyelshalom: USD 200 mn.; (in addition: branch to Bratislava M15)	- M1 the only concession project without state guarantees realized in Eastern Europe; start of operation: 1996, financial insolvency: late 1998 - transferred to the National Highway Agency
	- M3 Budapest-Gyöngyös (59 km)	- idea of project financing abandoned - user tolls replaced by vignettes
	- M5 Budapest-Kecskemét-Szeged (27 km Budapest-Kiskunfélegyhàza: reconstruction; 29 km 2nd lane; 40 km: new construction; USD 300 mn.	- concession to Hungarian-Austrian consortium (Aka Rt.); no project financing, but classical credit-financing with state participation - user tolls have remained thus far (only ones in Eastern Europe)
	- M7: Budapest-Székesféhérvàr (USD 700 mn.)	- first tender in September 1995 failed; new tender in preparation
	- toll bridge over Danube at Szekszàrd, plus 20 km highway access (USD 120 mn.)	- mixed private-public financing was planned, state-guaranteed loan by EBRD - the concessionaire was unable to prepare financial package; project abandoned
	- toll bridge over Danube at Dunaujvàros	- current status unclear in general: Hungary abandoned private financing based on user tolls in 1998-99, created instead a State Highway Company and introduced a general highway-vignette (except for M5)
Poland	- A1 North-South connection (Gdansk-Katowice)	- no financially viable concept was developed, no concession attributed - state contribution remains unclear
	- A2: Frankfurt/Oder-Warsaw (USD 1.5-2 bn.)	- concession initially given to Autostrada Wielkopolska SA (364 km section from Frankfurt/Oder to Lodz), but no financing scheme adopted thus far (tender planned for 2002) - planned toll of 4 US cents/km not cost-covering

Poland (continued)	- A4 Kattowice-Cracow (USD 590 mn.)	- concession given to trading company Stalexport (1997)
		- first toll highway in Poland, extension planned for the trunk Opole-Wroclaw
Czech Republic	- BOT-project D5 highway Prague-Nuremberg	- private project financing abandoned
		- traditional state financing
	- BOT D8 Prague-Aussig (-Dresde)	- not yet realized
		- general highway vignette was introduced in the Czech Republic (for some sections)
Croatia	- highway Zagreb-Gorican (HungarF) (USD 400 mn.)	- construction contract with Astaldi SpA (1997)
	- highway Krapina-Maceliy (17.4 km, USD 150 mn.)	- construction contract with Walter Bau (1998)
		in both cases user tolls have not been introduced as planned
Romania	- private financing of new highways (1,080 km in 10 sections; USD 4.4 bn.)	- no concessionaire found, little state support available for individual sections
	- introduction of user tolls on all highways (old and new)	- no tolls nor vignette introduced thus far
Bulgaria	- E85 North-South highway Gabrovo-Skipska	- build-operate model planned (1995), but not realized thus far
	- Trans-European toll motorway (East-West, 128 km)	- not developed, no toll introduced
Ukraine	- development of the highway L'viv-Polish border (Krakovets) to a toll highway	- project is tendered to a private Ukrainian concessionaire, but little investments undertaken thus far
	- 6 further projects, e.g. Kyiv-Vinnitsa and Charkiw-Russian border	- no project financially viable
Russia	- project toll highway Moscow-St. Petersburg	- project on hold
	- Moscow-Minsk-Brest toll highway (1,080 km, USD 1,5 bn.)	- project on hold

Sources: World Bank, EBRD, European Commission, Hauptverband der deutschen Bauindustrie (1992), Judge (1998), BfAI

Figure 8.1 Planned project financing of highways in Central and Eastern
        Europe (late 1990s)

3.2 Explication I: Wrong Model

One attempt to explain the difficulties of introducing private financing was to call into question the very instrument of toll roads. Thus it was argued that the East European experience was a logical consequence of applying the wrong model.[182] Road pricing has the following effects: i) the reduction of congestion on the toll road is welfare increasing, as users with a higher willingness to pay face less congestion; ii) the switch of users from the toll road to the non-toll road may increase the social costs on the latter and may thus be welfare reducing in total. Gronau (1997, 171) shows analytically that under certain assumptions, the pricing of a road can be welfare reducing. A profit-optimizing private operator can charge a toll above the socially optimal rate, since the operator does not take into account the social costs that occur on the free road. The private toll increases with lower price elasticity of demand and this increases the share of users that will switch to the free road, thus increasing the social costs on the free road. Therefore, the probability of choosing a welfare-reducing toll increases

– with reduced congestion on the toll road;
– with increasing congestion of the free road; and
– with decreasing elasticity of demand.[183]

Critics of private financing of highways have argued that precisely these conditions existed in the East European transformation countries. The danger of congested toll roads was small, and so was the price elasticity of demand. In that case imposing road pricing might indeed *not* be welfare increasing. However, this argument neglects the potential benefits of private road financing:

– The knowledge on future traffic flows, willingness to pay and other determinants of demand was very low in the early phase of transformation. The mobilization of private financing could have contributed to the collection of decentralized, private information, while at the same time, this more restrictive approach had the advantage of avoiding uncontrolled highway development through state financing ('white elephants');
– road pricing was the only way to avoid peaks in the use of highways and inter-urban roads, which have become not uncommon in some Eastern European regions, as well;

---

[182] This opinion was expressed by John Hansen, Economist at the World Bank, arguing against the introduction of highway tolls in Ukraine (Conference on 'Fiscal Policy for Ukraine', International Center for Policy Studies, Kiev, March 1999).

[183] The Gronau model assumes full substitutability between the two roads and homogeneous users; that is, with similar opportunity costs of travel time. In reality, the toll road will be of better quality and individuals will have different willingness to pay for toll road usage. The stronger these two effects, the higher the socially optimal toll will be.

– last but not least, road pricing and private participation in the supply of road infrastructure *are* compatible, if the state is willing to contribute additional resources. One supposedly successful model is the British shadow toll, where the private highway operator is paid directly by the state, dependent on traffic flows and quality parameters (Ewers and Tegner, 2000, 32).[184] Thus, private participation in the construction and operation of the project and an efficient distribution of risk *can* increase the productive efficiency of highway supply.

Private concession models based on user tolls are likely to be less profitable in Eastern Europe than in Western Europe or other industrialized countries, but no conclusive argument can be found *a priori* against the use of private financing. There is no reason why Eastern Europe, following the (more successful) Latin American examples, should not introduce private highway financing and tolls.

3.3 Explication II: Transformation-Specific Obstacles

3.3.1 Economic aspects
In this section, we enquire about the *transformation-specific* factors that might explain the low degree of success of concession models in Eastern Europe.[185] Among the economic aspects are the following:

– The depressed growth in the transformation process led to much *lower traffic volumes* than those forecast. For example, the Polish concession models were based on calculations of 20,000–60,000 paying vehicles per day, densities which were not even reached in the late 1990s on toll-free roads (Judge, 1998, 396);

– *low willingness to pay*: per capita income of the Central and Eastern European transformation countries in the first half of the 1990s was as low as about EUR 3,000–4,000, about 20 percent of the EU average. Thus, the opportunity costs of lost time were much lower than in EU countries. Subsequently, the marginal willingness to pay was low. Exceptions were the few East-West transit corridors used to a large extent by foreigners with a relatively high willingness to pay;

---

[184] Shadow tolling can be combined with a flat user charge ('vignette'), which is a second-best solution: if the flat charge covers total costs (the sum of the shadow tolls), equivalence is reached; it is second-best only because the fee is unrelated to the social marginal costs of highway use.

[185] According to EBRD (2001b, 22) 'several projects in the region have stalled, ... or concession tenders cancelled, ... or market-priced limited-recourse financing rejected in favor of other options for various financial and legal reasons. ... The reasons vary from project to project, but the most important actors seem to be: poor financial viability (particularly for motorway projects); public affordability and political acceptability; level and equitable allocation of risks; lack of equity; lack of local funding; regulatory and legal constraints; and lack of convincing examples in Western Europe.'

- the availability of *free parallel roads* further reduced potential demand for the toll road;
- the *high inflation rates* of the first post-socialist years and the risk concerning future inflation affected the interest on credits in a particular way and therefore increased the necessary tolls.[186] More generally, risk and uncertainty abounded with regard to domestic determinants of demand (such as GDP-growth and regional economic development) as well as external developments (such as the speed of EU integration, or economic and political relations with Russia). Under these conditions, a risk-averse investor was likely to require a particularly high pay-off from projects in transformation countries, which again increased the required user toll.

3.3.2 Institutional aspects

The institutional framework of the early years of transformation in Eastern Europe did not correspond to the reference model for private project finance. This concerns both formal and informal transformation-specific institutions:

- *Missing administrative competence* in the development, tender and control of private project financing was widespread in the early years of reform. The learning process and the adaptation to project-specific procedures within the bureaucracies had to take place in the midst of a radical restructuring and redefinition of tasks;[187]
- *underdeveloped domestic capital markets* obliged investors to take foreign-currency denominated credits on the international capital markets. Domestic real interest remained high in all transformation countries (two-digit);
- the *historical legacy* of free socialist infrastructure led to a low acceptance of highway user tolls in the transformation countries. Timid attempts by governments to improve public acceptance (such as in Poland and Hungary) were largely unsuccessful;[188]
- *transaction costs* in transformation countries grew exponentially due to missing or incomplete legal texts (laws, decrees, directives) and the lack of experience of domestic agents in dealing with international technical and legal standards.

---

[186] Dailami and Leipziger (1997) show that the relation between inflation and the interest spread (for example, compared to LIBOR) is not linear, but convex: countries with high inflation rates, among them the transformation countries, pay over-proportional interest rates on infrastructure credits.

[187] Anecdotal evidence of the difficulties of adapting administrative structures is described by Joosten (1999), and Sundakov, Alex (1999, 'Transition Crisis: Is Crisis Management Delaying Transition?' In Siedenberg and Hoffmann (eds), 111-118).

[188] Evidence of this comes from Hungary (M1, see below) and Poland, where the project Lodz-Warsaw was delayed for many years by the resistance of local communities *against* the toll highway project.

3.3.3 Political aspects

The high political risk in the early phase of transformation was an additional obstacle to private project financing. The political risk consisted of three elements:

– A low time-consistency of political decision making within a given organization (for example, the regulatory agency);

– contradictory behavior between organizations at a federal level (such as conflicts between the regulatory agency and the Finance Ministry); and

– inconsistent decision making between different federal levels (for example, contradictory decisions by the central state and regional governments).

High political risk in Eastern Europe thus increased the interest rates on credits even further. As in the case of inflation, political risk, too, was likely to have a non-linear impact on the interest rates of credits.[189]

The analysis of transformation specifics implies that private financing of toll highways in Eastern Europe was difficult. Given the persistent economic, institutional and political risks, pure project financing was not adequate to accelerate infrastructure development in Eastern Europe, or to render the process more efficient. This does *not* mean that private concession models cannot be applied at all in a transformation context. An up-front separation between private financing on the one hand and a state-supported toll scheme on the other hand (such as shadow tolls or lump-sum payments), for example, could have led to a more efficient outcome.[190] Furthermore it has become evident that institutional path dependency prohibited radical reforms, such as the jump from socialist state financing to private project financing. A *gradual* reform process would have been likely to yield better results; for example, first the commercialization of the highway system and subsequently the gradual privatization and introduction of private financing.[191]

---

[189] Dixit and Pindyck (1994, 6 sq.) report empirical evidence according to which the required profitability of investment projects often exceeds real capital costs (*hurdle rate*) by a factor of three to four; this corresponds to an implicit risk assessment. In the case of long-term infrastructure investment non-insurable political risk plays a particularly important role.

[190] The World Bank recently recommended a combination of private and public financing to Eastern Europe; see for example, the 'Strategic Priorities for the Polish Transport Sector' (World Bank, 1999, Infrastructure Unit, Europe and Central Asia Region Report No. 19450-POL); the document also states states that 'the assumption that the motorway program could be built without significant government financing has turned out not to be viable.'

[191] One positive aspect of the radical approach was that it blocked the state financing of overdimensioned highway expansion plans in East European countries (white elephants). Had sufficient funds been available, a lot more highways would have been constructed, not necessarily efficiently.

4. EMPIRICAL EVIDENCE: PRIVATE PROJECT FINANCING OF THE M1 (HUNGARY)

The private project financing of the highway trunk of the M1 between Györ (Western Hungary) and the Austrian border (Figure 8.2) was the first of its kind in Eastern Europe and the only one that has been realized in the region in the 1990s. This section presents the specific sectoral and institutional conditions of the project and aims at understanding its difficulties.[192]

4.1 Development and Failure of the Project

Hungary was the first East European country that decided to rely almost entirely on private concession models for its highway development. In order to overcome financing gaps for infrastructure programs, Parliament voted the first concession law in Eastern Europe, law No. XVI/1991 in 1991; this law was complemented by Directive XXXIX/1992. The required investments for highway construction alone were estimated around EUR 3 bn., which was to be raised through concessions to private investors, domestic and foreign. The project M1 had a pilot character for the subsequent projects that were in fact made conditional upon its success (Timàr, 1992, 32). After a two-step international tender, the Hungarian government concluded a concession contract with the project company Elmka Rt., led by the French Transroute International, in April 1993.[193] The project company obtained a concession for 35 years and had to commit to constructing and operating the highway under certain technical conditions.[194]

The total costs of the M1 were estimated at USD 250 mn.[195] The Hungarian government was *not* involved in the financing scheme, nor did it

---

[192] The discussion is based on expert interviews, the specialized press and the available literature, mainly Timàr (1992), Joosten (1999), Léderer (1998), Ewers and Tegner (2000, 33), and Franz, Otmar (1996, 'M1/M15 – Stellungnahme'. In: Bundesverband der Deutschen Industrie (ed.): *Projektfinanzierung und Betreibermodelle auf Auslandsmärkten: Das Geschäft der Zukunft*. Köln, 50-52).

[193] Further participants in the concession company were West European and Hungarian banks and construction companies (among others Caisse de Dépôts et Consignations, BNP, Commerce and Credit Bank of Hungary, Hungarian Savings Bank, Strabag Austria).

[194] In addition to the M1, the same consortium obtained a lump-sum contract for extending the highway from Györ in the direction of Bratislava (M15, investment sum approx. USD 130 mn.), on which no tolls were levied (the total project is sometimes referred to in the literature as M1/M15).

[195] Cost breakdowns were 15 percent financed through equity of Elmka, 42 percent through project financing by an international banking consortium, and 43 percent through Hungarian banks, the Hungarian capital market and other sources. There is contradictory information on the investment volume: EBRD (1997) mentions USD 329 mn., EBRD (2000) EUR 326 mn. for the M1/M15, respectively. BfAI (1999, *Möglichkeiten für Konzessionsverträge noch nicht ausgeschöpft*. Press release) calculates USD 200 mn. for the M1 alone. The

provide any guarantees on minimum revenues or similar (except for a HUF 30 bn. – USD 20 mn. – bond).[196] In January 1996, the first toll highway in Eastern Europe was opened to the public. The unitary, undifferentiated tariff for the 42.4 km was HUF 1,000 for cars (corresponding to USD 6.6 in 1996 HUF), HUF 3,500 for lorries and HUF 4,000 for buses. The toll of about 16 US cents/km for cars was among the highest in Europe; it exceeded the tolls on Latin American roads by far (which averaged 3 US cents/km).[197] The expected number of daily users was 11,500, and up to 15,000 according to the optimistic scenarios (Léderer, 1998, 252).

Contrary to expectations, the financial results of the first two years of operation were so bad that the concession company became illiquid in early 1998. The real number of users turned out to be lower than expected, at an average of 6,400 users per day (of which 90 percent were cars and 80 percent foreign users). Thus only 50 percent of the expected revenues were attained. The 'market share' of the highway within the transport corridor was 47 percent, implying that more than half of the users chose the toll-free parallel country road. In addition, in late 1997, a local court in Western Hungary forced the concession company to refund up to 40 percent of the toll to clients demanding this, after the Hungarian Automobile Club had filed a complaint against the concession company.[198] Contrary to its initial position, the Hungarian government did bail out the bankrupt concession company. In January 1999, the government decided to nationalize the concession and guarantee 89 percent of the outstanding loans (Joosten, 1999, 54).[199]

The difficulties with the M1 project led to a reorientation of Hungarian highway development policy. The government seized the occasion to introduce a general highway user fee (vignette), the only exception being the

---

[196] figure used here is calculated as the share of the M1 (42.4 km/50.9 km) in the overall costs of the M1/M15 of USD 329 mn. In 1998, EBRD provided a further credit, initially agreed as a *stand-by* option, of EUR 66.8 mn. for the financial restructuring of the M1/M15 project. The only direct government contribution to the project was the sovereign supply of land, financed by the Highway Fund (approximately 5 percent of total investments) and in addition, the concession company was exempted from import tariffs. Thus, the project was as private as any other 'private' project financing. Strictly speaking, the project was not purely private, as public banks contributed to the financing: EBRD: USD 3.9 mn. in the project company, and US 135 mn. in credits, Caisse des Depots et Consignations, and Kreditanstalt für Wiederaufbau (KfW).

[197] Estache, Romero and Strong (2000, 37), this figure does not include an extreme price of a private toll road, of 27 UScents/km.

[198] Joosten (1999, 54) reports that only two letters claiming a refund were received, whereas the concession company maintained its former tariffs, and even increased them to the summer tariffs in 1998; thus, the financial results of the concession company were not directly affected by the court decision.

[199] On September 20, 1999, the concession was transferred to the *National Highway Company*, a joint creation of the Hungarian Development Bank and the Ministry of Transport. It thus turned out that, just as in the Mexican case, the Hungarian government had given an *implicit* guarantee to the lenders.

M5, 70 km from Budapest to Kecskemet, which continued to be managed as a toll road. In the subsequent national highway development program (1999), priorities were switched from expensive four-lane highways to cheaper and faster-to-build two-lane freeways. The Ministry of Transport provided investment funds to the tune of USD 2.5 bn. for the period 2000–10 for major road development.[200] Besides the general highway vignette, a 10 percent highway tax was levied on gasoline sold in Hungary. The initial project of private highway financing was abandoned.

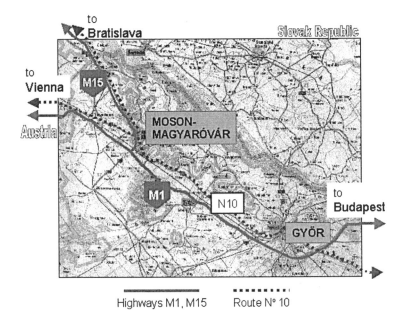

Highways M1, M15   Route N° 10

Figure 8.2 Planned toll highway M1 (Hungary)

4.2 Wrong Project Design?

The difficulties of the project can be explained to a certain extent by its inadequate design:

– A major reason is the *overestimation of future traffic flows*, which was used in the feasibility studies. The traffic flows on the toll highway during the first years of operation were overestimated by up to 100 percent. The best-case scenario (15,000 vehicles per day) was based on observed traffic flows from 1992 *without* tolls; thus, it was assumed that the price elasticity of

---

[200] Source: EBRD (2000, *Hungary – Country Investment Profile*. London, 18).

demand would be zero. The standard scenario (11,500 vehicles per day) unrealistically assumed high growth rates of GDP and tourism (Léderer, 1999, 252 sq.);[201]

– the assumption that *Hungarian* users would have a significant willingness to pay for the high quality of the highway and time economies turned out to be wrong. It also did not take into account earlier market research. The price for one car trip on the toll road, HUF 1,000, corresponded to as much as 1.7 percent of average monthly income. This contrasts with an average willingness to pay as low as HUF 258 (Léderer, 1998, 254 sq.);[202]

– *missing complementary activities* by the Hungarian state also contributed to the low traffic volume. In particular, the traffic of heavy trucks on the parallel free road was not forbidden, as had been specified in the concession contract (Ewers and Tegner, 2000, 33);

– the danger of a *competing parallel free road* was particularly high in the case of the M1. The country road from Györ to the Austrian border runs parallel to the M1 and ends at the same border station (Figure 8.2). Thus the degree of substitutability was particularly high and should have been taken into account in the pricing of the highway;

– last but not least, the very choice of the auctioning mechanism may have been inappropriate for a transformation context; that is, high demand uncertainty and little experience with highway concessions. The concession was auctioned among four competing groups to the highest bid and with a *fixed* concession period of 35 years. This mechanism reduced the flexibility to adjust the conditions in the (likely) case of unexpected developments. Under

---

[201] According to an insider, the over-optimistic forecasts relied on a sample of highway use on a summer vacation day with high traffic. There was also substantial political pressure on the forecasters: 'The Ministry of Transport, who had a clear interest in assuming high forecasts, supported these projections and seemed to consider a more conservative approach to traffic growth as a lack of trust in the Hungarian economy (Joosten, 1999, 52).' Whereas the forecasts assumed growth rates of 5–6 percent per year, 'traffic declined during 1995 and 1996, and remained constant thereafter.' (Joosten, 1999, 53). It was admitted that 'although some of this decline can be attributed to the serious economic recession in 1995, most of it is probably caused by an optimistic view of traffic developments supported by a misunderstanding of the traffic purposes and the reasons for traffic growth' (Joosten, 1999, 53).

[202] A survey carried out by a Hungarian market research institute had predicted a low use of the toll road: in the survey, 73 percent of the population considered the planned toll of HUF 800–900 as 'excessive', 17 percent as 'too high' and only 8 percent as 'acceptable'. The estimated willingness to pay was far below the planned price: the average willingness to pay in the group considering the toll as 'excessive' was HUF 173, the group 'too high' HUF 432 and the group 'acceptable' HUF 669, still 30 percent below the actual price of HUF 1,000 giving an average willingness to pay of HUF 258 (Léderer, 1998, 254 sq.) Note also that 61 percent of the population expected organized protest against the toll highway, and 76 percent were willing to sign a petition declaring free highway use for Hungarian citizens.

these conditions, a more flexible auction mechanism would have been appropriate.[203]

4.3 Transformation-Specific Reasons for Failure?

Apart from the technical aspects, the difficulties of introducing private infrastructure finance can also be explained by the specific conditions prevailing in the Hungarian economy in the early 1990s:
- The underdeveloped *formal* market economy institutions led to high transaction costs, in both the planning and the implementation of the project. In particular, the interpretation of the concession law and the directive on concessions turned out to be complex. According to insiders' estimates, transaction costs between the 34 participating parties accounted for *one-fourth* of total project costs;
- the unclear distribution of competencies between the central and the regional government increased the regulatory uncertainty. For example, both the central *and* the regional authorities had the right to sell concessions (Timàr, 1992), which led to a conflict of interests. Whereas the central government dominated in the first international tenders, resistance against toll roads was formed mainly at the *local* level (in the Western region against the M1, as well as in the South-East against the M5). In addition, the role of the central government within the process was not clearly defined (Joosten, 1999, 53);
- a lack of constraint in the regulator may have implicitly contributed to the realization of the project, and may thus have increased the probability of its failure. The Hungarian government had formally refused to take over any guarantee for credits or bonds. However, given the political exposure of the project, the project company may have *de facto* relied on support by the central government in the case of commercial distress;
- the fact that the regulatory risk was high is evidenced by the political and legal decision to oblige the concession company to a 40 percent rebate on its toll rates. This corresponds indeed to the classical hold-up situation, where the regulator tries to extract the quasi-rent from the private investor once the latter has sunk his or her investment;[204]

---

[203] On the flexibility of auctions, see also Trujillo, Lurdes, Emile Quinet, and Antonia Estache (2000, *Forecasting the Demand for Privatized Transport – What Economic Regulators Should Know, and Why.* Washington, D.C., World Bank, World Bank Institute, Policy Research Working Paper 2446, 5-8).

[204] A tacit agreement between the central government in Budapest and the local government might have been struck, as both could benefit politically from the hold-up. In particular, the central government could reject the responsibility for the decision, which it was in favor of but did not dare to endorse publicly, and push responsibility off to the regional court.

– *informal* aspects furthermore complicated the introduction of private highway financing in Hungary. The willingness of society to accept the concession of formerly free roads to toll highways was low.[205] Thus the campaign of the Hungarian Automobile Club against the pricing of the M1 could rely not only upon support by the directly affected population (such as the private car owners planning to take that route), but also on public opinion.

4.4 Financial and Risk Analysis

In addition to the descriptive analysis of risk related to project financing in a transformation context, a *financial* simulation analysis provides further insight. This section provides a rough analysis of the financial feasibility of the highway project M1, based on very simplified assumptions. First, a simulated mean-variance analysis of the project is performed; second, using the real option theory of investment, we test whether the decision to build the highway as early as 1993 was premature.

4.4.1 Mean-variance analysis of the M1 project

The mean-variance analysis is the simplest microeconomic analysis of the portfolio choice between different financial instruments (see Figure 8.3; see also Varian, 2000, chapter 13; Brealey and Myers, 2000, chapter 8).[206] In order to obtain real numbers for the mean-variance analysis, it is necessary to make several simplifying assumptions: the risk-free asset can be taken as the triple-A U.S. government bond for 30 years in 1993 (the starting year of the project), approximately 6 percent. As for the risky market asset, we take the average expected return of the German stock markets over the last 30 years; that is, an expected value of 10.2 percent and a standard deviation of 2.1 percent.[207] As for the expected return and the risk of the M1 project, we have

---

[205] Already in the late period of socialism (1988), an attempt by the government to introduce a general user fee for road use (vignette) had failed (Timàr, 1992, 30).

[206] In essence, the properties of financial titles are reduced to two parameters: the expected revenue (mean, μ) and the risk (standard deviation, σ). It is assumed that an investor has the choice between two assets, a *risk-free* asset (such as a triple-A government bond issued by the U.S. or a West European government), and a *risky* asset, for example, an index title representing an average mean-variance of a stock market. The respective points in the μ-σ diagram are (r_f/0) for the risk free title, and (r_m/σ_m) for the market title (Figure 8.3). The budget line gives the possible combinations of return and risk that an investor can attain, and the slope of the budget line, called the price of risk, is given by (r_m – r_f) /σ_m. A risk-averse agent will chose a portfolio so as to reach the tangency between a convex indifference curve and the budget line (point (r_x/σ_x) in Figure 8.3), while a risk-neutral agent will select any point on the budget line. If one introduces an additional asset, for example, the infrastructure project (M1), the question is where it is positioned with respect to the market index – whether it is above or below the budget line.

[207] Source: Deutsches Aktieninstitut (2000, *Factbook*, Frankfurt, page 09.1-3-a), we assume that there is no exchange rate risk between the USD and the DEM (EUR).

to perform a feasibility study with different scenarios reflecting the uncertainty on key parameters, such as GDP, the number of users, the exchange rate, and so on. The main parameters of the feasibility study and the basic assumptions concerning the scenarios are summarized in Table 8.4.

Table 8.5 shows one section of the cash-flow analysis for one of the 27 scenarios. If one weights each scenario with its probability (and assumes independence between the variables), it turns out that even under rather conservative assumptions, the M1 project had an expected return of investment of 12.5 percent with a risk (standard deviation) of 7.5 percent. Figure 8.4 shows the result of the mean-variance analysis: although the expected return of the M1 project is slightly above the expected market return, its high risk makes it unattractive for risk-averse *and* for risk-neutral investors.

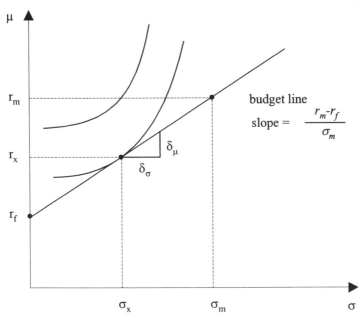

Source: Varian (2000, 354)

Figure 8.3 Mean-variance model

Table 8.4 Parameters for feasibility study and scenarios of M1 highway

Investments: USD 250 mn., spent in project years 1–3
Equity: USD 30 n., debt: USD 220 mn.
interest on debt: 15%
Discount factor: 0.9090 (= 1/(1+r), r = 10%)
Initial exchange rate: HUF/USD = 152.6
Initial users: cars: 11,000
Initial users: lorries/buses: 1,500
Lottery:

Annual exchange rate devaluation (HUF/USD): $\begin{pmatrix} 0\% & 5\% & 10\% \\ 0.2 & 0.7 & 0.1 \end{pmatrix}$

Operating costs (of revenues): $\begin{pmatrix} 5\% & 15\% & 25\% \\ 0.2 & 0.6 & 0.2 \end{pmatrix}$

Annual increase of users (cars, lorries and buses): $\begin{pmatrix} 0\% & 6\% & 12\% \\ 0.2 & 0.4 & 0.4 \end{pmatrix}$

Sources: EBRD, Timàr (1992), Léderer (1996), scenarios based on expert interviews and author's own assumptions

Table 8.5 Cash-flow analysis of the M1 highway project

	1993	1994	1995	1996	1997	1998	1999	2000 ..
Investment (mn. USD)	-100	-100	-50					
Debt (mn. USD)	-70	-100	-50	0	0	0	0	0
Current debt (mn. USD)	-70	-181	-258	-296	-275	-250	-221	-188
Activated interest (mn. USD)	-11	-27	-39	-44	-4	-37	-33	-28
Annuity (mn. USD)	0	0	0	-66	-66	-66	-66	-66
Operating costs (mn. USD)	0	0	0	-6	-6	-6	-6	-6
Revenues (mn. USD)	0	0	0	40	40	41	41	41
Net cash flow (mn. USD)	-30	0	0	-32	-32	-32	-31	-31
Discount factor	1.00	0.91	0.83	0.75	0.68	0.62	0.56	0.51
Present value of cash flow (mn. USD)	-30	0	0	-24	-22	-20	-18	-16
NPV (mn. USD)	-32							
Internal rate of return	8.34 %							

Sources: Author's calculations, based on the assumptions explained above

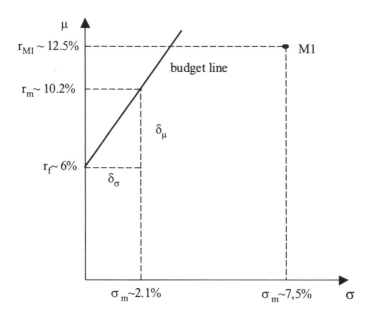

Figure 8.4 Mean-variance analysis of the M1 highway project

4.4.2 The option value of waiting

One major drawback of any project financing in the early years of transformation is the high *uncertainty* regarding future demand and other parameters. As we saw in the previous section, this uncertainty affected the feasibility study of the M1 significantly. In addition, the project was decided upon under heavy time pressure which may have favored premature decisions.[208] An indication whether the decision to build the M1 was premature is provided by the real option theory of investment (see Dixit and Pindyck, 1994, Brealey and Myers, 2000, chapter 21). In essence, this approach considers a project to be similar to any other financial option which *may* be executed but does not *have* to be. Thus, the possibility to *delay* the project and wait for more information has a positive value; this value of

---

[208] The project M1 was in fact the designated pilot infrastructure project for the preparation of the World Exposition 1996 that had been awarded to Budapest. This put pressure on the time frame: all contracts had to be signed and construction work had to start in 1993 to assure the timely opening of the highway. The Austrian government had promised to finish the remaining 20 km of highway and a by-pass around Vienna; on the Hungarian side, too, a 15 km circular road around Budapest was part of the infrastructure built for the World Exposition (Timàr, 1992, 32). The irony of history is that the World Exposition in Budapest was cancelled in late 1995, due to insufficient financial funds and the delay caused by technical preparations.

waiting may be so high that foregoing it by executing the project immediately may be inefficient in terms of expected net present value.

When applied to the M1 highway project, the real option theory would suggest that constructing it as early as 1993 might have been premature, as it destroyed a relatively high value of waiting, and the option *not* to carry out the project at all (which, as the former section has shown, would have been the best solution from a financial perspective). In particular, the high uncertainty regarding the macroeconomic parameters (GDP, traffic volumes, exchange rate) might have favored a delay of the project. As more information became available about the modest GDP development and demand for the road, for example, it might have become evident that the project would not pay for its investment.

The following simulation relies on very restrictive assumptions and serves for illustrative purposes only:

– The Hungarian government and the investor have the option to start the project in 1993, or to delay the project by one year;

– during that year of waiting, information on the realization of all three uncertain variables (devaluation, operating costs, traffic flows) becomes available (that is, the realization of the high-, medium-, or low-scenario);

– for the rest of the project duration, the variables are stationary.

Given these assumptions, the net present value of the project including a delay of one year is:

$$NPV^{delay} = \frac{1}{(1+r)} \sum_{i=1}^{27} q_i \cdot \max\left\{ \sum_{t=0}^{35} (1+r_f)^{-t} \cdot cash\ flow, 0 \right\} + I \cdot r = USD\ 197.03\ mn.$$

The expected present value of the project without waiting is only US 191.01 mn., that is, lower than the calculated net present value of delaying (USD 197.03 mn.), which implies that the investment decision on the M1 should have been *delayed*.

5. CONCLUSIONS

This chapter has highlighted the difficulties of implementing innovative instruments of infrastructure financing in Eastern Europe, taking the example of private project financing. In the early years of reform, private project financing of highways was considered a serious option to strengthen the underdeveloped infrastructure, to relieve the state from additional expenditures, and also to increase the efficiency of infrastructure projects. International experience from industrial *and* emerging countries indicates that the success of private financing models hinges upon the efficient participation of the state, including an optimal distribution of risks. Positive experiences are manifold, mainly in Latin America (Chile, Argentina), showing that private highway financing is feasible even under difficult macroeconomic and institutional conditions.

The attempts to introduce private financing models for highway construction in Eastern Europe in the early transformation period have to be assessed critically. Among the 20 projects conceived initially, only one has been carried out as planned, whereas the other ones were either transformed into more traditional state financing, or put on hold altogether. Evidence suggests that the specific conditions of financing, planning and executing highway projects in Eastern Europe were not sufficiently taken into account: among these factors are economic ones (low traffic volumes, low willingness to pay, high inflation) and institutional ones (low administrative competence, resistance against price differentiation, underdeveloped financial markets). The case study of the first project financing across Eastern Europe, the M1 highway in Hungary, highlights some of the difficulties. Although the qualitative jump into purely private financing failed, the countries attempting innovation (such as Hungary and Poland) have succeeded better in introducing toll highways than those rejecting any institutional innovation (such as Romania and Ukraine). One major lesson from Eastern Europe is that a *gradual* approach is more conducive to success in the transformation context than a radical approach.

It is not too late for institutional reforms in East European highway development. In fact, this remains an area where EU-accession countries can outpace their fellow West European neighbors in reforms. In order to do so, the East European governments should introduce gradually, if they have not yet done so, the following:

– Separation of the sovereign functions from the commercial functions, for example, the creation of a state highway fund alongside private project companies,

– gradual integration of private financing and operation in the framework of private-public-partnerships,

– introduction of a highway toll including distance-related and congestion elements, or, if this proves unfeasible, at least

– introduction of a shadow toll system, accompanied by a general highway toll (vignette).

9. Power Utility Re-regulation

... if I didn't tell her, I could leave today,
California dreaming, on such a winter's day ...

The Mamas and the Papas.

1. INTRODUCTION

Power sector restructuring is among the most complex, and certainly the most politically sensitive fields of infrastructure sector reform in any developing, emerging, and industrial country.[209] This applied to Eastern Europe, where the power sectors had to be entirely reorganized after the end of socialist planning. This chapter provides an institutional interpretation of power sector re-regulation in Eastern Europe during the decade of systemic transformation. The available empirical literature on Eastern Europe, such as Newberry (1994), Stern and Davis (1998), Kennedy (1999, 2002a, b), Opitz (2000) and EBRD (2001b), reports evidence on the difficulties of restructuring and privatizing electric utilities in Eastern Europe, but does not converge on the question as to *why* progress has been relatively slow thus far.

The analysis is, once again, based on a comparative institutional approach. In particular, the *transaction costs* of implementing and running different organizational models vary both with respect to the institutional endowment of a country and the technical state of its infrastructure (Bickenbach et al. 1999). The hypothesis that we pursue in this chapter is that, given the systemic and institutional change in Eastern Europe and the worn-out state of the infrastructure, it may not have been possible to implement 'best-practice' Western reform models in Eastern Europe. Section 2 discusses the options for regulatory reform in the power sector; Section 3 identifies the specific conditions of power sector reform in Eastern Europe, both institutional and technical. Section 4 presents a survey of power sector reform, appended by three country case studies (Poland, Hungary and Ukraine). Quantitative indicators are wholesale and retail prices, cost coverage ratios, investment

---

[209] The interaction between institutions and public policy in different regional/national and sectoral settings has been studied in depth for the power sectors in the USA (Joskow, 1997), Western Europe (Glachant, 1998), Latin America (Spiller, 1993) and Asia (World Bank, 2000).

levels and the degree of unbundling and privatization. Section 5 concludes with policy recommendations.[210]

2. OPTIONS FOR REGULATORY REFORM IN THE POWER SECTOR

2.1 Models for a Competitive Power Sector

This section briefly recalls the options facing East European countries desiring to reform their power sectors in the early 1990s (for surveys see Kennedy, 1999, or Kumkar, 1999). The power sector can be considered as consisting of four distinct activities:
- Generation (in power plants)
- high-voltage transmission (about 110–500 kV)
- low-voltage distribution (about 0.4–30 kV)
- sales and trading.

Transmission and distribution are considered natural monopolies. The hypothesis of market-oriented regulatory reform is that by introducing competition in power generation, by liberalizing trade and by installing an efficient regulation on the remaining monopolies, total welfare can be increased. The reform models which are implemented world-wide in order to introduce competition in the power sector can be classified into four groups, the difference being
- the degree of vertical integration;
- which stage in the value added chain is opened for competition (generation and/or wholesale and/or retail trade); and
- the regulation of the remaining activities (mainly transportation).

The following description of the reform models takes as reference the *status quo ante* prevailing both in Eastern Europe and in continental Western Europe, that is, vertically integrated monopolists subject to some rate-of-

---

[210] This chapter originates from a joint paper with Petra Opitz prepared for the Annual Conference of the International Society for New Institutional Economics (ISNIE), September 13-15, 2001, Berkeley (USA), which also appeared as DIW Discussion Paper No. 246 (2001) and TU-WiWi-Dok Discussion Paper 2001/10. Particular thanks are due to Petra Opitz for the permission to reprint parts of the latter. The chapter has benefited from the participation in a long-term advisory project to the government of Ukraine, the EU-Trans-European-Network project 'Baltic Ring', and an EU-DGII-ACE project on infrastructure policies in Eastern Europe. Thanks to Paul Gregory, Christoph Hassel, William Hogan, Ken Koford, Wolfgang Pfaffenberger, Russel Pittman, Barbara Praetorius, Wolfram Schrettl, Reimund Schwarze, Jon Stern, Thomas Waelde, and seminar participants at the University of Deleware and Berlin University of Technology for comments.

return regulation, often owned by the state (we follow Kumkar, 1999, 14 sq.):[211]

a) In the *single buyer* model, competition is introduced only in generation, via negotiations between the single buyer and the independent power generators or importers. The single-buyer is a monopsonist upstream and a monopolist downstream;

b) the *pool* model allows competition in generation and retail trade. Wholesale trade is organized by a pool which becomes a re-regulated monopoly (such as in the English and Welsh model). The pool dispatches load on the basis of a merit order (supply) and the forecast demand; it charges a fee for transmission, service and capacity. All stages of the value added chain are vertically disintegrated and organized within separate companies. If one assumes full information and a benevolent regulator, the pool model yields a welfare optimizing price mechanism;

c) the model of *Third Party Access (TPA)* abolishes the wholesale trade monopoly and allows competition in generation, wholesale and retail trade. Access to the transportation and distribution lines may be *negotiated* or *regulated*. Disintegration may be structural (full unbundling) or formal (accounting unbundling only, which implies the danger of transfer pricing);

d) the *common carrier* model (also general access model, market model) is generally considered the most liberalized model. Common carriage is a system implying vertical disintegration, free access to the network, and a full range of trading institutions at the wholesale and the retail level; there may be, but does not have to be, a centralized trading floor where short-term or long-term contracts are struck. In its pure form, competition prevails at all levels, only transportation remains a regulated monopoly. Commercial and physical transactions are separated; traders play the most important role for optimizing capacity use.[212]

2.2 A Transaction Cost Based Comparison Between Regulatory Models

The last 15 years have witnessed a lively debate about the efficiency of different models of power sector deregulation (Kumkar, 2000). Traditional

---

[211] Note that none of these models exists in reality in its pure form described below. Within the European Union (15 member states), there are no less than six distinct modes of regulation; with further liberalization, the variety of industry structures is likely to increase (source: Eurelectric; for an institutional interpretation see Glachant, 1998).

[212] The market for differences, that is, the quantities not contracted in advance, remains the monopoly domain of the system operator. For this reason, the common carrier model and the pool model are much less different in practice than they are in theory. Thus, in the PJM-model (Eastern United States) which is generally considered to be a centralized pool, 85 percent of the transactions are simple bilateral agreements. (I am grateful to William Hogan for this remark.)

competition theorists had argued that structural vertical disintegration was necessary to yield optimal results from liberalization.[213] By contrast, new approaches in microeconomic theory insist on the importance of information asymmetries in the definition of a regulatory model.[214] Also, the dangers of *collusion* and *double marginalization* that deregulation may bring about in the absence of efficient regulation have to be addressed. Thus, Meran and Schwarze (1998) have shown that if the natural monopolist, the system operator, cannot be forced to supply its transport capacity efficiently, then 'vertical disintegration with competition of power supply and reregulation of the power distribution does not beat the old fashioned system of vertically integrated electricity supply under regulation.' (p. 279).[215]

New institutional economics also argues that there is no simple solution to the conflict of interest that the regulator faces between creating conditions for socially optimal private investment (and thus assuring a stable and efficient supply and safeguarding investments), while at the same time forcing the monopolist to pass a maximum of his or her rent on to the consumers. The *hold-up* problem, where the regulator expropriates the quasi-rent from the private investor once the latter has sunk his or her investment, is particularly acute in a context where institutional structures are unstable, political strategies are short-term and external sanctions (such as reputation losses for an unstable regulator) are not well established.[216] Spiller (1993, 393) even argues that in a context characterized by political instability, weak judiciary and regulatory institutions and slow economic growth, *state ownership* of utilities and state investment may be (socially inefficient) default responses, as no private investor accepts the risk of expropriation.

---

[213] Cf. Gröner, H. (1965, 'Ordnungspolitik in der Elektrizitätswirtschaft'. *ORDO*, 333-412).

[214] Indeed, if there was no informational asymmetry and one assumed a stable institutional environment, *any* of the regulatory schemes described above, and even the vertically integrated monopoly, yielded the same, efficient result; in reality, information asymmetries and unstable institutions make all the difference between efficient and inefficient regulation.

[215] The reason is that by structurally separating transmission from generation and distribution, the efficient supply of energy *within* the vertically integrated firm is no longer assured, which leads to lower quantities supplied to the final consumer at higher prices.

[216] Traditionally, the issue of safeguarding investment has been dealt with in the definition of incentive-based versus cost-based regulation. Laffont and Tirole (1993, 19) have proposed that a low-powered 'cost of service regulation offers more protection of measurable investment than [high-powered] price cap regulation.' The reason for this is that under a rate-of-return regulation, prices can be adjusted instantaneously, whereas in price cap regulation there is a certain lag (until the next review). *De facto* price cap regulation can be considered as a lagged rate-of-return regulation, thus the problem of safeguarding investment can be reduced by shortening review periods. Armstrong and Vickers (1996, 305) argue in the case of Eastern European transformation countries for a 'regulatory lag shorter than the four or five years of British price caps but longer than under traditional U.S. regulation.'

In transformation countries, or other emerging and developing economies, there is no such thing as a smoothly functioning judicial system that respects property rights and contracts. 'Independent' regulatory agencies are neither conceivable nor even desirable in countries where this independence might either be curtailed overnight, or be misused for other purposes (such as for the individual enrichment of the regulator). Nor can the regulator be expected to invest in reputation building if his or her time horizon is short. We therefore propose to move away from the traditional welfare-oriented debate of 'first-best' models and concentrate on the *transaction costs* of different reform models in a transformation or developing context.[217] Following Kumkar (1999, 134 sq.), these transaction costs can be related to:

– safeguarding specific investments,

– defining optimal price structures (regional differentiation of power and network prices),

– regulating the market for differences (a natural monopoly of the system operator), and

– developing competing institutions of trading.

The difference between Eastern European power sectors and developed market economies lies mainly in the large investments that the former require for upgrading their worn-out equipment to international standards.[218] We shall therefore concentrate on the first aspect, safeguarding of investments. Bickenbach et al. (1999, 34 sq.) propose two types of criteria with regard to which the transaction costs of safeguarding in the different models can be compared: technical ones (market size, state of the transmission network) and institutional ones:

– the *market size* determines the extent to which real competition can be expected after deregulation. If the market is small, collusion between producers is likely. The market size also impacts the discretionary power of the regulator: if the market is small, there will be less external usage of the grid (TPA), which complicates the standardization of access conditions and increases the risk of discrimination;

– the *density of the transmission networks* also determines the maximal level of competition between regions and the degree of discretionary regulatory power. Only as long as a dense, redundant transportation network is available can different power plants really be put in competition without

---

[217] Kumkar (1999, 51) defines transaction costs in a pragmatic way as the difference between total costs of supply (including the cost of regulation) and the minimal production costs in the (hypothetical) 'first best' case; an optimal regulation model is one with regard to which no superior model, that is, implying lower transaction costs, can be defined.

[218] The investment needs of the Eastern European power sector were estimated at several tens of bn. USD by the European Commission, other estimates went as high as hundreds of bn. USD (see Chapter 4).

reducing system security.[219] An underdeveloped network also increases the heterogeneity of TPA, implying a complication of the regulation of the grid company, but also a lower degree of controllability of the regulator (Kumkar, 1999, 71).

Other things being equal, the transaction costs to safeguard specific investments are inversely related to the market size and the network density. In a small market with low network density, the single buyer model minimizes transaction costs, whereas transaction costs are relatively high in a common carrier model, as all possible complications of trade relations have to be integrated in the contracts. With increasing market size and network density, the relation is inverted: the common-carrier model features the lowest transaction costs of safeguarding in a large market without technical constraints (Table 9.1, upper part).

On the other hand, the *stability of the institutional environment* also has an impact on the transaction costs. In an unstable institutional environment, transaction costs depend crucially upon the discretion of the regulator: the wider the competencies and the fields of action of the regulator and the degree of vertical integration of the power sector, the higher the regulatory risk. Thus, in the absence of institutional checks and balances, a policy limiting the scope of activity of the regulator is a measure of reducing the regulatory risk. In this respect, the common carrier model has relatively low transaction costs, whereas the single-buyer model is most exposed to regulatory risk, due to the breadth of regulated activities and the high degree of vertical integration (Table 9.1, lower part).

The institutional interpretation of reform models implies that the chance of success in introducing competition into the power sector is positively related to the existence of a considerable market size, the availability of sufficient network capacity (grid and distribution net) and the stability of the institutional framework (reliable politics, independent judiciary, economic growth and the like). Bickenbach et al. (1999, 34) draw concrete conclusions on the appropriateness of different regulatory regimes:

-- The single buyer model seems adequate for countries with a less developed, relatively small power sector;[220]

---

[219] The quantification of the network density is technically difficult, as it not only includes the structure and capacity of the network itself, but also of the associated metering and communication system. Fintzel, Andreas (2001, *Stromsektorreform in Osteuropa – Ein Vergleich*. Berlin University of Technology, Master Thesis) suggest to take the degree of synchronization (ϕ) as an indicator for network efficiency.

[220] Lovei (2000) argues on the contrary that the single-buyer model is a 'dangerous path towards competitive electricity markets', and that it has major disadvantages in developing and transformation countries: 'It invites corruption, weakens payment discipline, and imposes large contingent liabilities on the government. These disadvantages in most cases overshadow the higher short-term costs of a "bilateral contract model" where generators contract with customers.' (p. 1).

– the common carrier model is suited for large, highly-developed industries, but also in an unstable regulatory framework;

– the advantages of these two 'extreme' forms (single buyer and common carrier) are related to the transaction costs of securing specific investments in generation and distribution against the hold-up problem and the administrative costs of regulating access prices;

– the pool model and the (regulated or negotiated) access are suitable intermediate solutions (on the path to common carriage) in growing economies; in medium-sized, less dynamic power sectors they can be the ultimate solution in and of themselves (note that for developed power sectors, the differences between the pool and the common carrier model largely disappear).

The institutional approach, when applied to Eastern Europe, reveals a *paradox*: first, given small market sizes and technically underdeveloped networks in most countries of Eastern Europe, the approach would suggest the application of a single buyer model; on the other hand, given substantial institutional instability and regulatory risk, a common carrier model or a non-obligatory pool seem to be most suitable. Second, the advantage of the common carrier model may disappear when the transaction costs of enforcing individual contracts are high, which is likely in a transformation economy; in that case, standardized contracts might be preferable and thus the single buyer model with supply obligation may be most appropriate.

The discussion shows that if one takes the transaction-cost approach seriously, it is not possible to prescribe a first-best regulatory model, independent of institutional and technical specifics. Based on these theoretical findings, we now shed some light on the *specifics* of power sector reform in East European transformation countries.

Table 9.1 Comparative evaluation of reform models with respect to
transaction costs

Model Specification	a) Single Buyer	b) Pool	c) Third Party Access	d) Common carrier
	Transaction costs of safeguarding specific investments			
low market size, low network density	+	0	0	–
medium market size, medium network density	0	0	+	–
large market size, large network density	–	+	0	+
	Transaction costs related to the institutional environment			
high stability of the institutional environment	0	0	0	0
low stability of the institutional environment	–	0	0	0

+ = low transaction costs
0 = medium transaction costs (or undefined)
– = high transaction costs

Source: based on Kumkar (1999, 141)

3. SPECIAL CONDITIONS OF POWER SECTOR REFORM IN EASTERN EUROPE

3.1 The Institutional Aspects

The restructuring of power industries in Eastern Europe took place within a process of *radical* political, institutional and economic change (for details see Chapter 4). The implications of system transformation on *power sector* restructuring can be traced at three different levels:

   i) The *formal* institutions required for reforming the energy sector were largely missing in the first years of transformation. These include the legal framework and the technical prerequisites to operate and control markets, and budget constraints on enterprises (such as bankruptcy procedures, banking and financial sector regulation, social security);[221]

---

[221] For example, it took until the late 1990s for most transformation countries to vote new energy laws (Poland: 1997, Estonia: 1998, Russia: 1998, the only exception being Hungary: 1994).

ii) the reform of the *informal* institutions could not be decreed by law, but had to emerge 'from below', though to a certain extent driven by external economic constraints, mainly relative prices. Concerning energy, an important informal institution in the post-socialist context was the idea of energy, in particular electricity, being a basic 'human right', a heritage of socialist times and the strong ideological role of electricity therein. As a result, there was a particularly strong discrepancy between supply of and demand for competition-oriented regulation in the power sector;[222]

iii) at a *technical* level power sector reform in Eastern Europe required the transformation of a system shaped by socialist equipment and standards, into one consistent with international cutting edge technology and standards prevailing in next door Western Europe (such as security, frequency stabilization, metering and communication equipment, environmental requirements).

3.2 Technical Parameters

In the early 1990s, the former socialist countries of Eastern Europe possessed a quantitatively well-developed power sector with serious qualitative insufficiencies (security standards, environmental pollution, and so on). Table 9.2 summarizes the main technical characteristics of the Central and East European EU-accession countries and the largest CIS countries (Russia and Ukraine). The following aspects merit attention:
– The power industry in the Central and East European countries was relatively small, only Russia featured a 'large' power sector. In all former socialist countries, specific electricity consumption (kWh/USD GDP) was among the highest in the world. Capacity utilization was below international standards;
– the network density was relatively high; however, the technical state of the network was bad throughout the region (problems of system security, frequency stabilization, insufficient measuring and communication equipment); this limited the extent to which competitive trading could take place;
– the unexpected drop in aggregate economic production (GDP) led to a sharp drop in electricity consumption throughout the transformation

---

[222] Stern (1994, 392 s.q.) explicitly introduced the notion of demand for and supply of economic regulation in CEE countries. He concludes that 'the key reason why so little progress has been made on instituting legally based, independent economic regulation of the energy sector in CEE countries is that the demand for it is concentrated on foreign and private investors and, indeed on a subset of them. Supply factors are also important, particularlry in practical terms, but could probably be overcome if the demand were sufficiently high.'

countries, and particularly in the republics of the former Soviet Union (Russia: by 30 percent, Lithuania: by 45 percent);

– the share of nuclear power was small, but had risen significantly during the last decade of socialism. In the 1990s and even until today, Eastern Europe, Russia and Ukraine are the only European countries that are constructing new nuclear power plants, with a projected increase of capacity from 49 GW to 59 GW (Kreibig et al., 2001). This implies an even higher political importance of power sector reform;

– a further constraint on restructuring was the slump in domestic primary energy production (hard coal, lignite, peat, wood, oil shale, etc.), and the dependence upon formerly subsidized oil and gas deliveries from Russia. In some countries, power sector restructuring was linked to the restructuring of the upstream coal industry (Poland, Czech Republic, Hungary, Ukraine), in part through forced vertical integration. Thus, short-term political constraints limited the scope of reform options.

Table 9.2 Basic technical data of East European power sectors (1999)

	Poland	Czech Republic	Hungary	Slovak Republic	Slovenia	Estonia
Net electricity generation (TWh)	130.3	60.3	34.3	20.0	13.2	8.7
Electricity import (TWh)	4.6	8.4	3.9	5.0	0.5	0.1
Electricity export (TWh)	8.1	10.8	3.3	2.5	2.1	0.7
Net electricity consumption (TWh)	111.5	52.9	30.1	21.1	10.7	7.6
Population (Mill.)	38.7	10.3	10.1	5.4	1.9	1.4
Consumption per capita (kWh per capita)	3470	1954	3359	3915	1777	5315
Electricity consumption/GDP (kWh/USD)	1.427	2.001	0.852	1.739	0.415	1.225
Year of lowest net electricity consumption since 1990	1992	1993	1994	1993	1993	1993
Drop of consumption in relation to 1990 (in %)	- 9	-10	-12	-10	- 10	-33
Installed Capacity (GW)	29.9	13.9	7.9	8.3	2.5	2.7
of which:						
Thermal Electric Power	27.9	11.3	6.2	3.3	1.1	2.7
Nuclear Electricity	0.0	1.8	1.8	2.6	0.7	0.0
Hydroelectricity	2.0	0.9	0.0	2.4	0.7	0.0
International grid connection	UCTE	UCTE	UCTE	UCTE	UCTE	UES

Table 9.2 (continued)

	Lithu-ania	Latvia	Ro-mania	Bulgaria	Russia	Ukraine
Net electricity generation (TWh)	15.6	4.8	52.5	38.4	771.9	157.9
Electricity import (TWh)	0.3	0.8	1.2	1.8	5.8	4.1
Electricity export (TWh)	4.2	0.3	0.5	2.0	21.0	7.0
Net electricity consumption (TWh)	7.8	4.9	49.6	35.5	702.7	144.0
Population (Mill.)	3.6	2.7	22.6	8.6	146.5	50.5
Consumption per capita (kWh per capita)	4615	5510	2195	4128	4795	2851
Electricity consumption/GDP (kWh/USD	1.278	0.704	1.647	2.426	2.006	2.262
Year of lowest net electricity consumption since 1990	1994	1995	1994	1994	1998	1997
Drop of consumption in relation to 1990 (in %)	-40	-45	-25	-20	-30	-33
Installed Capacity (GW) of which:	6.3	2.1	22.6	12.1	205.6	55.3
Thermal Electric Power	2.6	0.6	16.1	1.4	140.5	36.7
Nuclear Electricity	3.0	-	0.6	3.5	21.2	13.9
Hydroelectricity	0.7	1.5	5.9	7.1	43.9	4.7
International grid connection	UES	UES	-	-	UES	UES

Sources: EIA; IEA: Electricity Information 2000, Paris, 2000; IEA: Energy Balances of Non-OECD Countries 1996-1997, Paris, 1999; IEA: Energy Statistics and Balances of Non-OECD Countries, Paris, various issues; IEA: Electricity in European Economies in Transition, Paris, 1994; Lietuvos Energija

4. RESULTS OF POWER SECTOR REFORM: SURVEY AND COUNTRY CASE STUDIES

4.1 Survey: Little Competition After a Decade of Reform

Ten years after the inception of economic transformation, and just before many East European countries accede to the European Union, power sector reform has resulted in relatively *little* competition. Indeed almost all Eastern European and CIS countries had opted for the introduction of competition in power generation and trade, mainly based upon the pool model (Poland, the Baltic countries, Russia, Ukraine, initially even Hungary). Other countries, although tending toward some form of vertical integration, had also committed themselves to competition in generation and wholesale trading (for example, the Czech Republic and Slovakia). Table 9.4 (at the end of this chapter) presents the main results of ten years of power sector reform in Central and Eastern Europe and the CIS. They can be summed up as follows:

– *Industry structures* have not been sufficiently transformed to allow real competition. Few competitive measures were introduced in power generation, where the plants sell mainly to a state-owned reseller (for example, in Hungary and Ukraine) or have remained vertically integrated for a large part (such as in the Czech Republic). None of the projects for independent power production (IPP) has materialized. Regional monopolies persist in Hungary, the Czech Republic and, to a large extent, in Poland and Ukraine;

– the countries had a difficult time forming *regulation agencies* capable of introducing a competition-oriented, transparent regulatory framework. Where energy regulatory bodies exist (such as in Poland, Hungary, Russia and Ukraine), they have either remained under the influence of the respective branch ministry (economics, trade and industry, energy) or have been under severe political pressure (such as in Russia or Ukraine);

– *privatization* did not proceed as rapidly as expected. The privatization of power plants was sluggish (Poland, Estonia, Czech Republic) or even forbidden (Ukraine) in phase I of transformation. The privatization of the power grid was not seriously considered by *any* transformation country for strategic reasons.[223] Where privatization was partly carried out, it did not lead to more efficient governance structures (an example being Russia). The major exception to this rule was Hungary, which completely privatized generation and distribution.

4.2 Slow Price Adjustment

A sign that reforms have not attained their objectives is the development of absolute and relative electricity prices. As of 2001, none of the Eastern European countries had achieved price rebalancing, in other words, the adaptation of household and industry prices according to the true cost relation. Figure 9.1 shows household to industry price ratios: some countries have gradually raised the cost ratio (such as Poland and Slovenia), whereas others continue the subsidization of household consumption through industrial consumers and/or the state budget (Czech and Slovak Republics, Russia).[224] In addition, *cost-coverage* ratios of electricity prices remain low (Figure 9.2). Long-run maginal costs are attained in no East European

---

[223] There is one exception, Kazakhstan, with a (failed) attempt to privatize the grid to a foreign company (see Kennedy, 2002b).

[224] Full rebalancing is achieved when both household and industrial prices correspond to their respective long-run marginal costs. For comparison: in OECD and EU countries, the household-to-industry price ratio in equilibrium is estimated between 1.8 and 2, the reason being much higher distribution costs in the residential and household sectors.

country. This applies in particular to household prices, that were below 50 percent cost-coverage in *all* transformation countries. Industry prices fared somewhat better, but they, too, did not exceed 70 percent cost coverage.

The low cost coverage can be interpreted in two ways: either prices remain subsidized directly or indirectly, which hampers the adaptation of consumer behavior to the true costs, keeps consumption artificially high and thus contributes to further distortions of long-term investment projects. On the other hand, Stern and Davis (1998, 444) argue that as long as monopolistic structures prevail, and given that the power plants have earned their depreciation, adapting prices to long-run marginal costs would 'allow electricity companies to embark on large and potentially wasteful investment programs'.

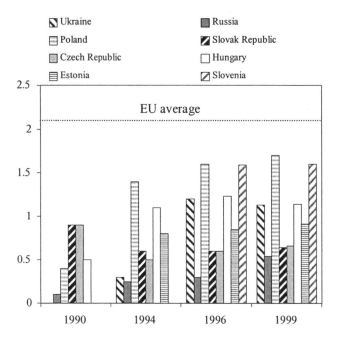

Sources: Stern and Davis (1998); IEA: Electricity Information; 2000; Eesti Energia AS; Eles Slovenija; RAO EES Rossii

Figure 9.1 Ratio of household to industry prices (1999)

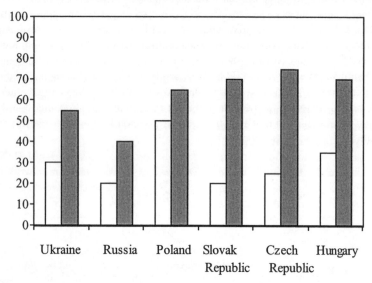

Sources: Stern and Davis (1998); IEA: Energy Prices and Taxes, various issues, author's own
calculations

Figure 9.2 Cost-coverage ratios of electricity prices (1990–99)

4.3 Poland: Much Talk, Little Competition

In the remainder of this section, we elaborate on the specific experiences of
three countries (Poland, Hungary and Ukraine), representing quite different
approaches to the choice of models and implementation of reforms, and
widely divergent outcomes. The *Polish* power sector reform is an example of
the difficult implementation of an ambitious reform project, mainly due to
resistance from interest groups. The Polish power sector is the largest in
Central and Eastern Europe, including 34 larger, mainly coal-fired plants
(total capacity of 32 GW) that produced almost 150 TWh in 1998 (capacity
utilization around two-thirds). The grid is quite developed quantitatively, with
bottlenecks in some peripheral regions (such as the North-East); however, the
equipment is largely worn-out, leading to reduced reliability and power
losses. The main technical, political and economic problem is the dependence

upon domestic hard coal and lignite, which are both expensive and environmentally damaging (Kuba, 1998). From the inception of reforms, this problem led to substantial pressure on the coal and power industry to delay the liberalization of the power sector and price rebalancing. Nonetheless, the Polish reform project was among the more ambitious of the East European countries. In its preliminary form it was a combination of a British-style pool model with competitive bidding between generators, and non-discriminatory access to the grid for direct contracts between generators and large customers (above 40 GWh/a). The project included structural unbundling of the power plants, the grid company (renamed PSE SA) and the regional distribution companies.[225] Price rebalancing and full cost-coverage were supposed to be achieved before the year 2000.

However, the implementation of the reform project was slow. Until 1997, when the Polish Energy Law finally came into force, the system worked according to a single-buyer principle. The Energy Law included various measures of liberalization. An independent regulatory body was created (ERO, Energy Regulatory Office) and given substantial discretion, including wholesale and retail price regulation. In 1998, a contract market was created, whereas trading on the so-called exchange market ('stock market') started in late 2000, at modest levels only. Regulated third party access to the grid (rTPA) for consumers above 40 GWh was introduced, on paper, in 2000. Thus, not only did it take ten years to implement the first significant reform steps, but the original reform model was in fact substantially altered to avoid the effects of competition on the power industry and upstream coal mining – see similar criticism by Kuba (1998) and Yarrow (1997):

– There is hardly any competition in generation or at the level of wholesale or retail trade. At the wholesale level, the grid company PSE continues to act *de facto* as a single buyer, negotiating long-term power contracts with the generating companies, and selling it on to the 32 quasi-monopolistic regional distributors.[226] Trading on the stock market remained marginal (average trading volume in October 2000 was 3,500 MWh). None of the three projects for independent power production has been implemented;

– privatization has proceeded slowly. As of mid-2001, among the 34 power plants to be privatized, only eight had been sold to a new owner, most

---

[225] Independent power producers were offered generous conditions for obtaining licenses: three (foreign) investors purchased licenses for independent power production: Enron in Nowa Warzyna (synchronization was initially planned for late 1999), Eurogas/National Power International in Zielona Gora (gas) and a third company in Belchatow (coal).

[226] In 1999, two-thirds of electricity was managed by PSE; only few direct contracts were made between generators and large customers, mainly state-owned companies. This modification of the initial project was justified with the necessity of keeping the coal-burning power plants in the market in order to cushion the drop of demand for domestic coal.

of them partially.[227] Only one of the 32 regional distribution companies was sold to a foreign investor (Warsaw, sold to the Swedish Vattenfall). The grid company PSE, projected to be 49 percent privatized, has remained in 100 percent public ownership;

– the Energy Regulatory Office did not develop into an independent agent and has remained under strong government influence thus far, and thus subject to interest group lobbying;

– though relative prices were almost rebalanced (1999 household over industry prices: 1.6), the absolute price level remains well below long-run marginal costs.[228]

Delayed liberalization does not seem to have favored private investment, nor is there evidence that the sale prices of public generation and distribution companies have benefited from the delay. The state continues to maintain a central position in the Polish power sector, as the supplier of inputs (coal), the dominant generator, the grid company, and the final distributor, a situation already prevailing in 1994 (IEA, 1995a, 117). The idea that the obstacles to Polish power sector reform were due to an overly ambitious reform approach, as some argue, can be rejected on the grounds that the technical conditions favored a competition-oriented model (34 quasi-independent power plants, a medium-sized market and a relatively well developed network, relatively stable institutional framework after the 1997 Energy Law). Rather, the development should be explained by the broad coalition of anti-reforming interest groups (coal mining, state-owned power industry, parts of the government, large parts of public opinion): the political costs of pursuing a competition-oriented reform were too high, given the low political yield.

4.4 Hungary: Privatization and Investment Rather than Competition

The restructuring of the power sector in Hungary is an intriguing case of a deliberate decision *against* competition, and in favor of a rapid modernization of the sector, largely financed by foreign private investment (see for different interpretations, Bakos, 2001, Stern, 1999, IEA, 1999). Hungary is a country with a small power sector, with only 7 GW installed capacity, one dominant

---

[227] CHP-Krakow: 55 percent to EdF; the PAK-complex (Patnow-Adamow-Konin) to Polish Elektrim, furthermore power plants Bedzin, Bialystok, Warsaw, Wroclaw, Gdansk and Zielona Gora.

[228] Long-run marginal costs are estimated at 4–5 UScents/kWh for industrial customers and 8–10 UScents/kWh for households (derived from analysis by Stern and Davis, 1998). Reichel, Markus, J. Malko, and D. Woiciechowski (1998, *Deregulation of the Electricity Market and its Influence on Local Energy Markets – The Example of Poland*. Paper presented at the fourth European IAEE Conference, Berlin, September) report average production costs of 0.039 Pf/kWh (about 1.8 UScents/kWh) for lignite, and 0.057 Pf/kWh (about 2.5 UScents/kWh) for hard coal, which is rather on the high side.

nuclear power plant (Pak, 1,840 MW, 40 percent of generation capacity), and eight larger power plants with capacity above 100 MW.[229] In socialist times, the state-holding company MVMT (Magyar Villamos Müvek Tröszt) was organized in 11 generating plants, six regional distributors and a grid company. In the early days of reform, Hungary claimed to follow a British-style reform model designed in close cooperation with British and US consultants (Newberry, 1994, 298/299). However, after resistance from the management of MVMT, the government decided to keep the sector in its former, quasi-monopolistic structures, and give priority to private, foreign investment as the driving force of modernization. The Electricity Act of 1994, the first of its kind in Eastern Europe, left the choice of the reform model open, so that the subsequent governments were free to install a *single-buyer* model. The State Energy Office was established, which was responsible for issuing licenses for respective business activity in the power sector, for construction of power plants, safety issues and for negotiating electricity tariffs.

Once the formal regulatory structure was set up, the government proceeded quickly with the privatization of generation and distribution. Investors were offered a rate-of-return regulation (on average, 8 percent on capital), they had to commit to significant investments in the modernization of capacities in generation, transmission lines and distribution. Table 9.3 shows the ownership structure of the Hungarian electricity supply industry, the predominance of large Western European utilities is evident (see also Bakos, 2000).[230] Even after privatization of generation and distribution, the single-buyer model was maintained.[231] Until 2000, there was no real competition, either in generation, where dispatch was organized by long-term contracts, or in distribution, given away to regional monopolies that enjoyed exclusive supply licenses.[232]

---

[229] In 1990, the installed capacity of 7 GW satisfied 70 percent of the county's electricity demand (39 TWh), the rest was imported (IEA, 1999). Due to economic decline, demand decreased until 1995 and was stabilized since 1997 (around 32 TWh). Traditionally, fossil-fuelled power plants were integrated with lignite mines in the Northern part of the country (27 percent of capacity), the rest being oil- and gas-fuelled plants (17 percent of capacity each).

[230] Between 1994 and 1996, almost USD 3 bn. were received for selling majority stakes in 7 (of the 8) large power plants, all six regional power suppliers and six regional gas supply companies. The Hungarian state, represented by the State Privatization Holding Company, retained a golden share in all of them, giving it control over mergers and acquisitions.

[231] MVM, the renamed corporatized state company (Hungarian Electricity Companies, Ltd.) continued to operate the grid and to act as the single buyer, it continued to hold stakes in generation (mainly the nuclear power plant at Pak), and also in some distribution companies; export and import activities remained exclusively with MVM as well.

[232] Large final consumers can conclude so-called individual public utility contracts with a distribution company; these contracts are freely negotiated without price control.

The Hungarian approach has been criticized for its conservatism (see for example, IEA, 1999, 123; Stern, 1999, 6 sq.; Lovei, 2000). MVM, the corporatized state company, is *de facto* a vertically integrated supplier. Foreign investors that have acquired stakes in generation *and* distribution are *de facto* vertically integrated as well (as long as they maintain good relations with the grid company MVM). Transmission prices are not clearly established, nor are non-discriminatory grid access rules defined as a precondition for competition. However, one may interpret the Hungarian case more positively: given substantial regulatory risk in the early phase of transformation (first half of the 1990s), the Hungarian approach was perhaps a second-best solution to attract investment to the sector and quickly approach European technical standards. The synchronization of the CENTREL-grid with the Western European UCTE-grid was assured in Hungary ahead of schedule (1995). In contrast to the electricity industry in Poland, the Hungarian electricity industry is now able to participate in European competition on a level playing field. Figure 9.3 shows the structure of the Hungarian electricity sector as of 1999.

The second aspect of the Hungarian story is the stabilization of the regulatory environment in the second half of the 1990s, leading to a reduction of regulatory risk. Regulation has proven to be reliable in phase II of transformation: the Hungarian Energy Office has taken a firm stand on the rate-of-return regulation, withstanding pressure of foreign investors to increase generation capacity and to overcapitalize.[233] The Hungarian government has made a binding commitment to market opening according to the EU-Power Directive. All investment contracts make reference to the 15 percent market opening required since 2001, and further increases of freely tradable electricity according to EU-Directive 96/92/EEC. Given a small market and an increasingly stable institutional framework, the single buyer model may have been conducive to modernizing the sector and to privatization.

---

[233] In 1997, the Hungarian Energy Office forced the industry to accept a lower increase of prices than planned, on the grounds that capital expenditures had risen less than expected. In 1998 the Energy Office recalled a license sold to RWE for the construction of the Bukrabany power plant and won the subsequent court case. Thus Hungary was able to avoid the investment ruin that developed in East Germany under a similar regulatory regime, but with heavy subsidies by the government and without a binding commitment to liberalization.

Table 9.3 Ownership structure of the Hungarian electricity supply industry (1999)

		Foreign ownership	Hungarian ownership
Elmü	75.6 %	RWE: 50.6 % EnBW: 25.0 %	24.4 %
Edasz	51.2 %	EdF: 27.4 % Bayernwerke: 23.8 %	51.8%
Titasz	74.9 %	Isar-Amperwerke	25.1%
Emàsz	71.4 %	RWE: 50.0 % EnBW: 21.4 %	28.6 %
Dédàsz	75.0 %	Bayernwerke[1]	25.0 %
Démàsz	50.0 %	EdF	50.0 %

[1] Bayernwerke belongs to EON Energie AG since 2000.

Source: IEA (1999)

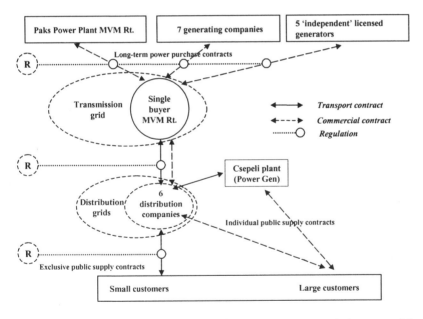

Figure 9.3 Structure of the Hungarian electricity sector: single buyer model (1999)

4.5 Ukraine: Institutional Obstacles to a Competitive Pool System

The Ukrainian power system was designed as an integral part of the Unified Energy System (UES) of the Soviet Union.[234] In 1994, inspired by foreign advice, the Ukrainian government decided to implement bold reforms, including the separation of production, transmission and distribution and the introduction of competition between producers through the creation of a pool (Ryding, 1998).[235] A National Energy Regulation Commission (NERC), officially an independent organization, and a pool-organization (Energorynok, part of the Ministry of Energy) were established. On paper, the regulatory framework indeed looked *more* advanced than the UK model, with at least four production associations and potentially additional independent producers competing with each other, against a duopoly in the UK. Formally, the wholesale market started to operate in April 1996.[236] Privatization was *not* part of the initial reform package.

In practice, the pool system never did function and the Ukrainian power sector was often close to collapse during the subsequent years. Prices were not fixed by the market but by the National Energy Regulatory Agency. A quota system for state consumers was maintained, obliging regional distributors to supply mainly local consumers at low prices. The regulator was controlled politically by the Energy Ministry. Unpaid bills of the customers resulted in a lack of payment to the pool and finally in non-payment to the generators, which became unable to pay for their inputs, most of all for fuel; payments to Oblenergos rarely exceeded 40 percent in the 1990s.[237] System frequency became unstable (down to 49.7 Hz on some days), and users had to be cut off temporarily for security reasons arising in the nuclear power plants.

The main reason for the failure to reform the Ukrainian power sector must be sought in the specific institutional situation that the country faced from 1992 on, in particular the low monetization of the economy, and the

---

[234] Total installed generating capacity in Ukraine amounts to about 55 GW. After a sharp decline of generation from 279 TWh in 1991 to about 172 TWh in 1998, electricity production and consumption seem to have stabilized. Thus, notwithstanding the fact that some of the plants are inoperable, there are large overcapacities (estimated at 12–15 GW, about 25 percent of capacity).

[235] The eight vertically integrated regional utilities were split up in 1993 and transformed into seven generation companies – one for nuclear power, two for hydropower and the remaining four for thermal power, in the four regions of the country: Center, West, South, East – and 27 regional supply companies ('Oblenergos').

[236] The pool's purchasing and selling prices were regulated on a cost-plus basis by the NERC. Only thermal power plants were allowed to bid into the pool; selling prices differed for every region. In addition, prices for the final customers and transport tariffs were also defined by the NERC.

[237] Source: Ministry of Energy. Independent traders developed and started to arrange complex barter-chains in order to solve the fuel problems and to settle payment on the basis on give-and-take contracts. Transaction costs rose and prices became even less transparent.

inconsistency of a legal basis and a rule of law.[238] Ukraine was basically a barter economy. Neither a legal framework nor law enforcement were developed to settle the conflicts of interest; during 1992–99, no private investment took place.[239] The most basic market rules (fulfilment of contracts) did not work. In addition, the absence of an adequate metering and communication system able to control and bill inflows and outflows of the grid implied the impossibility to introduce user-specific prices. The case of Ukraine shows the importance of the institutional environment upon the outcome of power sector reform. Due to highly unstable conditions, the well-intended reform project did not have a chance to succeed. It may be argued that the short-sighted implementation of an overly ambitious reform project has prevented a more gradual restructuring of the industry.

Referring to the theoretical discussion in Chapter 4, one may ask whether the observed delay of reforms in the East European power sector has rendered the restructuring process more sustainable, as some theoretical approaches had implied. Yet we see *no* indication that transformation countries delayed reform deliberately with a specific objective in mind (for example, to spur private investment), with the exception of Hungary. Instead, it seems that competition-oriented reform was resisted by influential *interest groups* rather than held back by far-sighted regulators. Kocenda and Cabelka (1999);[240] Kuba (1998); Opitz (2000); Yarrow (1997); IEA (1996); Stern (1999) and others somewhat converge in reporting evidence on the dominant role of incumbent monopolists, the liability of an ailing coal industry, and the request for monopolistic protection made by foreign investors. Whether or not this conservative policy has spurred investment is doubtful.

---

[238] The roots of this problem are complex. First, a lot of de facto value-subtractors (companies producing non-competitive products) in industry were not closed and were unable to pay their bills. Second, the state itself aggravated non-payment, two-thirds of unpaid bills having been caused by organizations financed from central and local budgets, and the government's debt of wages and pensions continued to increase. Third, certain business groups of political influence benefited from the existing situation.

[239] The electricity law which, after several years of political bargaining in Parliament, was approved in 1997 lacks regulation of the contractual mechanism of the wholesale market. A law on the wholesale market was brought into Parliament in mid-2000, but has been modified regularly since. Corruption and rent-seeking efforts, even within government structures, undermined the first steps of privatization (see Ryding, 1998). Some large potential foreign investors (such as EdF, RWE, Tractebel) which had shown some interest in taking over regional suppliers, turned their backs on Ukraine in 1998 (this was also caused by the August 1998 financial collapse). Only during 1999 were the first nine regional suppliers privatized via auctions, a decision reversed by Parliament in 2000. Privatization of the National Dispatch Center and the nuclear power stations remains forbidden by law.

[240] Kocenda, Evzen, and Stepan Cabelka (1999, 'Liberalization in the Energy Sector in the CEE-Countries: Transition and Growth'. *Osteuropa-Wirtschaft*, 44. Jhg., Nr. 1, 196-225).

5. CONCLUSIONS

This chapter has analyzed a decade of power sector reform in the countries of Eastern Europe and their attempts to adhere to international technical and regulatory standards. The available evidence seems to contradict the hypothesis according to which a competition-oriented approach, such as the British pool model, provided the best option for Eastern European countries to follow. On the theoretical foundation of the new institutional economics, no unequivocal recommendation could have been given to East European countries in the early phase of systemic transformation. While the small market size and the need to catch up technologically favored a single buyer model, high institutional instability implied a reduction of the scope of regulation and, thus, favored a common carrier or pool model. However, neither the technical nor the institutional requirements for competition in the power sector were available in most East European countries in the inception phase of reform.

The empirical evidence also suggests an inverse relationship between the scope of attempted reforms and the real outcome. Strangely, the most radical reforms in Eastern Europe have been attempted by countries with a particularly weak institutional framework (Russia, Ukraine), but with little success. The countries opting for a gradual reform approach (for example, Hungary and the Czech Republic) show no worse, and sometimes even better results than the potentially radical reformers in terms of price rebalancing, investment and regulatory stability. The Hungarian case of a seemingly successful single buyer model combined with rapid privatization and investment is particularly intriguing.

In the second phase of transformation, roughly speaking 1996 and thereafter, one observes a divergence between the state of the power sectors in East European candidates for EU accession and the CIS countries. The latter still suffer from institutional instability and thus rapid liberalization requiring stable regulation is difficult. By contrast, there is no reason to delay the next reform steps in the EU-accession countries any longer. Price rebalancing should be done quickly, and prices should reflect long-run marginal costs in order to give the correct price signals to consumers. Privatization of generation and distribution should now be carried out rapidly. The single buyer model restricts competition in an unnecessary manner; the choice between the two remaining competition models, the pool or generalized network access (common carriage), does not really matter as long as regulation is transparent and pricing non-discriminatory. Assuming that these reforms will be carried out, European enlargement in the power sector should succeed smoothly.

Table 9.4 Main institutional results of power sector reform in Eastern Europe (2001)

	Poland	Hungary	Czech Republic	Slovakia	Slovenia
Market description Generation	35 generating comp.	8 generating comp. and 5 licensed generators	CEZ a.s. [1] (74 %) and Elektrany Opatovice a.s.	SE a.s. [2] (87 %) and some IPP	8 generating comp.
Transmission	PSE SA [3]	MVM Rt. [4]	CEZ a.s.	SE a.s.	Eles [5]
Distribution	33 distribution comp.	6 distribution comp.	8 distribution comp.	3 distribution comp. [6]	5 distribution comp.
Market model/ TPA	rTPA	single buyer model	nTPA	single buyer model	rTPA
Restructuring	unbundling and separation	separation	distribution was separated from generation and transmission	distribution was separated from generation and transmission	separation
Ownership Generation	state and private owned	foreign and Hungarian shareholders; municipalities; MVM Rt.	67 % state owned; some foreign shareholders	mostly state owned	state owned
Transmission	state owned	state owned	67 % state owned; some foreign shareholders	mostly state owned	state owned
Distribution	mostly state owned	mostly foreign shareholders; golden share by the state	46-48 % state owned; municipalities and some foreign shareholders	state owned	state owned
Liberalization Wholesale market	gradually since 1998 – 2006; pool-trading since June 2000; 2006 all customers	MVM as single buyer;	gradual opening planned from 2002	gradual opening planned between 2001-2006	gradual opening planned from 2001
Retail market		small: between retailers and large customers	not yet	not yet	not yet
Regulatory authority	Energy Regulatory Board: URE [7] (Council of Ministers)	Energy Regulatory Board: MEH [8]; Ministry of Economic Affairs; Hungarian Atomic Energy Authority	Energy Regulatory Board as part of the Ministry of Industry and Trade; Ministry of Finance	Ministry of Finance; Ministry of Economy; Antimonopoly Office	some Ministries; Energy Agency (plan)
Legitimization	Energy Law 1997	Electricity Act 1994	Energy Law 1995	Energy Act 1998	Energy Law 9/1999

193

Table 9.4 continued

Market description	Estonia	Lithuania	Latvia	Bulgaria	Romania
Generation	Eesti Energia AS	Lietuvos Energija AB; NPP Ignalina; PP Vilnius and Kaunas	Latvenergo	NEK AG[9)], some separated power plants and industrial generators	Termoelectrica, Hidro-electrica; Nuclear PP; 10 licensed power generators, Transelectrica, Electrica
Transmission	Eesti Energia AS	Lietuvos Energija AB	Latvenergo	NEK AG	Transelectrica
Distribution	5 distribution comp.	7 distribution comp. (Lietuvos Energija AB)	Latvenergo	7 distribution comp.	Electrica
Market model/TPA	rTPA	rTPA	single buyer model	single buyer model	rTPA
Restructuring	separation	some separation		first separation steps	separation
Ownership					
Generation	private and state owned	85 % state owned; 9.8 % foreign shareholders; 4.4 % others	no privatization is planned	state owned; privatization until 2010	state owned
Transmission	state owned				
Distribution	private and state owned				
Liberalization					
Wholesale market	none; gradually as of 2003	gradually as of 2001	none	none	none
Retail market					
Regulatory authority	Energy Market Inspectorate	Energy Agency; Energy Inspectorate; National Control Commission for Energy Pricing and Energy Activity	Energy Regulation Council (Ministry of Economic Affairs)		Energy regulation Authority
Legitimization	Energy Law 1998	Energy Law 2000	Energy Law 1998	Energy and Efficiency Law 1999	2 acts from Energy- Regulatory Authority

[1)] CEZ a.s.: České Energetičke Zavody. – [2)] SE a.s.: Slovenské elektrárne. – [3)] PSE SA: Polskie Sieci Elektroenergetyczne SA. – [4)] MVM Rt.: Magyar Villamos Müvek Részvénytársag. – [5)] Eles: Elektro Slovenia. – [6)] Zapádoslovenské energetičké závody (ZSE); Stredoslovenské energetičké závody (SSE); Vychodoslovenské energetické závody (VSE). – [7)] URE: Urzad Regulacji – [8)] MEH: Magyar Energia Hivatal. – [9)] NEK AG: Natsionalna Električeska Kompania.

Sources: IEA(1995a and 1999); IEA: Electricity in European Economies in Transition, Paris, 1994; IEA: Energy Policies of the Czech Republic, Paris, 1994; IEA: Energy Policies of Slovenia, Paris, 1996; Kennedy (1999); Stern and Davis (1998); Ministry of Economic Affairs of Slovak Republic, Energy Policy of Slovak Republic: http://www.economy.gov.sk/mh/angl2htm; Eesti Energia: Annual Report 1999; Eles: 1999 Annual Report; Lietuvos Energija AB; http://www.cire.pl; http://www.strom.de

10. Gas Sector Restructuring – A Political Economy Approach

To state it clearly: In transformation countries, you first need a
well-functioning monopolistic market in order to approach liberalization.
Mr. Genge, Economic Director, Wintershall AG, 4 April 2001.[241]

1. INTRODUCTION

Having dealt with the power sector in the previous chapter, we now turn to a similar sector in which structural reforms were still more complex in the transformation countries. *Gas sector* restructuring is particularly important in the large CIS producer countries Russia, Ukraine, Turkmenistan and Uzbekistan. Although international organizations regularly push towards deregulation in the gas sector, the national gas industrialists have resisted the introduction of real transparency and competition, while domestic politicians have proven unwilling – or unable – to impose a more market-oriented regulatory regime. Industry structures and the distribution of monopolistic rents remain opaque, a problem which is particularly pronounced in the case of the world's largest gas supplier, Russia's Gazprom.

In this chapter, we adopt a *pragmatic*, political economy point of view to interpret gas sector reform in transformation countries. Our thesis is that gas sector restructuring in the CIS countries will *not* proceed along the lines of either the competition-oriented British model or the gradual reforming West European systems. Instead, the particular political and economic role of the gas industry in these countries will lead to a specific reform trajectory, the result of which is still open. Section 2 describes the evolution of the gas sector in the main CIS producer countries (Russia, Ukraine, Turkmenistan and Uzbekistan) between 1992 and 2001. In Section 3 we make the argument that a specific reform trajectory exists in these countries, and therefore analyze the unrealistic demand projections, the peculiar role of Parliament, and the absence of separation between politics and business. Section 4

---

[241] Wintershall headquarters (Kassel): Presentation 'Liberalization of Gas Markets' given to a Ukrainian governmental delegation.

describes process-oriented policy measures which could help overcome reform obstacles, and Section 5 concludes.[242]

2. THE EVOLUTION OF THE GAS SECTOR IN CIS COUNTRIES

2.1 The Structure of the CIS Gas Sectors

Under socialism, gas sector development was dominated by *political* objectives, be they local (such as providing free energy supply to industry or households) or geopolitical (such as expanding Russia's influence on the rest of the Soviet Union or the CMEA countries). Gas production, transmission and supply were carried out independently of cost and efficiency criteria. In particular, constraints upon production were absent: gas was produced in the most remote, permafrost regions of Siberia, even with the complete absence of local infrastructure. The Russian and Turkmen Soviet Republics subsidized other Soviet Republics through cheap gas deliveries.[243] The gas industry was organized in multifunctional combines which, besides exploring for gas, took care of all social and political aspects of their members' lives; this was particularly true of the remote gas areas developed in the 1970s.

Once socialism had ended, the traditional patterns of gas production and consumption underwent significant change. Table 10.1 shows the natural gas balances for Russia, Turkmenistan, Ukraine, and Uzbekistan for 1985 and for the period 1990–99. In *Russia*, production dropped significantly between 1991 and 1995, and has more or less stabilized since then; domestic consumption was seriously curtailed, which led to increased gas exports to Central and Western European countries, the main solvent clients. Still, the sector remains the most important one in the economy.[244] In *Turkmenistan*, the second largest producer in socialist times, production literally imploded, plummeting by 80 percent between 1991–97; however, since the late 1990s,

---

[242] This chapter originates from a policy paper for the Ukrainian government; an earlier version has appeared in Hirschhausen and Engerer (1999).

[243] See Krasnov, Gregory V., and Josef C. Brada (1997, 'Implicit Subsidies in Russian-Ukrainian Energy Trade'. *Europe-Asia Studies*, Vol. 49, No. 5, 825-843). Only once exporting to Western countries commenced, did gas become a commercial good sold against hard currency.

[244] The figures on the gas industry's importance to the Russian economy are indeed impressive: it contributed no less than 10 percent of total tax revenues. Gas export are about one-sixth of total exports. In terms of employment, too, the gas industry stands out as the 'mother of Russian industries': direct employment of Gazprom, Itera, Sibur, and some smaller companies exceeded 400,000, with indirect employment estimated at 1.5–2 mn. The value of the remaining state-owned shares of Gazprom (37.5 percent of the total) is about USD 30 bn., which would suffice to cover 1.5 years of the Russian government budget deficit alone.

gas production in Turkmenistan has been rising. *Ukraine's* role has diminished and it is now merely a transit country (Balmaceda, 1998). Gas consumption has remained relatively high at 80 percent of the 1991 level; combined with a price increase, this has led to a steep increase in the gas import bill. *Uzbekistan* was able to avoid an output reduction and even succeeded in increasing production slightly; but owing to low energy efficiency and relatively stable domestic consumption, the country has not become a significant net exporter and is unlikely to do so in the future.

In none of the countries have gas prices been fully liberalized thus far. In particular, household gas prices remain low, and the Turkmen government still offers gas to end-users for free. In Russia, the Federal Energy Commission was established in 1995, and given some regulatory authority as well.[245] Table 10.2 shows some structural indicators for the CIS gas industry: the payment ratio for gas deliveries in 1997 was as low as 15 percent and 25 percent in Russia and Turkmenistan, respectively. Barter trade has increased in domestic as well as in intra-CIS trade.[246] Finally, the gas industry is among the largest employers in all CIS countries, a fact that does not commend restructuring. It is estimated that if the CIS gas sectors were restructured and modernized according to the British model, labor requirements would be reduced by between one- and two-thirds.

---

[245] In 1997, gas prices in Russia were differentiated between regions, taking into account transport costs. Prices for households were increased gradually in order to reduce cross-subsidization of industry. However, as in most CIS countries, the main problem of non-payment remains unresolved in Russia as well.

[246] In all countries, the gas sector is heavily involved in the inter-enterprise arrears problem. Furthermore, while the gas industry is, on paper, a major tax payer, the gas concerns have accumulated large tax arrears to the budget (the net position of the gas industry being unknown).

Table 10.1 Gas Balance for Russia, Turkmenistan, Ukraine and Uzbekistan (1985, 1990, 1996–2001)

	1985	1990	1996	1997	1998	1999	2000	2001
				Russia				
Supply	529.9	705.7	..	..	..	..	..	..
Production	462.0	640.5	601.0	570.0	551.3	551.0	545.0	542.4
Imports	67.9	70.2	..	..	..	..	..	..
Stock Increases a	n.a.	5.0	..	..	..	..	..	..
Domestic Consumption	n.a.	456.5	402.5	369.1	364.7	363.6	377.2	372.7
Exports	n.a.	249.2	198.5	200.9	186.6	187.4	167.8	169.7
C.I.S	n.a.	140.2	70.5	80.0	66.3	61.9	..	..
Non-C.I.S	n.a.	109.0	128.0	120.9	120.3	125.5	..	..
				Turkmenistan				
Supply	83.2	87.8	35.2	17.3	12.4	21.3	43.8	47.9
Production	83.2	87.8	35.2	17.3	12.4	21.3	43.8	47.9
Imports	0.0	0.0	0.0	0.0	0.0	0.0	0.0	0.0
Domestic Consumption	14.8	15.9	10.9	10.8	10.3	11.3	12.6	12.9
Exports	68.4	71.9	24.3	6.5	2.1	10.0	31.2	35.0
				Ukraine				
Supply	n.a.	115.1	86.1	80.5	68.8	73.0	68.5	65.8
Production	n.a.	25.5	18.4	18.1	16.7	16.8	16.7	17.1
Imports	n.a.	87.3	68.7	62.4	52.1	56.2	51.8	48.7
Stock Increases a	n.a.	2.3	-1.0	0.0	..	..	..	..
Domestic Consumption	n.a.	115.1	82.5	74.3	68.8	70.6	68.5	65.8
Exports	n.a.	0.0	3.6	6.2	0.0	2.4	..	..
				Uzbekistan				
Supply	34.6	40.8	43.2	53.0	52.3	52.9	52.2	53.5
Production	34.6	40.8	49.0	51.2	51.1	51.9	52.2	53.5
Imports	0.0	0.0	0.0	2.0	1.0	1.0	..	..
Stock Increases a	n.a.	n.a.	-4.8	-0.2	n.a.	n.a.	..	..
Domestic Consumption	30.0	37.9	38.3	43.9	47.0	49.3	49.8	46.0
Exports	4.6	2.9	4.9	9.1	5.3	3.6	2.4	7.5

a – Stock increases refer to gas that has been withdrawn from or added to underground gas storage facilities (Decreases: +; Increases: -). Where data on stock increases is not available (n.a.), it is treated as 0.0

Sources: Compiled from IEA (1995b); Statistical Yearbook of Russia 1996, p. 347 ff., 516; Statistical Yearbook of Russia 1997, p. 345 ff; Russian Economic Trends, 1997, Vol. 3, p. 78 and 85; Rossija v cifrach 1997g., p. 166 and 167; Ukrainian Economic Trends, September 1997, p. 10 and 11; BP Statistical Review of World Energy 2000, author's own calculations and estimates

Table 10.2 Structural indicators of the CIS gas industry (1997)

	Russia	Turkmenistan	Ukraine	Uzbekistan
Employment	375,000	n.a.	110,000[a]	90000[b]
Gas prices (% of international prices)				
- households	25%	0%	77%	67%[c]
- industry	80%	2%	104%	67%
Gas payment ratio	15%[d]	>25%[e]	55%[d]	n.a.

[a]: own estimate based on Ukrainian State Committee for Oil and Gas
[b]: Uzbekneftegaz [c]: wholesale price [d]: share of gas deliveries paid for in cash (Ukraine: including barter) [e]: share of gas exports paid for

2.2 Maintenance of Monopolistic Market Structures

Most *enterprise structures* in the CIS countries have so far resisted attempts to deregulate or unbundle. Vertically integrated monopolies still dominate the gas industry. They came into being in 1992 with the disappearance of the Soviet State Gas Concern Gazprom, founded in 1989 to replace the Soviet Ministry of the Gas Industry. The new national concerns (Gazprom, Turkmengas, Ukrgazprom and Uzbekneftegaz) inherited almost the entire exploration, production, transmission and some distribution activities, engineering and other elements of their respective Republics, not to mention all 'social assets'.[247] If the state is not the sole owner of the company, as is the case with Russia's Gazprom, ownership remains unclear.[248]

---

[247] Thus, Gazprom consists of the headquarters with the international marketing department, nine exploration and production enterprises, five processing enterprises, and 14 gas pipeline transportation enterprises. Furthermore, it owns enterprises in mechanical engineering, transport, an airline, agriculture and food processing, hotels and housing, holiday resorts. Gazprom has also acquired shares in gas companies in all major Central and Western European countries (except the Czech Republic), such as Panrusgas (Hungary), Wingas (Germany), and Promgas (Italy) (see IEA, 1995b, 178; Pleines, Heiko, und Kirsten Westphal (1999, *Rußlands Gazprom – Teil I: Die Rolle des Gaskonzerns in der russischen Politik und Wirtschaft*. Bericht des Bundesinstituts für ostwissenschaftliche und internationale Studien, Nr. 33), and Heinrich, Andreas (1999, *Rußlands Gazprom – Teil II: Gazprom als Akteur auf internationaler Ebene*. Bericht des Bundesinstituts für ostwissenschaftliche und internationale Studien, Nr. 34).

[248] Formally, in 2001, 40 percent of its shares belonged to the Russian State, 33 percent to domestic investors (individual and investment funds), 15 percent to employees and management of Gazprom itself, 9 percent to foreign investors, and 3 percent to others. None of the ministers *not* coming from the gas lobby were successful in increasing the transparency of Gazprom (Tchubais, Nemzov, Kirienko). In mid-2001, the apparatchik Rem Viakhirev was replaced at the top of Gazprom management, and President Putin proposed a vertical unbundling of the group; chances that the project will succeed this time are low.

The structure of Ukraine's Neftegazukraine (the gas branch of which corresponds to the former Ukrgazprom) resembles that of Russia's Gazprom, except that its core activity is transportation rather than production. Neftegazukraine has four main gas activities (exploration and production; transmission; mechanical engineering; technical services), to which social assets have to be added. In contrast to Gazprom, Neftegazukraine is wholly state-owned. Similar industrial structures also prevail in Turkmenistan (Turkmengaz), where the gas industry is directly subordinate to the President via the Ministry of the Oil and Gas Industry, and in Uzbekistan, where the Deputy Prime Minister controls the Uzbekneftegaz Corporation and prescribes its long-term development plans (IEA, 1998).

Thus, the results of ten years of 'reform' have in general been deceptive. Almost all CIS countries had formally agreed to implement bold reform programs. Russia had even conceded to integrate market-oriented gas sector restructuring in its 1996 memorandum of understanding with the International Monetary Fund.[249] But, in reality, monopolistic and opaque industry structures dominate. Gas sector reform in the CIS countries thus differed from the gradual, though slow, approach to reform in the advanced reforming countries in Central and Eastern Europe which was characterized by some vertical unbundling, price liberalization, access of foreign investors, and an improving regulatory environment.[250]

3. THE SPECIFICS OF GAS SECTOR RESTRUCTURING IN THE CIS COUNTRIES

Why has gas sector reform been progressing so slowly thus far in the CIS countries, despite much lip service from governments in favor of reform? We believe that this is due to specific conditions affecting these countries:

– *Lack of a market environment*: as was shown in Chapter 3, many CIS countries still lack fundamental elements and institutions of a market economy. Although attempts have been made thus far to establish and to improve the economic environment, examples such as non-payment indicate that important elements of a market economy have still not been introduced.

---

[249] Concerning the ordinance on structural reforms in the field of natural monopolies enacted in spring 1997, competition in the gas sector should be promoted; for example, new gas enterprises should be given access to the transport network. (*Rossiskaja gazeta*, May 7, 1997, 3).

[250] This is not to say that deregulation in Central and Eastern Europe has made much more progress than, say, in continental Western Europe. However, the binding commitment of Central and Eastern European countries to EU membership, and thus the obligation to apply, *inter alia*, the EU gas directive of 1998, does provide a yardstick for further reform, which is lacking in the CIS.

Unresolved issues of debt arrears often serve as an argument to delay gas sector restructuring;[251]
– *unrealistic demand projections:* reforms are also obscured by unrealistic energy demand projections. Most governments like to issue demand forecasts that assume a return to the production and consumption levels of the 1980s. Also, demand projections are still based upon the assumed *physical* needs of industrial and household consumers, rather than on their *economic* willingness and ability to pay for gas at cost-based prices;[252]
– the role of *parliament:* most of the national parliaments have opposed major changes in gas legislation; where changes were introduced, they were only partially put into practice. Many members of parliament considered the gas industry to be an important lever of political power, and are therefore largely in support of domestic gas concerns;
– '*politonomics*': in Western-type capitalist market economies, a certain separation exists between state action (called politics) on the one hand, and individual, profit-oriented business activity on the other (called economics). Even in the gas sector, which has been a highly politicized sector in most countries, a certain separation exists between Western economically oriented (albeit state-owned) enterprises and governmental action. This does not hold true for most CIS countries, least of all for the new autocratic regimes of Central Asia and the Caspian region. Instead, a combination of the two – 'politonomics', as we call this phenomenon – abounds; state intervention is still dominant, be it at the industrial or the regional level. Even if it were politically desired, regulatory reform is difficult to push through, for in many cases, the owner of the protected industry is also the regulator;[253]

---

[251] Typically, governments are afraid of cracking down on non-paying consumers thus attempting to avoid the social hardship that would result from such crack-downs. But, instead of continuing to subsidize 'bad consumers' directly or indirectly, in the long run they will be forced to take steps against the worst of them. At the same time, a social security system needs to be developed allowing for subject-oriented instead of object-oriented transfers.

[252] Thus, the 'Russian Energy Strategy' of 2001 expects production to increase to 700 bcm by 2020, a rise of 15 percent. Ukrainian gas consumption was still projected at 92 bcm by 2010, that is, at 113 percent of the 1995 level. Uzbekistan estimated gas consumption to increase by 18 percent between 1995 and 2020. These projections ignore the fact that even with the resumption of economic growth, price increases and energy savings may lead to further reductions of current energy consumption levels.

[253] 'Politonomics' has become obvious in the 'auto-privatization' of the world's richest gas reserves in *Russia*: the former Gas Minister, Victor Chernomyrdin, simply became the CEO of Gazprom, and then Prime Minister later on. Since then, Gazprom has been a major agent in Russia's foreign policy (see Rutland, 1996, 'Energy Rich, Energy Poor - Russia's Energy Empire Under Strain - Russia's Natural Gas Leviathan', In: *Transition*, 3 May, 5-13, 63; Pleines and Westphal, 1999, op. cit.).

– *technical 'obstacles' which do not exist*: finally some of the claims of technical 'obstacles' frequently cited by some CIS countries to show that 'reforms cannot work' in a post-Soviet context have to be exposed as false:

i) Third Party Access (TPA) to high-pressure transmission facilities is *technically* feasible. Traditionally, high-pressure and low-pressure networks were not always separated from each other, so that network management is a major problem. However, the fact that individual, negotiated TPA already exists for individual gas traders (although on an informal basis) shows that the technical problems can be overcome;

ii) gas metering and billing is possible even with the existing, rudimentary equipment. There is no reason to wait for state gas meter programs as a condition for solving the issue of unpaid gas bills;

iii) unbundling and enterprization of the national gas monopolies is possible. The splitting-up has so far been delayed with reference to the 'technological interdependence and uniqueness' of the gas sector. Yet, there is no *technical* argument why transport activities could not be separated from the rest of the concerns, which themselves could be split up into different independent companies; that is, exploration and exploitation, mechanical engineering and technical services (such as R&D and maintenance).

4. PERSPECTIVES FOR GAS SECTOR REFORM

4.1 The Political Economy of Gas Sector Reform from a Western Perspective

Western governments, international organizations and enterprises have shown a tremendous interest in gas sector reform in the CIS; considerable financial and publicity efforts have been invested so far. Financial engagement mainly includes commercial loans by private banks, but also by the IMF, World Bank, EBRD and other multi- and bilateral organizations, all in all amounting to several billion USD between 1994–2001. The Western interests in gas sector reform in Russia and other CIS countries are driven by concrete interests, the main ones being geopolitics, business and 'pro-deregulationism':

– Geopolitical stabilization in Russia and the CIS: the West in general, and the European Union in particular, are interested in maintaining good relations with the world's largest gas supplier (Russia), while trying to avoid its dominance in other geopolitical areas (such as Central Europe, the Caspian region and Central Asia);

– business opportunities: *consulting* in the CIS gas sector (and the energy sector at large) was a most profitable short-term business opportunity for law firms, accountants, researchers, consultants and the like during the first years of reform. In the medium term, *trade agreements* may offer high returns, be they for importing gas from Russia, or obtaining licenses for regional distribution within the country;[254]

– the interest in deregulation is based on the idea that a liberalized market and competition in network industries such as gas, is welfare enhancing. After the success of the Anglo-Saxon model of gas liberalization and upcoming reforms in the EU countries and East European EU-accession countries, the CIS countries still lag significantly behind. In these countries, deregulation can also be justified on political grounds, such as diminishing the political power of the gas industry ('abandon politonomics').[255]

Figure 10.1 presents a concrete case study on the political economy of gas sector reform in post-Soviet countries: it gives an overview of the attitude of different interest groups on gas sector deregulation, taking the situation in *Ukraine* in the late 1990s as an example. The horizontal axis measures support for reform and deregulation from the relevant organizations. The vertical axis measures the control of the respective organizations over gas and information flows. Not surprisingly, the propensity to deregulate was inversely related to the current control of gas and/or information in the old system. We have marked those groups that could contribute to a turnaround of structural reform:

– The reform-oriented *Deputy Prime-Minister for Economics* who could gain politically by showing that a large part of consumers can, in the medium term, benefit from gas sector reform;

– the National Energy Regulation Commission (*NERC*) that could become the main regulating body;

– *potential wholesalers* that could benefit from liberalization of licensing procedures and market access; and

– the *gas consuming industries* that could obtain lower gas prices.

---

[254] *Joint ventures* between Western and CIS companies have so far concentrated on trading, too, but some industrial cooperation is also underway, for example, in equipment production, exploration and processing. *Direct investment* is of interest to those enterprises seeking direct control over Russian resources or transit pipelines.

[255] Note that the three interest groups mentioned (geopolitics, business, deregulation) are dedicated to gas sector reform to varying degrees. In political terms, the unbundling of the large gas concerns is first and foremost an attempt to weaken the industrial lobby and to strengthen reformist movements. The pro-deregulation faction is also clearly in favor of deregulation. However, when it comes to business, interests diverge: consultants can gain the most from continued deregulation; portfolio investors would also benefit from a separation of profitable activities (transportation) from unprofitable ones (for example, engineering, or the social sphere). On the other hand, direct investors may be rather critical of unbundling their business partners: indeed it may be easier to negotiate with one centralized, powerful monopoly than with several spin-off companies. Long-term supply contracts might be put at risk.

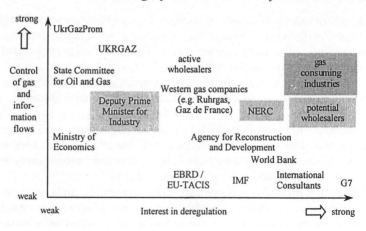

Figure 10.1 The position of the main interest groups on gas sector reform in Ukraine (1997)

4.2 Elements of a Process-Oriented Gas Sector Reform

So far, several energy reform projects in CIS countries have encountered substantial difficulties, be they bureaucratic obstacles at central and operational level, long delays, difficulties in monitoring project progress and misuse or even disappearance of funds. It seems reasonable, then, to devise gas sector reforms which are as simple as possible, with a down-to-earth, *process-oriented* project design. The immediate introduction of an ambitious deregulation model, such as the British model, to any CIS country would be incompatible with the two aforementioned conditions (process orientation and political feasibility), and would therefore most likely fail. The short-term goal should be to establish *transparency* as a precondition for structural reform. The first reform measures could be those that can be introduced *rapidly*, at practically *no cost*, and that have a significant effect in introducing transparency, reducing uncertainty and improving predictability in the sector:

– *Publish gas tariffs and their composition.* At present, only Russia has introduced a formal procedure for publishing gas tariffs, but it is not applied throughout the sector by the Federal Energy Commission. In other CIS countries, gas tariffs for state deliveries are fixed by the price-department of the Economics Ministry, while tariffs for private deliveries are unknown. It seems reasonable, then, to require that *all* CIS countries publish extensive tariff information;[256]

---

[256] a) composition of end-user prices: import price; cost of high-pressure transport (divided into

– *publish detailed consumption figures.* At present, gas consumption figures are not widely available. In order to monitor gas consumption and energy savings, each country should regularly publish the following data in its respective statistical bulletins: supply (imports, production, storage out) and demand (domestic: by user group: industry, power plants, residential, and so on; exports, storage in). Similar information should be provided at the level of the Oblasts as well;

– gather and *publish information on domestic gas payments.* At present, domestic gas payments are still irregular (cf. Table 10.2). The absence of reliable information on non-payments not only obscures economic analyses of the gas sector; other economic policies may also be adversely affected, such as measures against the non-payment crisis, balance of trade analyses and macroeconomic projections. A thorough monitoring of the recovery ratio and the main default clients is a precondition for improving payment discipline;[257]

– *establish a public information campaign on gas sector reform issues.* At the same time, an information campaign should be designed to inform the public. It might also be argued that a large part of the population will benefit from the reform process (an aspect which is largely misunderstood today). As Spiller and Vogelsang (1997) have shown, public awareness is also conducive to containing regulatory risk.

Only once a minimum of transparency is institutionalized may reforms proceed through establishing new structures of industry governance. For this, structural change in administration is inevitable.[258] First of all, inconsistent governance structures within the gas industry should be abolished.[259] A second, even more difficult task, is to establish some form of *external governance structures.* Initial attempts have been made, such as the Federal Energy Commission (FEC) in Russia or its pendant (NERC) in Ukraine. If structural reform is to succeed in the gas sector, governance structures have to be created which are as politically independent as possible, yet sufficiently

---

fixed costs and variable costs); cost of low-pressure transport/distribution (fixed and variable costs); storage, other; taxes; b) prices for standard household and industrial consumers: a set of 'standard' consumers has to be defined and prices published on a quarterly basis. For comparison: in the EU, five domestic standard consumers and seven standard industrial consumers are chosen for comparative price publications; cf. European Council Directive 90/377/EEC on 'A Community Procedure to improve the transparency of gas and electricity pricing charged to industrial end-users.'

[257] For each consumer group (households, budgetary organizations, communal services, industry), the following information should be collected and published by the respective Economics Ministry: arrears outstanding; amount due, amount paid (of which: in cash/in barter); overall collection ratio.

[258] Fifteen years of struggle on reforms in the Western European gas industry provide evidence of the magnitude of the task.

[259] At present, several bureaucracies claim authority over the gas industry. This is not the result of a voluntary energy policy, but stems from the power struggle between different administrations.

powerful to impose their decisions. The task is to ensure not only tariff control, but also consumer protection, public information and, eventually, the gradual introduction of competition.[260]

5. CONCLUSIONS

This chapter has given an overview of gas sector reform in transformation countries, with particular emphasis on the obstacles to reform in the CIS countries. We contend that, under certain conditions, competition can work in the gas market; yet, for the time being only Anglo-Saxon countries have proven this (the UK, USA, Canada, Australia, New Zealand). Continental Western and Eastern European countries have also committed themselves to introducing competition and are taking the first steps to implement the EU Gas Directive of 1998. By contrast, empirical evidence indicates that the conditions are unfavorable for reforms in the large CIS gas countries (Russia, Turkmenistan, Ukraine, Uzbekistan). More than ten years after the demise of socialism, the gas sectors in these countries show stagnation – such as low consumer prices, lack of enterprise control structures, or unrealistic demand projections – rather than signs of market-oriented restructuring.

For the Western world, in particular Western Europe, gas reform in the CIS countries will remain an unknown variable for some time to come. In the current geopolitical context, and given rising EU import dependence on Russia, supporting these countries' gas sectors will remain a key element of any cooperation strategy. Today, the time for bold reform experiments is over, both in the CIS countries and the EU-accession countries. A realistic, process-oriented approach to gas sector reform is the only feasible strategy both for national, reform-minded decision makers and for foreign actors.

---

[260] For this, three conditions are necessary (though not sufficient): i) to attract decision makers with a strong industrial and political background, not necessarily coming from the gas industry; ii) to staff the new structures with qualified personnel from other institutions (for example, the Energy Ministry, the State Committees, the Economics Ministry; in order to attract good staff and motivate them, incentive structures should include the possibility of higher wages than average public service wages); iii) to create a corporate identity within the new structures, backed by a public campaign explaining their role.

11. The Russian Gas Reserves – A New Perspective

Russian Gas Resource Base: Large, Overstated, Costly to Maintain.
Grace, John D. (1995a).

1. INTRODUCTION

Following the political economy analysis of gas sector reform, this chapter addresses a slightly different aspect of infrastructure development in Eastern Europe, but one that is also highly relevant for the enlarged European Union: the assessment of the Russian gas reserves, and its export potential. The thrust of this chapter is that the systemic transformation requires a *reassessment* of the economic evaluation of the gas sector. This has direct implications; for example, on the financial valuation of the East European gas companies and on the estimation of their gas export potential. This applies particularly to Russia, which boasts the world's largest gas reserves (47 tcm). That is, one-third of the world total and more than the entire Middle East (BP Amoco Statistic Review of World Energy).

As was shown in the previous chapter, the Russian gas industry, too, has experienced problems. From a macroeconomic perspective, it was argued that the 'Dutch disease' might reduce the benefits of a resource-based development strategy (Götz, 1995). Given decreasing gas output from the large existing Russian gas fields, a reorientation of gas exploration and the commissioning of new fields is imminent. Central and Western Europe depend increasingly upon Russian gas exports, and thus have a genuine interest in this issue.[261]

This chapter discusses the economics of Russian gas reserves, by linking technical arguments to the overall topic of this book, infrastructure policies under systemic transformation. We argue that under market economy conditions, Russia may *not* be as well endowed with natural gas as is

---

[261] See Nail (Jim,1997, 'Gazprom – the Cash-Man Cometh'. *Deutsche Morgan Grenfell: Focus Eastern Europe*, July 3: 7-11), Pauwels (1994), and Quast, O., and C. Locatelli (1997, 'Russian Natural Gas Policy and its Possible Effects on European Gas Markets'. *Energy Policy*, Vol. 25, No. 2 (February), 125-133).

generally assumed. The reason being that the Russian gas industry does not have sufficient effective demand to sell the gas and still make a decent profit. Section 2 reviews the difference between the socialist and the market economic notion of 'reserves'. Section 3 presents different estimates of Russian gas reserves and resources, opposing the 'socialist' figures to updated estimates under market economy conditions. Depending upon which category is used, reserve figures vary as much as between 18–47 tcm. A depletion scenario shows that gas production from existing fields will diminish significantly in the second half of this decade (2006–10). Section 4 discusses some issues related to the gas reserve estimates and Section 5 concludes.[262]

2. DEFINITIONS OF GAS RESERVES

That the estimation of gas reserves can vary in different economic systems may sound odd. Yet it is an important consequence of the systemic transformation process in Eastern Europe: under *socialism*, a reserve was defined by the *physical availability* of a natural resource (expressed in m^3, kg, t, etc.). There was a formal nomenclature for the classification of gas resources, from best to worst: A(best)-B-C1-C2-C3-D1-D2. However, once the political decision was made to develop a certain gas field, there were only physical but no more economic constraints on exploiting, transporting and distributing the resource. For international comparison, gas reserves were defined as the resources included in groups A to C1. The Soviet Union boasted by far the largest gas reserves in the world.[263]

In contrast, in a *market economy*, the idea of a reserve is linked to the ability of a profit-oriented enterprise to exploit, transport and *sell* a natural resource in such a way as to cover its costs and obtain an appropriate return on capital. Only a natural resource that can be sold at a profit is considered a valuable reserve. Hence, it is not the physical availability and production that count, but the *monetary value*, expressed in costs and profits. The simplest definition identifies reserves as 'those quantities which geological and engineering information indicates with reasonable certainty can be recovered

---

[262] Thanks to Hans-Jürgen Wagener, Hella Engerer, Petra Opitz, Wolfram Schrettl and Eirik Svindland for comments on earlier drafts, furthermore to participants at the 22nd International Conference of the International Association of Energy Economists (IAEE, Rome, June 1999), and the 10th Ukrainian-German Economic Symposium in Kyiv (June 2000) for comments and questions.
[263] In 1976, the Soviet Union's share of world gas *reserves* was estimated at 40 percent, in 1988 at 32 percent; the Soviet Union's share of world gas *production* was slightly lower: 37 percent (1986) and down to 24 percent in 1988 (BP, 2001).

in the future from known reservoirs under existing economic and operating conditions.' (BP, 1997, p. 20).[264]

The point is that the energy reserves of any given country are not defined by nature. The characterization of a country as reserve-rich or reserve-poor also depends upon the economic system operating in that country at the point in time in question. A country that was considered to be reserve–rich under socialism – for example, the Soviet Union – may appear otherwise when it adopts an economic system based on market criteria and sanctions. As a consequence, the gas reserves of all transformation countries, and in particular Russia, should have been re-evaluated in the context of their new economic environment. However, owing to the technical difficulties of this exercise, the high costs and also some resistance from the Russian gas industry, this did *not* happen. In the gas sector, the socialist categories A-C1 continued to be translated into Western-type 'reserves'. This continued use of the socialist reserve figures may, however, have been a mistake, as it underestimated the change of economic conditions that the gas industries went through. The question then is: are the Russian gas reserves really as promising as official statistics suggest?

3. ESTIMATES OF RUSSIAN GAS RESOURCES AND RESERVES

A closer look at the composition of gas resources and reserves in Russia reveals not only some data inconsistency, but above all the necessity for an in-depth technical *and* economic analysis. The dominant source of information is still data from Soviet times. The first comprehensive study carried out by a Western geological company (by De Golyer and MacNaughton in 1999) checked the *technical* feasibility of existing Russian data on proven and probable stocks of Gazprom; but it did not provide a judgement on the *economic* feasibility of producing and distributing this gas. In the following pages, we review the estimates of Russian gas resources and gas reserves.

3.1 Resources

There is some debate on the volumes of gas for which technical and economic feasibility is uncertain, that is, gas *resources*. Gazprom (1998, 63) puts Russian gas resources at 226 tcm (total initial resources of 236.1 tcm minus

---

[264] For a brief overview of the problems of Western and Russian conceptions of gas reserves, see Grace (1995a).

cumulative production of 10.1 tcm). On the other hand, Grace (1995a, 73) estimates the 'total Russian unproduced recoverable resource base' at only about 165 tcm (see Table 11.1).[265] A closer look reveals that a large part of what are considered to be gas resources in Russia would hardly fit into the Western, market economy-oriented definition of resources, which requires that 'the existence of assessed volumes be scientifically supported and that the economic and technological prerequisites to their recovery do not demand conditions clearly over the horizon' (Grace, 1995a, 73). About 70 percent of the Russian resource base exists in as of yet *undiscovered* fields. The 39 tcm of undiscovered gas offshore (categories D1 and D2) are also unlikely to become relevant even in the long run.

The Russian gas resources, then, realistically boil down to the existing 16 fields that are the basis of current production (Urengoy, Yamburg, Nadym regions) as well as non-producing fields in Western Siberia. Other regions have to be largely excluded from the resource base.[266] If one were to reduce the resource concept to the Soviet categories A1-C2, that is, explored and initially appraised gas, a reasonable estimate for Russian gas resources would be around 60 tcm.

Table 11.1 Estimates of Russian gas resources

In trillion cubic meters (tcm)	Grace	IEA	Gazprom
Total	165	212	226
Of which			
Onshore			68%
West Siberia			41%
Eastern Siberia			19%
Volga-Urals			6%
Northern European Part			1%
Northern Caucasus			1%
Offshore			32%

Sources: Grace (1995a, 73), IEA (1995b, 167), Gazprom (1998, 63)

---

[265] Grace (1995a, 73) explains how the Soviet concept of reserves stretches the Western concept beyond its normal limits: 'Soviet recoverable volumes are typically estimated based on virtually unlimited budgets and the presupposed application of almost any conceivable technology. Therefore, it is surprising, but not inconsistent, that gas recovery factors still used in official statistics from the FSU assume 100 percent recovery of gas in place.'

[266] The uncertain character of non-Western Siberian resources is confirmed by the composition of reserve additions in the first half of the last decade (1991–95): 80 percent of the onshore reserve additions of 2.9 tcm are from Western Siberia and less than 10 percent from Eastern Siberia (Gazprom, 1998, 67).

3.2 Reserves

The most commonly used figure on Russian gas *reserves* is 47.3 tcm.[267] These make up 32 percent of world gas reserves and make Russia the largest reserve base in the world, far ahead of Iran (16 percent) and Qatar (8 percent). The reserves are concentrated in Western Siberia, with minor spots in the Volga-Urals area and offshore (see Table 11.2). Doubts on the officially announced reserve figures have existed for quite some time, but no alternative evaluation has been undertaken.[268] In addition to the geological checks of the official reserve data, an *economic* valuation is required. Only when the Russian gas industry is able to bring its gas resources to the marketplace and sell them to solvent clients is the economic value of the resources proven, and only this gas can be called a reserve.[269]

The following is a rough back-of-the-envelope attempt to check which part of the official reserves can be upheld as reserves under market-economy criteria. Table 11.2 contrasts the official reserve figures for the largest fields with what we consider to be economically justified reserve levels (called *adjusted* reserves). The underlying adjustments are the following:

– Total reserves at *Yamburg* were estimated at 4,400 bcm in 1994 (Resunenko and Maichel, 1997, 1055); they fell to 3,900 bcm in 1998.[270] However, Cenomanian reserves in shallow, easy-to-extract horizons are only around 2,000–3,000 bcm, while production at deeper horizons (Neocomian, Valanganian) is generally considered to be uneconomic (Grace, 1995b). Thus we include only Cenomanian reserves in the adjusted reserve figure;

– official reserves in *Urengoy* are 3,700 bcm, including the North Urengoy field, and other satellites yield 5,100 bcm. Once again, the adjusted reserves should include only Cenomanian reserves. For Urengoy alone, these were estimated at 6,200 bcm in 1980; today, they are about 3,000 bcm for this area and 4,100 bcm for the entire region;

---

[267] This figure is provided by Gazprom (1998, 63) and regularly replicated, more or less, by international statistics, most notably the BP-Amoco Annual Statistical Review.

[268] The study by the company De Golyer and Mac Naughton on the gas reserves of Gazprom largely confirmed the physical existence of what Gazprom calls proven reserves; however, only two-thirds of the potential reserves were examined. Yamburg, Urengoy, Zapolyarnoye, Yamal, and other fields in Western Siberia, as well as Ural-Volga (sum of 18.8 tcm); *not* analyzed were the so-called reserves in Medvezhye, Astrakhan, Stockman, and others (total of 8.3 tcm). Some industry analysts concluded from this that 'the total amount of the proven and probable stocks of Gazprom is 18.8 tcm gas' (AK&M Information Agency, 1999, Otrasli rossijskoj ekonomiki: proizvodstvo, finansy, cennye bumagi, Nr. 304, 22.2., 32); if this estimate were to be generalized at the level of the entire country, it would imply a level of Russian reserves of around 33 tcm.

[269] For example, production costs in more complex spheres rise sharply and may thus prohibit an economic use of the gas. Thus, average production costs from Russian fields are expected to rise from the current 3–5 USD/th cm to 12–15 USD/th cm by 2015 (Grace, 1995b, 80).

[270] Gazprom (1998: *Annual Report*, Moscow).

– the *Medvezhye* field has already been in decline for some time. Gazprom itself estimates reserves at 640 bcm. Other fields in the *Nadym* area (mainly Yubiley and Yamsovey) are said to contain about 3,000 bcm, but their future development might be more expensive as well. A reasonable figure for other Nadym reserves is 1,500–2,000 bcm;

– *Yamal* is a very special case. Contrary to international conventions, Gazprom includes *undeveloped* fields in its reserve base. According to Western criteria, Yamal gas cannot be considered a 'reserve' since there are serious doubts about the economics of its exploitation.[271] Thus, neither the Bovan and Kharasevey fields under appraisal nor the undeveloped Kruzenstern and other fields seem to be economically viable at this point. Thus, Yamal should be subtracted from the reserve base;

– little information is available on the 10,000 bcm of *other West Siberian* reserves. One-third seems to be an optimistic estimate of this gas, most of which is only under appraisal;

– reserves in the *Astrakhan* region are officially estimated at 2,100 bcm. However, the site is under appraisal only as the gas is of an inferior quality (sulphurous) and thus production is likely to be expensive. It seems unlikely that more than 50 percent will be recovered;

– the *Stockman* reserves are estimated at 2,200 bcm by Gazprom, but it is unlikely that they will be developed in the medium term. Plans for the development of Stockman in the event of a Baltic Gas Ring have been shelved thus far. Hence, this resource, too, should be excluded from the reserve base;

– of the *other* reserves, about 5,000 bcm are still less explored than those in West Siberia. Therefore they are discounted to one-fifth, which still seems to be on the optimistic side.

When subtracting those elements from the official reserves for which economic feasibility is not clearly evident, the Russian gas reserve base shrinks to about 18–20 tcm. This is still a significant amount, but less than half of the internationally used figures.

---

[271] The objective of the Yamal-Europe project was to tap the gas on the Yamal peninsula in the Northern Urals, and to export about 70 bcm per year to Central and Western Europe (Resunenkeo and Maichel, 1997). Given the unexpected slump in Russian domestic consumption, more gas from existing fields is now available for exports, diminishing the chances that Yamal will be developed soon. The decision of Russia in 2001 to contract up to 30 bcm per year of Turkmen gas in the future has further reduced the necessity of large new field developments in Yamal. Nowadays, the Yamal project is even rated as inferior to Stockman, as 'Yamal is a difficult and inflexible project, which can not be built in a modular fashion.' (Stern, J., 1997, 'Will Gazprom Need Yamal Before 2010?' *Petroleum Economist* (May), 110-114, here: 112).

Table 11.2 Russian gas reserves by major regions and fields

Region/field and status	Official Reserve (bcm) Figure	Adjusted Reserve (bcm) Estimate
**** Yamburg	3900	2000-3000
**** Zapolyarnoye	3000	3000
*** Urengoij	3700	3000
*** Medvezhye	640	600
*** others Nadymgazprom	3000	1500-2000
** Yamal	10000	-
of which		
** Bovanenko	(4400)	-
** Kharasevey	(1300)	-
* Kruzenstern	(1000)	-
* others Yamal	(3300)	-
**West Siberia	10000	3000-4000
***Orenburg (Ural-Volga)	1000	1000
***Surgut	1000	1000
***Severgazprom	500	500
***Tyum	1000	1000
**Astrakhan	2100	1000
*Stockman	2200	-
Others	ca 5000	-
Sum	ca. 47000	ca. 18000-20000
of which		
Western Siberia	78%	
Volga-Urals	10%	
Eastern Siberia	2%	
Far East	2%	
Offshore	8%	

by state of exploitation:
**** in operation: plateau or rising
*** in operation: tail (falling production)
** under appraisal
* undeveloped

Sources: Official reserve figures: Gazprom (1998), Vyakhirev (1998),[272] BGR (1998),[273] author's own calculations based on specialized press and expert interviews

---

[272] Vyakhirev, Rem (1998, 'Gas Industry in Russia on the Threshold of the XXI Century'. In: Ministry of Fuel and Energy of the Russian Federation (ed.): *Proceedings of G8 Energy Ministerial Business Consultative Meeting on the World Energy Future*. Moscow).
[273] BGR (1998, *Reserven, Ressourcen und Verfügbarkeit von Energierohstoffen*. Hannover).

3.3 Reserve Depletion and Additions: A Stylized Scenario

The depletion of existing fields is of concern to the Russian gas industry in the medium term, in particular to Gazprom which owns two-thirds of the reserves. Indirectly it also concerns European gas imports. Gas reserve additions in Russia have fallen significantly since the early 1990s. In the latter half of the 1980s, average annual reserve additions exceeded 2 tcm, which is about five times the consumption level. However, this ratio was not only inverted after 1994 but fell to a mere 0.19 in 1998 (see Table 11.3): gas output of 564 bcm was compensated for by only 107 bcm in reserve additions.[274]

Most of the larger fields in operation have already passed their plateau rate and their yearly production is currently diminishing. This is the case most notably with the Orenburg field and in Siberia in Medvezhye and Nadym and Urengoy. Yamburg has nearly reached its plateau rate of 200 bcm and is likely to decline gradually. This leaves Zapolyarnoye as the only commissioned giant field where a significant production increase is to be expected. Figure 11.1 shows a depletion scenario for Russian gas reserves from producing fields.[275] We assume that about 75 percent of reserves are really recoverable.[276] Furthermore, we assume a 'long-tail' for all fields, that is, gradually decreasing production after the plateau phase.

The scenario shows that production from existing fields will gradually decline in the first half of this decade; in 2005, production will still be above 500 bcm. However, the fundamentals are likely to change afterwards: with the expected phase-outs of major fields in Orenburg and Western Siberia, gas production from existing fields will fall more significantly in the second half of the decade. By the year 2015, only the giant Zapolyarnoye field will still contribute significantly to Russian gas output. This evidently raises the issue of replacement capacity from other fields, be they new giant fields, new large fields, or satellites; this issue is amply discussed both inside and outside of the Russian gas industry (Gazprom, 1998; Mabro and Wybrew-Bond, 1999; and IEA, 2002).

---

[274] Since 1993 the reserve base has been reduced by over 1.5 tcm. No change in this tendency, which results from a lack of investment, is to be expected in the near future. Note that from an economic point of view, underinvesting is rational as long as the market is depressed and ample reserves already exist.

[275] 'Other' fields include those commissioned before 1995 (Vyngapurskoye, Komsomolskoye) and those commissioned more recently (Tarkosalinskoye, Yubilyeynoye, Yamsovey); fields to be commissioned in 2001–05 are not included (these are mainly satellite fields of South Russkoye, Pestcovoye, Gubkinskoye).

[276] According to Grace (1995b, 73), about 80 percent of quoted reserve figures can be considered recoverable whereas other specialists quote a ratio of two-thirds. We assume that reserve additions occur mainly in non-producing fields.

Table 11.3 Russian gas output and reserve additions (1990–98)

	1990	1991	1992	1993	1994	1995	1996	1997	1998
Production	613	618	620	601	581	570	575	571	564
Reserve Additions	2785	1741	1813	725	265	187	180	545	107
Ratio of Reserve Additions/Production	4.54	2.82	2.92	1.21	0.46	0.33	0.31	0.95	0.19

Sources: Gazprom (1998, 68), Gazprom Annual Reports (1997, 1998)

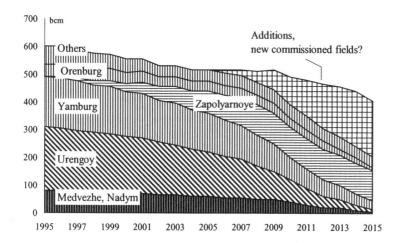

Figure 11.1 Depletion scenario for Russian gas reserves from existing fields[277]

4. FURTHER ISSUES: RUSSIAN GAS EXPORTS AND FINANCIAL INDICATORS

4.1 Perspectives of Russian Gas Exports to Western Europe

The issue of gas reserves and their depletion is to some extent linked to the perspectives of gas exports and the financial strength of Gazprom. Russian gas exports have contributed significantly to the country's trade balance,

---

[277] Historical data (1995–98) is adjusted and may not fully correspond to real production of non-associated gas.

accounting for about 15 percent of total exports. The total amount of exports has recovered in the late 1990s, after a slump in the early years of transformation. Whereas gas exports to CIS countries were significantly lower, non-CIS exports increased over the last several years (see Table 10.1).

One major factor determining exports is the structure and development of *costs*. Some authors have expressed doubts as to whether Russian gas exports to Western Europe will be economically sustainable over the long term. The reasons for this are not only the capital replacement expenditures required for upgrading equipment, pipelines and compressors. They also include the fact that gas transport over long distances is expensive and most Russian gas is located along the Urals (South and North) and in Western Siberia, thousands of kilometers away from the centers of effective demand, mainly Central and Western Europe.[278] Pauwels (1994) and IEA (1995b, 1995c) addressed the issue by estimating future European gas supply curves. Though based on 1993 data from the very beginning of the transformation process in Russia, they concluded that not Russian, but *Algerian* and *Norwegian* medium-cost fields would be able to supply the cheapest large additional quantities of gas to Europe.[279]

On the other hand, official import statistics of the European Union show import prices for Russian gas below the above estimates, in the same range as those of its competitors.[280] Only gas from the UK was somewhat cheaper at 2.00 USD/MBtu. If these figures reflect reality and if Russian gas exporters do not sell below their costs on a permanent basis (dumping), then Russian gas *is* competitive in Western Europe.[281]

---

[278] IEA (1994, *Russian Energy Prices, Taxes and Costs*. Paris, OECD) undertook an analysis of the hypothetical costs of gas delivery, assuming market economy cost accounting, including depreciation on capital. It concluded that under full-cost accounting, the Russian gas sector may *not* have been profitable in the early 1990s.

[279] According to IEA's (1995c) estimates, in the year 2020, the least-cost suppliers to the EU should be the Algerian Transmed pipeline at about 35 USD/th cm (or 1.06 USD/Mbtu) at EU-border, Algerian LNG from Montoir (65.3 USD/th cm, 1.96 USD/MBtu) and the Norwegian fields Ekofisk (44.6 USD/th cm, 1.34 USD/MBtu), Sleipner (51.9 USD/th cm, 1.56 USD/MBtu) and Troll (65.3 USD/th cm (1.96 USD/Mbtu) delivery Emden, 76.3 USD/th cm (2.29 USD/MBtu). Even the Norwegian Haltenbanken field, which is yet to be developed, would be cheaper (at 97.2 USD/th cm, 2.92 USD/ MBtu) than the cheapest Russian delivery from Western Siberia (107 USD/th cm, 3.22 USD/MBtu). In that scenario, Russian Yamal gas (112 USD/th cm, 3.37 USD/MBtu) and Turkmen gas (150 USD/thcm, 4.49 USD/ MBtu) were supposed to be significantly more expensive.

[280] In 1999, the natural gas import price into Europe was 62.3 USD/th cm (1.87 USD/MBtu) for Russian gas, similar to the 64.6 USD/th cm (1.94 USD/Mbtu) for gas from The Netherlands, 66.3 USD/th cm (1.99 USD/Mbtu) for Norwegian gas and 55.9 USD/th cm (1.68 USD/Mbtu) for non-specified sources (most likely Algerian gas). Source: IEA (2000, *Energy Prices and Taxes*, third quarter 1999, 32).

[281] High transportation costs from Russia to Western Europe are offset by lower production costs. Gas swaps can provide relief from high transport costs for a certain volume of gas. The 1998 devaluation of the Russian rouble has improved the competitiveness of Russian

Another issue is whether Russian gas exports can still increase significantly from the current levels of 120–130 bcm. Given capacity constraints on existing pipelines, increasing exports would require new infrastructure. For the time being, smaller export projects are carried out parallel to the two large-scale projects.[282] Among the large projects, the first line of the Blue Stream project was finished in 2002, allowing an increase of Russian gas exports to Turkey.[283] On the other hand, the Yamal project, under discussion for 15 years now, is not advancing on its critical issue, that is, the development of the Yamal peninsula gas fields and the connection to the Northern Light pipeline at Uchta. By contrast, work on the link between the 'Northern Lights' pipeline in Minsk (Belarus) and Poland (Kondratki-Wloclawek) is advancing: the 56 inches diameter connection has been completed in late 1999, and increases in capacity are expected from the present 10 bcm to 28 bcm or even 56 bcm. This provides Russia with not only additional export capacity, but also with a strategic alternative to gas transit to Central and Western Europe that circumvents the politically unstable Ukraine.[284]

4.2 Financial Indicators for Russia's Gazprom

Last but not least, the issue of gas reserves also directly affects the financial evaluation of the gas giant Gazprom. Should the true gas reserves be below 50 percent of the current estimates, the corporate value of Gazprom would need to be significantly discounted. On the other hand, the financial strength of Gazprom will determine the level and the speed of investing in new reserve additions. Due to the domestic non-payment crisis, the operating profit of the company and thus its capacity to invest have been curtailed. In late 1999, the

---

gas exporters. Note, however, that the price data may be severely distorted from costs because of oligopolistic pricesetting of the EU gas suppliers. Schostin ('Die Energiewirtschaft Russlands, Entwicklung und Perspektiven'. *IW-Trends*, November, 74-87, 1997, 81) assumes that Gazprom's exports to Western Europe are lossmaking even today.

[282] An example is the Balkan expansion project, which is supposed to expand export capacity onshore through Ukraine, Romania, Bulgaria and down to Turkey. Transit capacity is to be increased by 14 bcm by the year 2002; the first stretch between Ghust (Ukraine) and Satu Mare (Romania) has already been started.

[283] The 'Blue Stream' gas pipeline connects Russia with Turkey by underground. Whereas the Izobilnoe–Dzubga (Russia, 373 km) and the Samsun–Ankara (Turkey, 444 km) onshore stretches are conventional and modestly expensive (approximately USD 500–800 mn. each), the multi-billion USD crossing of the Black Sea (396 km, down to 2,150 m under water, between Dzubga and Samsun) is pushing even Western equipment companies to their limits.

[284] Opinions diverge on whether Central and Western European markets would be able to absorb large quantities of additional Russian gas exports. For a detailed discussion of the geopolitical aspects, see Opitz and Hirschhausen (2001); and for a simulation of the winners and losers from this new pipeline, see Chollet et al. (2001).

average domestic gas price fell to about 30 percent of the export price (against 55–60 percent pre-devaluation).[285]

The development of the *share price* can be considered as an indicator of the market's evaluation of Gazprom's strengths and weaknesses. Pre-August 1998 analysis showed that Gazprom was discounted by about 60 percent compared with the average Russian oil company on a *reserve* basis; on an *output* basis, the discount was 36 percent (Nail, 1997, op cit.). Things changed somewhat after the financial crisis, under which Gazprom stood up better than most other companies in the energy sector. The Gazprom share price on the Moscow Stock Exchange fell by 'only' 67 percent whereas the RTS-stock index dropped by 86 percent.[286] Since late 1998, the Gazprom share price has recovered more than half of its pre-crisis value and has thus become stronger than most oil titles. Yet when compared to the two most successful oil companies, Lukoil and Surgutneftegaz, the Gazprom share still seems to be lagging behind in the recovery process. In October 1999, Gazprom's market capitalization to reserve ratio was only 3.5 percent of the ratio of Lukoil and Surgutneftegaz.[287] The market capitalization over production ratio of Gazprom was in the same range, at about 7 percent.[288] If 'the market is right' in this case, it might be concluded that investors see Gazprom's development perspective as less promising than those of the oil champions. Part of this perception of Gazprom can be attributed to the collapse of the domestic market and to inefficient governance structures; however, another factor might be that the market players also consider the gas reserves to be overvalued.

---

[285] The normalization of relative prices that had made progress in 1996–97 was stalled for social reasons in 1998. The government had agreed to increase the gas price for residential consumers to at least 88 percent of the industrial wholesale price, which it was unable to attain.

[286] At the same time, the London quotation of the Gazprom depository share (ADR) fell by 37 percent, but the index of Russian issuers corporate securities dropped by 62 percent (Gazprom Annual Report, 1998).

[287] Gazprom: market capitalization (Moscow Stock Exchange): USD 3.2 bn, reserves: 295 bn. bbl (corresponding to the official 47 tcm), that is 0.011 USD/bbl reserve, against 0.32 USD/bbl for Lukoil and 0.36 USD/bbl for Surgutneftegaz. The average prices for oil and gas (per million BTU or one barrel) were quite similar in 1998: natural gas European Union c.i.f. import price: 2.27 USD/MBtu; crude oil OECD countries c.i.f. import price: 2.18 USD/MBtu, see BP-Amoco (1999, *Statistical Review of World Energy*, 29).

[288] Gazprom's MCAP/production ratio: 0.95 USD/bbl, against 12.3 USD/bbl and 13.8 USD/bbl for Lukoil and Surgut, respectively. See for a more detailed financial and strategy analysis of the Russian oil and gas sectors Opitz, Engerer and Hirschhausen (forthcoming).

5. CONCLUSIONS

This chapter has analyzed infrastructure policies in Eastern Europe from a different perspective than that of the preceding chapters, a resource economic perspective. For many East European countries, natural resources are an important ingredient of economic development; this is particularly true for Russia. For Western Europe, the Russian gas resources are of increasing importance, as Europe will soon depend for over 50 percent of its needs on Russia's gas supply. We have analyzed the effect of the transformation process on the evaluation of the Russian gas resources and reserves. The institutional approach suggests a distinction between the notion of reserves in *socialist* times and the reserves in a *market* economic environment. This implies that not all of the official Russian gas reserves of 47 tcm can be considered as real reserves in a market economic, Western sense. Our estimates rather hint at real, economically valid gas reserves of about 18–20 tcm, that is, only about 40 percent of the official figure.

The result of this analysis is that Russia may *not* be as gas-rich as it is generally considered to be. Russia's gas reserves should be re-assessed, taking into account undistorted cost and demand data. Western governments and export credit agencies should not give priority to the Russian gas industry by guaranteeing the economic risk of export credits; insuring the political risk would suffice. The analysis also suggests that the EU–Russian energy partnership should not be based on wishful thinking about what *might* happen, but on a more sober analysis of the economic determinants of Russian gas exports to Europe.

Part III
Summary and Conclusions

12. Lessons and Perspectives on the Way to European Enlargement

To everything, ..., there is a season.

Ecclesiastes 3:1–8.

1. INTRODUCTION

'Paving the way to European enlargement'. This book has addressed theoretical and policy issues on infrastructure policies in Eastern Europe on the path from socialism towards market economies and European enlargement. It has proven to be a controversial topic, both with respect to economic theory, where traditional static welfare economics contrasts with the new institutional economic approach, and with respect to economic policy, where a minimalist approach contrasts with demands for multi-billion USD 'Marshall Plan' type infrastructure polices. After the theoretical concepts were laid out in Part I, the preceding chapters of Part II have highlighted specific aspects of infrastructure policies over the last decade. When reforms started in the early 1990s, no generally valid policy guidelines could be given: former attempts at gradual 'reform' within the socialist countries provided no useful yardstick, nor could parallels be drawn from other emerging regions of the world, for example, Latin America. Today, it has become normal to think of most Central and Eastern European countries as upcoming EU members, and to apply concepts of developed market economies to the policies of these countries. This book is then an attempt to sketch out the infrastructural conditions of this process.

This final chapter summarizes the main results of the book and derives conclusions for economic research and policy on the path to European integration. Section 2 summarizes the main results, Section 3 synthesizes the empirical sector studies of Part II by relating them to the general questions formulated at the outset. Section 4 derives a set of theoretical findings and suggestions for further research, and Section 5 concludes with implications for infrastructure policies in and towards Eastern Europe, with particular attention to the issues of EU enlargement.

2. MAIN RESULTS

Among the different approaches to and results of infrastructure policies in Eastern Europe over the last decade, some common trends can be identified that appear more or less clearly across countries and across sectors:

1. *The systemic change in Eastern Europe from socialism towards a market economy required a substantial technical and organizational overhaul of the infrastructure.*

The collapse of socialism in Eastern Europe implied a drastic change of the infrastructure, in financial, organizational, and in many cases also in physical terms. Efforts to maintain the socialist infrastructure as such were bound to fail; the existing infrastructure was largely incapable of fulfilling the service functions required in a market economy. *New* mechanisms of planning, financing and operation needed to be set up all over Eastern Europe. This overhaul of the infrastructure had to be done under conditions of high uncertainty, ranging from the most basic economic parameters (GDP, inflation, structural change) to fundamental constitutional issues. In this context, the analysis of infrastructure policies must not be reduced to one particular factor of uncertainty, that is, partial analysis within a given set of rules ('choice within rules'); it also has to consider the options and decisions shaping the very institutional framework ('choice of rules').

2. *Early attempts at introducing competition-oriented infrastructure policies have met with little success.*

Many East European countries tried to utilize the window of reform opportunity of the early 1990s to implement market-oriented infrastructure policies. Examples are the private project financing of highways, the introduction of a market-oriented pool model in the power sector, or the separation of infra- and superstructure in the railway sector. However, these attempts have met with little success: whereas some far reaching reforms were already abandoned in the early phase of transformation, others were carried through but did not lead to the expected results. Evidence of this is provided by the mediocre infrastructure reform indicators of East European countries (see Chapter 5). The difficulties of implementing ground-breaking reforms is furthermore evidenced at the level of *individual projects*. Among the 30 or so first generation reform projects in Eastern European infrastructure, no clear success story emerges.[289] We have highlighted the institutional and political economic reasons for the difficulties. They are not *per se* a reason to reject

---

[289] Among them private highway financing, mainly in Hungary and Poland. Pool model or market system in the power sector: Hungary, Poland, Russia, Ukraine. Separation of superstructure and infrastructure in the railway sector: Estonia, Czech Republic. Market mechanisms in wholesale and retail gas markets: Ukraine, Russia.

the reformist approach. However, empirical evidence shows that the objectives conceived in a 'big bang' approach to infrastructure policy reforms have hardly ever been attained.

3.a *One explanation for the limited success of competition-oriented reform are formal and informal institutional obstacles specific to East European transformation countries.*

3.b *An alternative or additional explanation for the limited success of reforms is interest group lobbying against privatization and deregulation.*

The difficulties experienced by the transformation countries in implementing competition-oriented infrastructure policies can in general be explained by two factors: i) formal and informal institutional obstacles linked to the process of systemic transformation. This implies that the East European governments 'could not' achieve their objectives even if they were seriously trying to, due to the institutional path-dependency prevailing in the transformation period; ii) the particular political economy resulting from the socialist legacy. This latter explanation implies that the transformation countries, or some powerful interest groups therein, 'did not want to' implement truly market-oriented reforms. Whereas the institutional obstacles have rendered infrastructure sector reform more difficult in phase I of transformation, the dominant reason for delayed reform in phase II is to be sought in interest groups' lobbying against privatization and deregulation. An indicator for this is that, whereas in phase II of transformation the institutional constraints have largely abated, at least in most Central and East European countries, market-oriented infrastructure reforms remain weak.

4. *There is no clear evidence that choosing a gradual approach to reform at the outset would have led to superior results.*

From a theoretical perspective, an argument to explain the conservative attitude towards infrastructure policies is that rapid privatization and deregulation were not the optimal strategies in the first place, and that the transformation countries' governments knew this and acted accordingly. There are indeed several valid theoretical arguments for carrying out non-traditional infrastructure policies during transformation, both macroeconomic (for example, support economic recovery and growth) and microeconomic ones (for example, accelerate structural change, generate positive investment externalities, assure certain politically determined objectives). However, there is no clear-cut evidence that choosing a gradual approach in the first place would have led systematically to more consistent and successful reforms. In particular, there is no evidence that governments have explicitly chosen a gradual approach in order to reap the benefits suggested by theory.

5. *Direct state support to what were considered to be particularly strategic infrastructure sectors has met with little success.*

In many cases, East European transformation countries provided certain infrastructure sectors with direct support, mainly financial. There is little evidence that these selective attempts to favor certain infrastructure sectors have met the objectives in an efficient manner. Examples are the large Public Investment Programs, state support to national innovation systems, and overdimensioned highway development programs.

6. *The East European EU-accession countries need to accelerate their reforms in order to facilitate the enlargement process.*

The institutional framework provided by the EU-accession process was an essential determinant of infrastructure policies in Central and Eastern Europe, in that it has provided a framework for the modernization process. In general, the East European counties heading towards EU membership have adjusted their reforms to the requirements of the White Book on European Integration. Most East European EU-accession candidates have implemented the EU legal *aquis communautaire* in the infrastructure sectors, or have committed themselves to do so in the near future. However, there is still a wide gap between the formal implementation of reform, and the *implementation* in reality. Evidence of this comes from the modest success of implementing EU directives in the railway sector (91/440 EEC and subsequent), the power sector (96/92 EEC) and the gas sector (98/30 EEC). At a macroeconomic level, streamlining expenditures for infrastructure development also seems to be a condition for attaining the stability criteria required for accession to the European Monetary Union.

3. SELECTED EVIDENCE

This section summarizes the evidence from the empirical analysis carried out at the national and sectoral level, presented in Part II. Table 12.1 summarizes the empirical analyses with respect to the main hypotheses and stylized findings of this book. The following aspects are worth mentioning:

I. *Public Investment Programs* (PIP) do not seem to be an efficient instrument to enhance private infrastructure investments and thus to accelerate the economic recovery of Eastern Europe. In addition to the traditional factors of bureaucracy failure (such as inefficient supply of public goods, incentive problems, information asymmetries), PIP in transformation countries had to be implemented in the midst of profound administrative restructuring and quickly changing political and constitutional decisions ('shooting at moving targets from a moving platform'). The skepticism towards PIP in Eastern Europe is confirmed by case studies at the level of individual projects, which show that the integration of these projects into PIP guaranteed that neither the required financing nor the necessary political support would be obtained.

II. *Innovation policies* (in transformation countries sometimes also called S&T policies) had to cope with the implosion of the socialist innovation system and the devaluation of most of its potential, linked to the necessary adaptation of enterprises to international technological trajectories with which the socialist trajectory was incompatible. The East European governments faced the alternative of a) a market-oriented, demand-driven approach entailing introduction of competition and internationalization to the national innovation systems, and b) a more conservative approach entailing maintenance of the existing capacities through continued state financing (supply-orientation). For political reasons, most governments chose the latter approach. In contrast, the business sector attempted a catching-up process based on the integration into international innovation, production and sales networks. *Imitation* of existing technology was the key determinant for the catching-up process of the East European enterprises, and not their own R&D and innovation. A mere increase of state expenses for innovation policies is unlikely to have significant positive effects on future economic development.

III. The difficulties in implementing *private project financing* in the region can be explained in terms of the high political and economic risk prevailing in the early reform years, which added to the complexity of private project financing schemes already prevalent in Western countries. The implementation of innovative financing schemes in Eastern Europe also hinged upon the lack of a coherent legal system (extensiveness *and* effectiveness). Informal institutions may also have contributed to the difficulties; for example, the absence of a broad public consensus in favor of private infrastructure financing and the consequences thereof (such as cost-covering prices). A consensus has emerged in business and academia that purely private infrastructure financing is *not* a feasible option for most projects in East European transformation countries; however, this does not exclude an increasing private sector participation.

Table 12.1 Survey of main results and application to empirical tests

	1) Substantial overhaul of infrastructure required	2) Limited success of competition-oriented infrastructure policies	3a) Explanation I: institutional obstacles ('could not')
I) Public investment programs	Yes fundamental restructuring of economic system and public management necessary	yes decisions based on political bargaining, priority given to large-scale projects	yes low administrative capacities to implement innovative policy instruments
II) Innovation policies	Yes reorganization of innovation infrastructure necessary, due to new, market-economic technical trajectories	yes some privatization, few closures; public financing remains the dominant source	no less state financing was possible; successful low-cost strategies by some enterprises via international networking
III) Private project financing	Yes new financing mechanisms required, but high political and economic uncertainty	yes some attempts (e.g. M1, IPP), but not a single success	yes e.g. underdeveloped capital markets and legal system; also, low public acceptance
IV) Power sector de-regulation	Yes new standards of security, environment, system management, interconnection, etc. required	yes several attempts to introduce competition *ad hoc*, all of which have failed	yes legal framework, bad technical state, lack of minimal public consensus, little public support
V) Gas sector de-regulation	yes technical system stable but outdated; high investment requirements, strategic role of gas sector	yes hardly any competition prevailing in Eastern Europe	yes lack of legal framework, public support
VI) Estimate of gas reserves	yes necessity for full-fledged re-estimation of gas reserves under market conditions	..	no re-assessment of reserves and resources was possible

Table 12.1 continued

3b) and/or explanation II: political economy ('did not want to')	4) Superiority of a gradual approach?	5) Few positive effects of state involvement?	6) EU accession requires further reforms
yes self-interest of bureaucracy to maintain state planning procedures	..	yes loss of resources without significant effects at macro- or sectoral level	yes focus on few, critical projects necessary to relieve fiscal constraints
yes strong lobbying to maintain the presumed S&T 'potential'	no gradual redeployment of socialist innovation potential was nearly impossible	yes state financing (supply-side approach) less efficient than demand-orientation of new networks	yes stronger focus on demand may increase competitiveness of domestic innovation potential
unclear some pilot attempts, but many more would have been possible	yes fully private project financing seems impossible in a transformation context	no some state support is required , e.g. the takeover of demand-risk	yes improvement of institutional framework required to attract private capital
yes strong coalition of vested interests against deregulation and privatization	maybe given objective requirements for modernization; but problem of regulatory capture	..	yes EU power directive (96/92 EEC) fulfilled on paper in most countries, but not in reality
yes strong interest groups against reforms (mainly former monopolists)	maybe liberalization may require a sector in sound technical shape	..	yes EU gas directive (98/30 EEC) not fulfilled on paper by many countries, let alone in reality
yes re-estimation will lower the reserve-base, may therefore be rejected by incumbent gas companies	..	..	

IV. *Power sector re-regulation* has not made as much progress as hoped for a decade ago. Several East European countries attempted a 'big bang' reform, in other words the introduction of a market-oriented pool model. These attempts were not immediately successful in Central and Eastern Europe (Poland, initially also Hungary) and even less in the CIS (Russia, Ukraine). Whereas a combination of institutional factors (technical and legal standards, high regulatory risk, and also lacking public support) constituted one determining factor, solid resistance of vested interests against more competition and privatization also proved to be decisive. Transaction cost considerations also tend to favor a gradual approach to deregulation, in particular given the bad technical condition of the network. However, with the stabilization of the institutional environment, the technical modernization of the industry, and the necessity to adhere to the European directive on electricity (EU/98/92), no further reason exists to delay the liberalization of the sector any longer.

V. Structural reform in the *gas sector* was attempted by a few East European countries, and results were limited; market competition at the wholesale level has not truly been implemented, let alone at the retail level. Resistance to market-oriented reforms was particularly strong in the large CIS countries where gas sector reform was among the most highly politicized issues. In the EU-accession countries, gradual reforms towards the 1998 EU gas directive have begun very recently but no significant breakthrough towards a competitive system is to be expected.

VI. The institutional approach also highlighted the relevance of systemic transformation for seemingly purely technical issues, such as the estimation of a country's *gas reserves*. The *market* principles of calculating gas reserves should be applied to the transformation countries as well. The case of the Russian gas reserves, which would have to be discounted by over 50 percent, shows that this is not a purely academic debate but one with significant financial and policy implications. It also affects the perspectives of West European gas imports directly.

4. THEORETICAL FINDINGS AND SUGGESTIONS FOR FUTURE RESEARCH

One finding of this study is that infrastructure policies in Eastern Europe need to be evaluated in the light of their *specific* institutional frameworks, and that policy recommendations must likewise be tailored according to the specific conditions. The *real-world* comparative institutional approach suggested by Demsetz (1969) is superior to an approach seeking theoretically first-best solutions. Related to this is the need of *decentral* solutions brought about by the competition of models. While this is not a very surprising result for adherents of the institutional approach, it does contrast with the search for first-best reform proposals put forward in the early phase of transformation, both by practitioners and by part of the scientific community. The specific economic and institutional conditions in Eastern Europe have rendered the introduction of market-oriented infrastructure policies in transformation countries difficult, whereas these have been shown to work successfully in institutionally stable, developed economies (such as the UK).

Given the unique process of systemic change, a brief period of observation (<10 years) and unreliable data, a *bottom-up* approach is better suited to analyzing infrastructure policies than a top-down approach. In the terms of comparative economic system analysis, the infrastructure policies in transformation countries may usefully be compared with those of other *underdeveloped* and *emerging* countries. East European countries did indeed show a multitude of similarities to underdeveloped and emerging countries, at least in phase I of reforms, such as dualistic structures, the wedge between the formal and the informal sector, or the contrast between dominant state ownership and some 'islands' of privatized or newly created private enterprises, monolithic industrial and rural regions, and so on. Also, the separation between the state and the economic sphere that is a condition for economic development (Volckart, 1999, 8) was non-existent in many post-socialist transformation countries. In phase II, most Central and East European countries changed to become emerging market economies, having defined a path towards implementation of fundamental institutional and economic reforms. In that sense, the EU-accession countries' infrastructure policies may in the future be usefully compared with those of Latin America or some Asian countries in the 1990s.

One possible extension of the comparative institutional approach is to apply the institutional and sector-specific analysis to infrastructure policies in *other* countries undergoing system transformation. One obvious example is China, which thus far has not been the subject of in-depth analysis. Another interesting case is South Africa, where various models of developing infrastructure have been tested, among them the granting of quasi-unregulated monopolies, ESCOM.[290] A very specific European region undergoing transformation is that of the Balkan post-war countries, where infrastructure development was declared a top priority of the Stability Pact, but where opinions on *how* to implement this diverge.

A theoretical aspect that merits further consideration is the assessment of *sector*-specific transaction costs. The credo of the institutional approach, 'institutions matter', needs to be applied, and the specific nature of transaction costs be defined, at the *sectoral* level. The first application to Eastern Europe is Pittman (2001), deriving differentiated recommendations on the degree of vertical unbundling in the power, railway and telecommunication sectors, based on quantitative technical and institutional indicators.

---

[290] For an analysis of the South African power sector, see Praetorius, Barbara (2000, *Power for the People*. Hamburg, Lit Verlag).

5. POLICY IMPLICATIONS

The research program summarized in this book has addressed the policy question of how to design appropriate infrastructure policies in Eastern Europe. The concrete policy implications derived from the above analysis concern primarily the Central and East European countries on the path towards EU accession, but to a certain extent can also be applied to the CIS and other emerging countries:

– Delayed (instead of immediate) phasing out of monopolistic structures and public ownership may have been justified in individual cases, but the potential welfare losses have to be weighed carefully against the expected benefits. Immediate liberalization of infrastructure markets and privatization may not have been the appropriate choice for all East European transformation countries, in particular if politically defined objectives have to be met in the short term (such as EU quality standards) or investment requirements are high for some other reason (for example, to secure European infrastructure interconnection). However, prolonged state involvement comes at the risk of X-inefficiencies and the wrong investment decisions; thus, they have to be considered as an exception to the rule, and one that needs to be well-justified;

– attempts at introducing radical market-oriented reforms into infrastructure sectors, even if they do not succeed immediately, should not be dismissed as a strategy for transformation countries. The resulting long-term effect depends on the institutional capacity of a country to adapt to frequent policy changes, the technical and organizational state of the sector in question, and the nature of the reform window of opportunity. The case of the Hungarian highway projects has shown that even a failed radical reform may have positive effects if it paves the way for second-best solutions. In contrast, if the window of opportunity is tight, allowing for but one 'shot' of reform, radical solutions are too risky (for example, in the case of Ukraine);

– significant financial support to Eastern Europe from international financial organizations, for example, in the form of a second 'Marshall Plan', was unlikely to have substantial positive effects. As the potential impact of such programs diminishes over time, the discussion of a Marshall Plan for Eastern Europe or Russia (such as proposed by Steinherr, 1999) seems no longer to be of high relevance. During phase I of transformation, higher external financial flows may have cushioned the macroeconomic downturn, but they did not come about due to the organizational slack and low absorptive capacities in the recipient transformation countries. Today, there is no more need for macroeconomic regulation through external financial packages, and the obstacles to reform at the sector level are not financial but *institutional*;

– the EU integration of East European countries will be expensive, but it is unlikely to be fuelled significantly by massive financial support from Brussels. The financial resources of the (old) European Union (EU-15) are limited, and they should be concentrated on a small number of projects of trans-European relevance. Decentral infrastructure development in the accession countries can hardly be financed from the outside, and should not, in most cases. Infrastructure policies in Eastern Europe have become something different than a mere question of money and public support;

– as European enlargement is approaching, there are no (more) reasons for the East European accession countries to further delay liberalization and privatization in their infrastructure sectors. In general, these countries have attained sufficient institutional stability to implement market-oriented infrastructure policy, short-term technical bottlenecks have for the most part been overcome. Today, the main obstacle to market-oriented reforms is probably interest group lobbying; hence, efforts also need to be undertaken to prevent a coalition of East *and* West European lobbyists against market-oriented infrastructure reforms. EU accession is feasible, but the East European accession countries need to maintain the reform momentum on the long and winding road to European integration.

Bibliography

Aghion, Philippe, and Mark Schankerman (1999): 'Competition, Entry and the Social Returns to Infrastructure in Transition Economies'. *Economics of Transition*, Vol. 7, No. 1, 79-101.

Ahrens, Joachim (1994): *Der russische Systemwandel – Reform und Transformation des (post)sowjetischen Wirtschaftssystems*. Frankfurt am Main, Peter Lang.

Ahrens, Joachim (1996): *The Political Institutions of Economic Development*. Volkswirtschaftliches Seminar der Universität Göttingen, Diskussionsbeitrag Nr. 88.

Alston, Lee J. (1996): 'Empirical Work in Institutional Economics: An Overview'. In: Alston, Eggertson and North (eds).

Alston, Lee J., Thrainn Eggertson, and Douglass C. North (eds) (1996): *Empirical Studies in Institutional Change*. Cambridge, Mass., Cambridge University Press.

Apolte, Thomas (1992): *Politische Ökonomie der Systemtransformation*. Duisburger Volkswirtschaftliche Schriften 15. Hamburg, Steuer- und Wirtschaftsverlag.

Armstrong, Mark, and John Vickers (1996): 'Regulatory Reform in Telecommunications in Central and Eastern Europe'. *Economics of Transition*, Vol. 4, No. 2, 295-318.

Aschauer, David A. (1989): 'Is Public Expenditure Productive?' *Journal of Monetary Economics*, Vol. 23, No. 2.

Aslund, Anders (2002): *Building Capitalism: The Transformation of the Former Soviet Bloc*. Cambridge, Cambridge Univ. Press.

Autorenkollektiv der Hochschule für Verkehrswirtschaft Friedrich Liszt (1978): *Lehrbuch der Transportwirtschaft*. Berlin (Ost), Transpress VEB Verlag für Verkehrswesen.

Bakos, Gábor (2001): 'Privatizing and Liberalizing Electricity: The Case of Hungary'. *Energy Policy*, Vol. 29, 1119-1132.

Balmaceda, Margerita (1998): 'Gas, Oil and the Linkages between Domestic and Foreign Policies: The Case of Ukraine'. *Europe-Asia Studies*, Vol. 50, No. 2 (March), 257-286.

Beckers, Thorsten (2002): *Infrastrukturinvestitionen unter Unsicherheit.* Berlin, Diplomarbeit TU Berlin, Fachgebiet Wirtschafts- und Infrastrukturpolitik.

Berliner, James S. (1976): *The Innovation Decision in Soviet Industry.* Cambridge, Massachussetts, The MIT Press.

Bernholz, Peter und Friedrich Breyer (1993): *Grundlagen der politischen Ökonomie. Band 1 – Theorie der Wirtschaftssysteme.* Tübingen, Mohr Siebeck.

Bernholz, Peter und Friedrich Breyer (1994): *Grundlagen der politischen Ökonomie. Band 2 – Neue politische Ökonomie.* Tübingen, Mohr Siebeck.

Bickenbach, Frank, Lars Kumkar, and Rüdiger Soltwedel (1999): *The New Institutional Economics of Antitrust and Regulation.* Kiel Working Papers 961, December.

Biehl, Dieter (1995): 'Infrastruktur als Bestimmungsfaktor regionaler Entwicklungspotentiale in der Europäischen Union'. In: Karl, Helmut, und Henrichsmeyer, Wilhelm (eds): *Regionalentwicklung im Prozess der Europäischen Integration.* Bonn, Europa Union Verlag (Bonner Schriften zur Integeration Europas, Band 4).

Biehl, Dieter (2001): 'Infrastructure in Ukraine - An Evaluation with European Comparisons'. In: Hoffmann and Möllers (eds).

Bitzer, Jürgen (2000): 'An Evolutionary View of Post-socialist Restructuring: From Science and Technology Systems to Innovation Systems'. In: Hirschhausen and Bitzer (2000).

Bitzer, Jürgen, and Christian von Hirschhausen (1998): *Infrastructure Policies for Sustained Growth in Eastern Europe - The Cases of the Baltic Countries.* Berlin, Brussels, Final Report of the Phare-ACE project P-95-2111-R.

Bitzer, Jürgen, and Christian von Hirschhausen (2000): 'Reform of Innovation Systems in Eastern Europe: Structural Change Sluggish'. *Economic Bulletin,* Vol. 37, No. 6, 183-190.

Blanchard, Olivier, and Michael Kremer (1997): 'Disorganization'. *Quarterly Journal of Economics,* Vol. 112, No. 4, 1091-1126.

Bofinger, Peter, Heiner Flassbeck, and Lutz Hoffmann (1996): 'The Economics of Orthodox Money-Based Stabilizations: the Examples of Russia, Ukraine and Kazakhstan'. *Economic Systems,* Vol. 21, No. 1, 1-33.

Bolton, P., and J. Farrell (1990): 'Decentralization, Duplication, and Delay'. *Journal of Political Economy,* Vol. 98, 803-826.

Bolz, Klaus, und Andreas Polkowski (1996): *Lettland – Regulierung und Deregulierung im Transformationsprozess.* Hamburg, HWWA-Report Nr. 158.

Bomsel, Oilvier (1995): 'Enjeux industriels du post-socialisme'. *Revue d' Economie Industrielle.*

Boroch, Wilfried (1996): *Litauen – Regulierung und Deregulierung im Transformationsprozess.* Hamburg, HWWA-Report Nr. 157.

BP Amoco Statistic Review of World Energy (various issues). London. (formerly: *BP Statistic Review of World Energy).*

Braudel, Fernand (1979): *Civilisation matérielle, économie et capitalisme.* Paris, Armand Colin.

Brealey, Richard, A. and Stewart C. Myers (2000): *Principles of Corporate Finance.* 6th edition. New York, McGraw-Hill.

Breithaupt, Manfred, Horst Höfling, Lars Petzold, Christine Philipp, Norbert Schmitz und Rolf Sülzer (1998): *Kommerzialisierung und Privatisierung von Public Utilities – Internationale Erfarhungen und Konzepte für Transformationsländer.* Wiesbaden, Gabler.

Brenck, Andreas (1992): 'Theoretische Aspekte des Road Pricing'. In: *Berichte aus dem Institut für Verkehrswissenschaft an der Universität Münster 3* (Schwerpunktthema Road Pricing), 3-11.

Brenck, Andreas (1993): 'Privatisierungsmodelle für die Deutsche Bundesbahn'. In: Allemeyer, W., et al.: *Privatisierung des Schienenverkehrs. Beiträge aus dem Institut für Verkehrswissenschaft an der Universität Münster.* Band 130. Göttingen, Vandenhoeck & Ruprecht, 37-183.

Brücker, Herbert (1996): *Elf Thesen zur Privatisierung von Infrastrukturunternehmen in Transsformationsländern.* Berlin, Lecture concept for the Gesellschaft für technische Zusammenarbeit (GTZ), June 11.

Brücker, Herbert, Wolfram Schrettl, und Ulricht Weißenburger (1995), *Investitionsfinanzierung im Transformationsprozess – Der Konflikt zwischen monetärer Stabilisierung und Wachstumspolitik in den Nachfolgestaaten der früheren Sowjetunion.* Berlin, Gutachten im Auftrag des Bundesministeriums für Wirtschaft.

Buchanan, James M. (1965): 'An Economic Theory of Clubs'. *Economica,* Vol. 32, 1-14.

Buchanan, James M. (1975): *The Limits of Liberty: Between Anarchy and Leviathan,* Chicago, The University of Chicago Press.

Buchanan, James M., R.D. Tollison, and G. Tullock (eds) (1980): *Towards a Theory of the Rent-Seeking Society.* College Station, Texas.

Burger, Bettina, und Markus Lenzner (1996): *Estland – Regulierung und Deregulierung im Transformationsprozess.* Hamburg, HWWA-Report Nr. 156.

Carbajo, José, and Steven Fries (1997): *Restructuring Infrastructure in Transition Economies*. London, European Bank for Reconstruction and Development, Working Paper No. 24.

Chollet, Andreas, Berit Meinhart, Christian von Hirschhausen, and Petra Opitz (2001): *Options for Transporting Russian Gas to Western Europe*. Berlin, DIW Discussion Paper 261.

Cleaver, Kevin (2002): *A Preliminary Strategy to Develop a Knowledge Economy in European Union Accession Countries*. Washington, D.C., World Bank (Europea and Central Asia Region) Working Paper.

Clement, Hermann und Joachim Jungfer (eds) (1998): *Den Transformationsfortschritt messen: Die staatliche Einflußnahme auf die Wirtschaftstätigkeit in ausgewählten Transformationsstaaten. ifo Studien zur Osteuropa- und Transformationsforschung 29*. München, Weltforum Verlag.

Coase, Ronald H. (1937): 'The Nature of the Firm'. *Economica*, Vol. 4 (November), 386-405.

Coase, Ronald H. (1960): 'The Problem of Social Cost'. *The Journal of Law and Economics*, Vol. 3 (October), 1-44.

Cornia, Giovanni Andrea, and Vladimir Popov (1998): 'Transition and Long-Term Growth: Conventional Versus Non-Conventional Determinants'. Moct-Most, Vol. 8, 7-32.

Couderc, Marie-Laure (1996): *Entreprisation: Adaptation of Some Former Research Units to the New Economic Environment in Russia*. CERNA, Research Paper, 96-B-2.

Cowen, Peneolpe Brook, and Tyler Cowen (1998): 'Deregulated Private Water Supply: A Policy Option for Developing Countries'. *Cato Journal*, Vol. 18, No. 1 (Spring/Summer), 21-41.

Cullis, John, and Philip Jones (1998): *Public Finance and Public Choice*. 2nd edition. Oxford, Oxford University Press.

Dailami, Mansoor, and Danny Leipziger (1997): *Infrastructure Project Finance and Capital Flows: A New Perspective*. Birmingham Conference on Financial Flows and World Development, and World Bank (mimeo).

Dallago, Bruno (1999): 'Convergence and Divergence of Economic Systems: A Systemic-Institutional Perspective'. *Economic Systems*, Vol. 23, No. 2 (June), 168-172.

Davis, Christopher (2001): 'The Health Sector: Illness, Medical Care and Mortality'. In: Granville, Brigitee, and Peter Oppenheimer (eds): *Russia's Post-Communist Economy*. Oxford, Oxford University Press.

Demsetz, Harold (1968): 'Why Regulate Utilities?' *Journal of Law and Economics*, Vol. 11, 55-65.

Demsetz, Harold (1969): 'Information and Efficiency: Another Viewpoint'. *Journal of Law and Economics*, Vol. 12, 1-22.

Dewatripont, Mathias, and Gérard Roland (1992): 'The Virtues of Gradualism and Legitimacy in the Transition to a Market Economy'. *The Economic Journal*, Vol. 102 (March), 291-300.

Dewatripont, Mathias, and Gérard Roland (1995): 'The Design of Reform Packages under Uncertainty'. *American Economic Review*, Vol. 85, No. 5, 1207-1223.

Dewatripont, Mathias, and Gérard Roland (1996): 'Transition as a Process of Large-Scale Institutional Change'. *Economics of Transition*, Vol. 4, No. 1, 1-30.

Dewatripont, Mathias, and Gérard Roland (2000): 'Soft Budget Constraints, Transition, and Industrial Change'. *Journal of Institutional and Theoretical Economics/Zeitschrift für die gesamte Staatswissenschaft*, Vol. 156, No. 1, 245-260.

Dixit, Avinash K., and Robert S. Pindyck (1994): *Investment under Uncertainty*. Princeton, NJ, Princeton University Press.

Dodonov, Boris, Christian von Hirschhausen, Petra Opitz, and Pavlo Sugolov (2001): *Infrastructure Monitoring for Ukraine*. Kyiv, Institute for Economic Research and Policy Consulting (IERPC), Working Paper No. 8 (June).

Dodonov, Boris, Christian von Hirschhausen, Petra Opitz, and Pavlo Sugolov (2002): 'Efficient Infrastructure Supply for Economic Development in Transition Countries'. *Post-Communist Economies*, Vol. 14, No. 2, 149-167.

Duchêne, Gérard (1989): *L'économie de l'URSS*. Paris, Editions La Découverte.

Dutz, Mark A., and Maria Vagliasindi (1999): *Competition Policy Implementation in Transition Economies: An Empirical Assessment*. EBRD Working Paper No. 47, December.

Dutz, Mark, and James Silberman (1993): *Building Capabilities: A Marshall Plan Type Productivity Enhancement Program for Eastern Europe and the Former Soviet Union*. 'Osteuropa-Seminar' Institute for Advanced Studies, Vienna, and the Vienna Institute for Comparative Economic Studies; World Bank, Washington D.C.

Dyker, David (1997): *The Technology of Transition: Science and Technology Policies for Transition Countries*. Budapest, Central European University Press.

EBRD (1994): *Transition Report – Economic Transition in Eastern Europe and the Former Soviet Union*. London, European Bank for Reconstruction and Development.

EBRD (1995): *Transition Report – Investment and Enterprise Development*. London, European Bank for Reconstruction and Development.

EBRD (1996): *Transition Report – Infrastructure and Savings*. London, European Bank for Reconstruction and Development.

EBRD (1997): *Transition Report – Enterprise Performance and Growth*. London, European Bank for Reconstruction and Development.

EBRD (1998): *Transition Report – Financial Sector in Transition*. London, European Bank for Reconstruction and Development.

EBRD (1999): *Transition Report – Ten Years of Transition*. London, European Bank for Reconstruction and Development.

EBRD (2000): *Transition Report – Employment, Skills and Transition*. London, European Bank for Reconstruction and Development.

EBRD (2001a): *Transition Report – Energy in Transition*. London, European Bank for Reconstruction and Development.

EBRD (2001b): *Transport Operation Policy*. Internal Strategy Paper. London, European Bank for Reconstruction and Development.

EBRD (2002): *Transition Report Update*. London, European Bank for Reconstruction and Development.

Ees, Hans van, and Harry Garretsen (1994): 'The Theoretical Foundation of the Reforms in Eastern Europe: Big Bang Versus Gradualism and the Limitations of Neo-Classical Theory'. *Economic Systems*, Vol. 18, No. 1 (March), 1-13.

Eger, Thomas (2000): *Systemtransformation als umfassender institutioneller Wandel: Die fünf Dimensionen der Transformationsprozesse in Osteuropa*. Frankfurt/Oder, Diskussionspaper des Frankfurter Institut für Transformationsstudien No. 12/00.

Eichengreen, Barry (1995): 'Financing Infrastructure in Developing Countries: Lessons from the Railway Age'. *The World Bank Research Observer*, Vol. 10, No. 1 (February), 75-91.

Engel, Eduardo, Ronald Fischer, and Alexander Galetovic (1997): 'Highway Franchising: Pitfalls and Opportunities'. *American Economic Review*, Vol. 87, No. 2 (Proceedings), 68-72.

Engel, Eduardo, Ronald Fischer, and Alexander Galetovic (1999): *The Chilean Infrastructure Concessions Program – Evaluation, Lessons and Prospects for the Future*. Universidad de Chile, Center for Applied Economics (CEA), Discussion Paper No. 60 (September).

Engerer, Hella (2001): *Ownership in Transformation – Limits to Privatization in Central and Eastern Europe*. London, Macmillan.

Estache, Antonio (1995): *Decentralizing Infrastructure – Advantages and Limitations*. Washington, D.C., World Bank Discussion Papers 290.

Estache, Antonio, and José Carbajo (1996): *Designing Toll Road Concessions – Lessons from Argentina*. Washington, D.C., World Bank Viewpoint, Note No. 99.

Estache, Antonio, and Ginés de Rus (eds) (2000): *Privatizing and Regulation of Transport Infrastructure.* Washington D.C., World Bank Institute Development Studies.

Estache, Antonio, Manuel Romero, and John Strong (2000): *The Long and Winding Path to Private Financing and Regulation of Toll Roads.* Washington, D.C., World Bank, World Bank Institute, Policy Research Working Paper 2387.

European Investment Bank (various issues): *Annual Report,* Luxemburg.

Eucken, Walter ([1952] 1990): *Grundsätze der Wirtschaftspolitik. 6. Auflage.* Tübingen, Mohr. (1. Auflage, edited by E. Eucken und K.P. Hensel, 1952, Tübingen).

European Commission (1999): *Agenda 2000 – Final Document.* Brussels, Bulletin of the European Union.

Ewers, Hans-Jürgen (ed.) (1995): *Verkehrsinfrastrukturpolitik in Europa – Eine deutsch-polnische Perspektive.* Beiträge aus dem Institut für Verkehrswissenschaft an der Universität Münster, Band 137, Göttingen, Vandenhoeck & Ruprecht.

Ewers, Hans-Jürgen, and Henning Tegner (1997): 'What Type of Strategic Planning?' Paper presented at the 14th International Symposium on Theory and Practice in Transport Economics. (CEMT). Innsbruck.

Ewers, Hans-Jürgen, und Hansjörg Rodi (1995): *Privatisierung der Bundesautobahnen.* Beiträge aus dem Institut für Verkehrswissenschaft an der Universität Münster, edited by Hans-Jürgen Ewers, Band 134, Göttingen, Vandenhoeck & Ruprecht.

Ewers, Hans-Jürgen, und Henning Tegner (2000): *Entwicklungschancen der privaten Realisierung von Verkehrsinfrastruktur in Deutschland.* Berlin, Düsseldorf, Essen.

Falk, Martin, und Norbert Funke (1992): 'Zur Sequenz von Reformschritten: Erste Erfahrungen aus dem Transformationsprozess in Mittel- und Osteuropa'. *Die Weltwirtschaft,* Heft 2, 186-206.

Feldmann, Horst (1999): 'Ordnungstheoretische Aspekte der Institutionenökonomik'. *Volkswirtschaftliche Schriften,* Heft 499. Berlin, Duncker & Humblot.

Fischer, Stanley, and Alan Gelb (1991): 'The Process of Socialist Economic Transformation'. *Journal of Economic Perspectives,* Vol. 5, No. 4 (Fall), 91-105.

Frey, René (1970): *Infrastruktur – Grundlagen der Planung öffentlicher Investitionen.* Tübingen, Mohr Siebeck.

Fritsch, Michael, Thomas Wein und Hans-Jürgen Ewers (1999): *Marktversagen und Wirtschaftspolitik: Mikroökonomische Grundlagen staatlichen Handelns.* 3. Auflage. München, Vahlen.

Funke, Norbert (1993): 'Timing and Sequencing of Reforms: Competing Views and the Role of Credibility'. *Kyklos*, Vol. 46, 337-362.

Furubotn, Eirik, and Richter, Rudolf (1992): 'The New Institutional Economics – Eastern European Reconstruction Problems: Editorial Preface'. *Journal of Institutional and Theoretical Economics*, Vol. 148, 1-3.

Furubotn, Eirik, and Richter, Rudolf (2000): *Institutions and Economic Theory: An Introduction to and Assessment of the New Institutional Economics*. Ann Arbor, University of Michigan Press.

Gaddy, Clifford G., and Barry W. Ickes (1999): *Beyond a Bailout: Time to Face Reality About Russia's 'Virtual Economy'*. Washington, D.C., The Brookings Institution.

Gaspard, Michel (1996): *Transport Infrastructure Financing in Central and Eastern Europe*. Paris, Presses de l'Ecole Nationale des Ponts et Chaussées, and EU-Commission, DG VII.

Gazprom (ed.) (1998): *Strategic Development of the Russian Gas Industry*. Moscow, Gazoil Press.

Glachant, Jean-Michel (1998): 'England's Wholesale Electricity Market: Could this Hybrid Institutional Arrangement be Transposed to the European Union?' *Utilities Policy*, Vol. 7, No. 2, 63-74.

Götz, Roland (1995): *Structural Change, De-Industrialization and Structure Policy in Russia*. Cologne, Reports of the BIOST, No. 16.

Götz, Roland (1998a): 'Theorien der ökonomischen Transformation'. *Osteuropa-Wirtschaft*, 43. Jg., 339-354.

Götz, Roland (1998b): 'Weitere Theorien der ökonomischen Transformation. Die Rolle der Institutionen'. *Osteuropa-Wirtschaft*, 43. Jg., 1086-1100.

Grace, John D. (1995a): 'Russian Gas Resource Base Large, Overstated, Costly to Maintain'. *Oil and Gas Journal*, Feb. 6, 73-74.

Grace, John D. (1995b): 'Cost Russia's Biggest Challenge in Maintaining Gas Supplies'. *Oil and Gas Journal*, Feb. 13, 79-81.

Grais, Wafik, and Zheng, Kangbin (1996): 'Strategic Interdependence in European East-West Gas Trade: A Hierarchical Stackelberg Game Approach'. *Energy Journal*, Vol. 17, No. 3, 61-84.

Gramlich, Edward M. (1994): 'Infrastructure Investment: A Review Essay'. *Journal of Economic Literature*, Vol. 32 (September), 1176-1196.

Gregory, Paul (1999): *Ten Years of Transformation*. Frankfurt/Oder, Guest Lecture presented on Tuesday, July 13 (and FIT Discussion Paper).

Gronau, Reuben (1997): 'The Economics of a Single Toll Road in a Toll-Free Environment'. *Journal of Transport Economics and Policy*, Vol. 33, Part 2, 163-172.

Gros, Daniel, and Marc Suhrcke (2000): *Ten Years After: What is Special About Transition Countries?* HWWA Discussion Paper 86.

Gutmann, Gernot (1990): 'Euckens konstituierende Prinzipien der Wirtschaftspolitik und der ordnungspolitische Wandel Osteuropas'. In: Forschungsstelle zum Vergleich wirtschaftlicher Lenkungssysteme (ed.): *Zur Transformation von Wirtschaftssystemen: Von der sozialistischen Planwirtschaft zur sozialen Marktwirtschaft'. Arbeitsberichte zum Systemvergleich* Nr. 15. Marburg; Philipps-Universität.

Hainz, Christa (2001): *Project Financing in Transition Economies.* Paper presented at the Annual Meeting of the German Economic Association (Verein für Socialpolitik), Magdeburg, September 28.

Hauptverband der Deutschen Bauindustrie (ed.) (1992): *Private Finanzierung von Verkehrswegen in Osteuropa.* Bauverlag GmbH Walluf, Bauwirtschaft, Sonderteil (Oktober).

Havrylyshyn, Bogdan, Ivailo Izvorski, and Ron van Rooden (1999): 'Growth in Transition Economies 1990–97: An Econometric Analysis with Application to Ukraine'. In: Siedenberg, Axel and Lutz Hoffmann (eds): *Ukraine at the Crossroads – Economic Reform in International Perspective.* Heidelberg, New York, Physica.

Hayek, Friedrich A. (1944): *The Road to Serfdom.* Chicago, University of Chicago Press.

Hayek, Friedrich A. (1945): 'The Use of Knowledge in Society'. *American Economic Review*, Vol. 35 (September).

Hayek, Friedrich A. (1969): *Freiburger Studien.* Tübingen, Mohr Siebeck.

Hedtkamp, Günter (1995): 'Die Bedeutung der Infrastruktur in makroökonomischer Sicht'. In: Alois Oberhauser (ed.): *Finanzierungsprobleme der deutschen Einheit: Ausbau der Infrastruktur und kommunaler Finanzausgleich. Schriften des Vereins für Socialpolitik*, N.F. Bd. 229/III. Berlin, Duncker & Humblot.

Henisz, Witold J. (2000): *The Institutional Environment for Infrastructure Investment.* University of Pennsylvania (mimeo).

Henke (1999): *Efficiency Scrutiny of Financing Expenditures in Health Care in Novosibirsk and Rostov Oblast and Proposals for Reform.* Berlin, Discussion Papers on State and Economy, European Center for Comparative Government and Public Policy, No. 12/2000.

Heybey, Berta, and Peter Murrell (1997): *The Relationship between Economic Growth and the Speed of Liberalization During Transition.* Working Paper, University of Maryland.

Hirschhausen, Christian von (1996): 'Lessons from Five Years of Industrial Reform in Post-socialist Central and Eastern Europe'. *DIW Vierteljahreshefte zur Wirtschaftsforschung/DIW Quarterly Journal for Economic Research*, Vol. 65, No.1, Berlin, 44-56.

Hirschhausen, Christian von (1998): 'The Ukrainian Economy Six Years after Independence: From Socialism to a Planning Economy?' *Communist Economies and Economic Transformation*, Vol. 10, No. 4 (December).

Hirschhausen, Christian von (1999): 'What Infrastructure Policies for Eastern Europe? Lessons from the Public Investment Programs (PIP) in the Baltic Countries'. *Europe-Asia Studies*, Vol. 51, No. 3 (May), 417-432.

Hirschhausen, Christian von, and Hella Engerer (1998): 'Post-Soviet Gas Sector Restructuring in the CIS: A Political Economy Approach'. *Energy Policy*, Vol. 26, No. 15, 1113-1123.

Hirschhausen, Christian von, and Hella Engerer (1999): 'Energy in the Caspian Sea Region in the Late 1990s: The End of the Boom?' *OPEC-Review*, Vol. 23, No. 4, (December), 273-291.

Hirschhausen, Christian von, and Jürgen Bitzer (eds) (2000): *The Globalization of Industry and Innovation in Eastern Europe – From Post-Socialist Restructuring to International Competitiveness*. Edward Elgar, Cheltenham, UK and Northampton, MA, USA.

Hirschhausen, Christian von, and Michael Andres (2000): 'Long-Term Electricity Demand in China – From Quantitative to Qualitative Growth?' *Energy Policy*, Vol. 28. No. 3, 231-241.

Hirschhausen, Christian von (2001): *Infrastructure Policies in the East European Transformation Countries*. Berlin, European Centre for Comparative Government and Public Policy, Discussion Papers on Government and Economics, No. 31/2001 (December).

Hirschhausen, Christian von, and Thomas Waelde (2001): 'The End of 'Transition' – An Institutional Interpretation of Energy Sector Reform in Eastern Europe and the CIS'. *MOCT-Economic Policy in Transitional Economies*, Vol. 11, No. 1, 91-108.

Hirschman, Albert O. (1958): 'The Theory of Economic Development'. *Yale Studies in Economics*, Vol. 10, New Haven, CT, Yale University Press.

Hoffmann, Lutz, and Felicitas Möllers (eds) (2001): *Ukraine on the Road to Europe*. Heidelberg, New York, Springer.

Hoffmann, Lutz, und Axel Siedenberg (eds) (1997): *Aufbruch in die Marktwirtschaft - Reformen in der Ukraine von innen betrachtet*. Frankfurt, New York, Campus.

Hölscher, Jens (1998): 'Zur Formierung marktwirtschaftlicher Ordnungen in Zentralosteuropa. ('On the Formation of Economic Orders in East-Central Europe')'. *Applied Economics Quarterly (Konjunkturpolitik)*, Vol. 44, No. 4, 393-422.

Hulten, Charles R. (1996): *Infrastructure Capital and Economic Growth: How Well You Use it May be More Important than How Much You Have*. Cambridge, Mass., National Bureau of Economic Research, NBER Working Paper 5847 (December).

Hunya, Gábor (1995): 'Transport and Telecommunication Infrastructure in Transition'. *Communist Economies and Economic Transformation*, Vol. 7, No. 3, 369-384.

Hutschenreuter, Gernot, Mark Knell and Slavo Radosevic (1999): *Restructuring Innovation Systems in Eastern Europe*. Edward Elgar, Cheltenham, UK and Northampton, MA, USA.

Infrastructure Yearbook (various issues).

International Energy Agency (various issues): *Energy Prices and Taxes*. Paris, OECD.

International Energy Agency (1995a): *Energy Policies of Poland – 1995 Survey*. Paris, OECD.

International Energy Agency (1995b): *Energy Policies of the Russian Federation*. Paris.

International Energy Agency (1995c): *Natural Gas Security Study*. Paris, OECD.

International Energy Agency (1996): *Energy Policies of Ukraine – 1996 Survey*. Paris.

International Energy Agency (1998) *Caspian Oil and Gas, the Supply Potential of Central Asia and Transcaucasia*, Paris.

International Energy Agency (1999): *Energy Policies of IEA Countries*: Hungary 1999 Review. Paris, OECD.

International Energy Agency (2002): *Russia Energy Survey*. Paris, OECD.

Irwin, Timothy, Michael Klein, Guillermo E. Perry, and Mateen Thobani (1999): 'Managing Government Exposure to Private Infrastructure Risks'. *The World Bank Research Observer*, Vol. 14, No. 2 (August), 229-245.

Jochimsen, Reimut (1966): *Theorie der Infrastruktur*. Tübingen, Mohr Siebeck.

Johnson, Simon, Daniel Kaufmann, and Andrei Shleifer (1997): 'The Unofficial Economy in Transition'. *Brookings Papers on Economic Activity (Fall)*. Washington, D.C., The Brookings Institution.

Johnson, Simon, John McMillan, and Christopher Woodruff (1999): *Contract Enforcement in Transition*. London, Centre for Economic Policy Research (CEPR) Discussion Paper No. 2081.

Johnson, Simon, John McMillan, and Christopher Woodruff (2000): 'Entrepreneurs and the Ordering of Institutional Reform – Poland, Slovakia, Romania, Russia and Ukraine Compared'. *Economics of Transition*, Vol. 8, No. 1, 1-36.

Joosten, Rik (1999): 'M1/M15 – How a Successful Project Ended Unnecessarily in Tears'. *Project Finance International*, No. 179 (October 20), 52-55.

Joskow, Paul L. (1985): 'Vertical Integration and Long-term Contracts: The Case of Coal-Burning Electric Generation Plants'. *The Journal of Law, Economics and Organization*, Vol. 1, No. 1, 33-80.

Joskow, Paul L. (1994): *Privatization in Russia: What should be a firm?* Paris, Seminar at the University Paris 1 Sorbonne on 'Transaction Cost Economics', May 26.

Joskow, Paul L. (1996): 'Introducing Competition into Regulated Network Industries'. *Industrial and Corporate Change*, Vol. 2, 341-382.

Joskow, Paul L. (1997): 'Restructuring, Competition and Regulatory Reform in the US Electricity Sector'. *Journal of Economic Perspectives*, Vol 11, No. 3, 119-138.

Judge, E.J. (1998): 'State Participation in Toll Route Developments and Potential Development Benefits: The Situation in Poland'. In: Ecole Nationale des Ponts et Chaussées (ed.): *Road Financing*. Paris, Presses de l'Ecole Nationale des Ponts et Chaussées, 393-411.

Karnite, Raita (1998): 'Evaluation of the Public Investment Programs in Latvia'. In: Bitzer, Jürgen and Hirschhausen, Christian von (eds): *Infrastructure Policies for Sustained Growth in Eastern Europe – The cases of the Baltic Countries*. Berlin, Brussels, Final Report of the Phare-ACE project P-95-2111-R.

Kennedy, David (1999): *Competition in the Power Sectors of Transition Economies*. London, EBRD Working Paper, No. 41 (August).

Kennedy, David (2002a): *Liberalization of the Russian Power Sector*. EBRD Working Paper No. 69.

Kennedy, David (2002b): 'Regulatory Reform and Market Development in Power Sector of Transition Economies: The Case of Kazakhstan'. *Energy Policy*, Vol. 30, 219-233.

Kessides, Ioannis N. (ed.) (2000): *Hungary: A Regulatory and Structural Review of Selected Infrastructure Sectors*. Washington, D.C., World Bank Technical Paper No. 474.

Kilvits, Kaarel (1998): 'Evaluation of the Public Investment Programs in Estonia'. In: Bitzer, Jürgen and Hirschhausen, Christian von (eds): *Infrastructure Policies for Sustained Growth in Eastern Europe – The cases of the Baltic Countries*. Berlin, Brussels, Final Report of the Phare-ACE project P-95-2111-R.

Kinze, Hans-Heinrich, Hans Knop und Eberhard Seifert (eds) (1983): *Sozialistische Volkswirtschaft. Hochschullehrerbuch*. Berlin, Verlag Die Wirtschaft.

Kiwit, Daniel (1994): 'Zur Leistungsfähigkeit neoklassisch orientierter Transaktionskostenansätze'. *Ordo*, Bd. 45, 105-035.

Kiwit, Daniel, und Stefan Voigt (1995): 'Überlegungen zum institutionellen Wandel unter Berücksichtung des Verhältnisses interner und externer

Institutionen'. *Ordo. Jahrbuch für die Ordnung von Wirtschaft und Gesellschaft*, Bd. 46, 117-148.

Klugman, Jeni (1998): 'Uzbekistan: Institutional Continunity Helps Performance'. *Moct-Most*, Vol. 8, No. 1, 63-82.

Kornai, Jànos (1992): *The Socialist System: The Political Economy of Communism*. Oxford, Clarendon Press.

Koziolek, Helmut, Werner Ostwald und Hans Stürz (1986): *Reproduktion und Infrastruktur*. Berlin Verlag Die Wirtschaft.

Kreibig, Uta, Petra Opitz, and Christian von Hirschhausen (2001): 'The Power Sector in Central and Eastern Europe: More Competition Needed in the Run-Up to EU Membership'. *Economic Bulletin*, Vol. 38, No. 1 (January), 33-38.

Kuba, Elzbieta (1998): 'Die Umstrukturierung der polnischen Elektrizitätswirtschaft'. *Zeitschrift für Energiewirtschaft*, Nr. 2.

Kumkar, Lars (1998a): *Privatwirtschaftliche Koordinierungsstrukturen in vertikal strukturierten Industrien: Eine Analyse der Stromwirtschaft auf Grundlage der neuen Institutionenökonomik*. Kieler Arbeitspapier Nr. 928. Kiel, Institut für Weltwirtschaft.

Kumkar, Lars (1998b): *Regulierung vertikal strukturierter Industrien: Eine Analyse der Stromwirtschaft auf Grundlage der neuen Institutionenökonomik*. Kieler Arbeitspapier Nr. 928. Kiel, Institut für Weltwirtschaft.

Kumkar, Lars (1999): *Alternative Liberalisierungsmodelle für die Stromwirtschaft: Eine komparative Institutionenanalyse*. Kieler Arbeitspapier Nr. 928. Kiel, Institut für Weltwirtschaft.

Kumkar, Lars (2000): *Wettbewerbsorientierte Reformen in der Stromwirtschaft– Eine institutionenökonomische Analyse*. Tübingen, Mohr Siebeck (Kieler Studien 305)

Laffont, Jean-Jacques, and Jean Tirole (1993): *A Theory of Incentives and Procurement*. Cambridge, Mass. and London, MIT-Press.

Lau, Lawrence J., Yingyi Quian, and Gérard Rolland (2000): 'Reform without Losers: An Interpretation of China's Dual-Track Approach to Transition'. *Journal of Political Economy*, Vol. 108, No. 1, 120-143.

Léderer, K. (1998): 'After Two Years of Operation of M1/M15 the First Hungarian Concession Motorway: Dilemmas of Private Motorway Concession in the Transition Economies'. In: Ecole Nationale des Ponts et Chaussées (ed.): *Road Financing*. Paris, Presses de l'Ecole Nationale des Ponts et Chaussées, 251-257.

Levy, Brian, and Pablo Spiller (eds) (1994): *Regulations, Institutions and Commitment*. Cambridge University Press.

Lewington, Ilka (1997): *Framework Options for Electricity Utilities in Transition Economies: Attempting a Systematic Approach*. Centre for

Economic Reform and Transformation (CERT) Discussion Paper, Heriot-Watt University Edinburgh, March.

Lipton, David, and Jeffrey Sachs (1990): 'Creating a Market Economy in Eastern Europe: The Case of Poland'. *Brookings Papers on Economic Activity*, No. 1, 75-147.

Lovei, Laszlo (2000): 'The Single-Buyer Model'. Washington, D.C., World Bank, *Public Policy for the Private Sector,* Note No. 225.

Lunina, Inna (1997): *Infrastruktur im Sozialismus.* Kiev (mimeo).

Mabro, Robert, and Ian Wybrew-Bond (eds) (1999): *Gas to Europe: The Strategies of Four Major Suppliers.* Oxford, Oxford University Press.

Marin, Dalia, and Monika Schnitzer (1999): *Disorganization and Financial Collapse.* London, CEPR Discussion Paper No. 2245.

Meißner, Thomas (1999): *Verkehrsinfrastruktur und Wettbewerbsfähigkeit am Beispiel der Reformstaaten Mittel- und Osteuropas.* Halle, Institut für Wirtschaftsforschung, IWH-Forschungsreie Nr. 6/1999.

Melo, Martha de, and Alan Gelb (1996): 'A Comparative Analysis of Twenty-Eight Transition Economies in Europe and Asia'. *Post-Soviet Geography and Economics.* Vol. 37, No. 5, 265-285.

Ménard, Claude (ed.) (2000): *Institutions, Contracts and Organizations – Perspectives from New Institutional Economics.* Cheltenham, UK, Edward Elgar.

Ménard, Claude, and George Clarke (2000a): *A Transitory Regime: Water Supply in Conakry, Guinea.* Washington, D.C., World Bank Development Research Group (Policy Research Working Paper, 2362).

Ménard, Claude, and George Clarke (2000b): *Reforming the Water Supply in Abidjan, Cote d'Ivoire: Mild Reform in a Turbulent Environment.* Washington, D.C., World Bank Development Research Group (Policy Research Working Paper, 2377).

Meran, Georg, and Schwarze, Reimund (1998): *Transmission Access to Power Networks: A Microeconomic Analysis of Alternative Regulatory Regimes.* Berlin, Paper presented at the 4th European Conference of the IAEE.

Meske, Werner (1998): *Institutional Transformation of S&T Systems in the European Economies in Transition.* WZB Discussion Paper P98-403.

Milbrandt, Beate (2001): *Die Finanzierung der Europäischen Union: Perspektiven für eine Osterweiterung.* Baden-Baden, Nomos.

Mises, Ludwig von ([1932] 1951): *Socialism.* London. Jonathan Cape (Translation of the 1932 edition).

Mises, Ludwig von (1920): 'Economic Calculation in the Socialist Commonwealth'. In: F.A. Hayek (ed.) (1935): *Collectivist Economic Planning.* London, Routledge, 87-130.

Morkunaite, Rasa (1998) 'Evaluation of the Public Investment Programs in Lithuania'. In: Bitzer, Jürgen and Hirschhausen, Christian von (eds): *Infrastructure Policies for Sustained Growth in Eastern Europe – The cases of the Baltic Countries*. Berlin, Brussels, Final Report of the Phare-ACE project P-95-2111-R.

Müller, Jürgen (2000): 'Restructuring of the Telecommunications Sector in the West and the East and the Role of Science and Technology'. In: Hirschhausen and Bitzer (2000), 185-226.

Mummert, Uwe (1995): *Informelle Institutionen in ökonomischen Transformationsprozessen*. Baden-Baden, Nomos.

Mummert, Uwe, und Michael Wohlgemuth (1998): *Ordunkgsökonomische Aspekte der Transformation und wirtschaftlichen Entwicklung Ostdeutschlands*. Jena, Max-Planck-Institut zur Erforschung von Wirtschaftssystemen, Diskussionsbeitrag 03-98.

Murrel, Peter, Karen Turner Dunn, and Georges Korsun (1996): 'The Culture of Policy Making in the Transition from Socialism: Price Policy in Mongolia'. *Economic Development and Cultural Change*, Vol. 45, No. 1 (October), 175-194.

Musgrave, Richard A., and Peggy B. Musgrave (1996): *Public Finance in Theory and Practice*. 6th Edition. New York, McGraw-Hill.

Newberry, David M. (1994): 'Restructuring and Privatizing Electric Utilities in Eastern Europe'. *Economics of Transition*, Vol. 2, No. 3, 291-316.

North, Douglas C. (1971): 'Institutional Change and Economic Growth'. *Journal of Economic History*, Vol. 31, 118-125.

North, Douglas C. (1981): *Structure and Change in Economic History*. New York.

North, Douglas C. (1990): *Institutions, Institutional Change and Economic Performance*. Cambridge, M.A., Cambridge University Press.

North, Douglas C. (2000): 'Big-Bang Transformations of Economic Systems: An Introductory Note'. *Journal of Institutional and Theoretical Economics/Zeitschrift für die gesamte Staatswissenschaft*, Vol. 156, No. 1, 3-8.

North, Douglas, and R.P. Thomas (1973): *The Rise of the Western World: A New Economic History*. Cambridge.

Nuti, Domenico (1999): 'Comparative Economics after the Transition'. *Economic Systems*, Vol. 23, No. 2 (June), 155-159.

Olson, Mancur (1965): *The Logic of Collective Action*. Cambridge (Mass.), Harvard University Press.

Olson, Mancur (1969): 'The Principle of "Fiscal Equivalence": The Division of Responsibilities Among Different Levels of Government'. *American Economic Review*, Vol. 59, 479-487.

Olson, Mancur (1982): *The Rise and Decline of Nations*. New Haven and London, Yale University Press.

Olson, Mancur (1995): 'Why the Transition from Communism is so Difficult'. *Eastern Economic Journal*, Vol. 21, No. 4 (Fall), 437-461.

Olson, Mancur (1996): 'Big Bills Left on the Sidewalk: Why Some Nations are Rich, and Others Poor'. *Journal of Economic Perspectives*, Vol. 10, No. 2, 3-24.

Olson, Mancur (1999): *Power and Prosperity: Outgrowing Communist and Capitalist Dictatorships*. New York, Basic Books.

Opitz, Petra (2000): 'The (Pseudo-)Liberalization of Russia's Power Sector: The Hidden Rationality of Transformation'. *Energy Policy*, Vol. 28, No. 3, 147-155.

Opitz, Petra, and Christian von Hirschhausen (2001): 'Ukraine as the Gas Bridge to Europe? Economic and Geopolitical Considerations'. In: Hoffmann, Lutz, and Felicitas Möllers (eds).

Opitz, Petra, Hella Engerer, and Christian von Hirschhausen (forthcoming): 'The Globalization of the Russian Energy Industry – A Way out of the Financial Crisis?' *International Journal of Global Energy Issues*, Vol. 14.

Pauwels, J.-P. (1994): *Géopolitique de l'approvisionnement énergétique de l'Union européenne au XXIe siècle*. Brussels, Bruyant.

Peltzmann, Sam (1976): 'Toward a More General Theory of Regulation'. *Journal of Law and Economics*, Vol. 19.

Peltzmann, Sam (1998): *Political Participation and Government Regulation*. Chicago, University of Chicago Press.

Pfähler, Wilhelm, Ulrich Hofmann, and Bönte, Werner (1996): 'Does Extra Public Infrastructure Capital Matter? An Appraisal of Empirical Literature'. *Finanzarchiv*, N.F., Bd. 53, 68-112.

Piazolo, Daniel (1999): 'Growth Effects of Institutional Change and European Integration'. *Economic Systems*, Vol. 23, No. 4 (December), 305-330.

Piazolo, Daniel (2001): 'The Integration Process Between Eastern and Western Europe'. *Kiel Studies* No. 310. Berlin, Heidelberg, Springer.

Pittman, Russel (2001): *Vertical Restructuring of the Infrastructure Sectors of Transition Economies*. Background paper for the World Development Report 2002: Building Institutions for Markets. Washington, D.C., World Bank.

Radosevic, Slavo (1999): *Final Report on the TSER-Project 'Restructuring and Reintegeration of Eastern European S&T-Systems'*. Brighton.

Radosevic, Slavo and Auriol, Laudeline (1999): 'Patterns of Restructuring in Research, Development and Innovation Activities in Central and Eastern European Countries: An Analysis Based on S&T Indicators'. *Research Policy*, Vol. 28, 351-376.

Radosevic, Slavo, and Laudeline Auriol (1998): 'Measuring S&T Activities in the Post-socialist Countries of CEE: Conceptual and Methodological Issues in Linking Past with Present'. *Scientometrics*, Vol. 42, No. 3, 273-297.

Raiser, Martin (1997): *Informal Institutions, Social Capital and Economic Transition: Reflections on a Neglected Dimension.* European Bank for Reconstruction and Development, Working Paper 25 (December).

Raiser, Martin (1999): *Trust in Transition.* London, European Bank for Reconstruction and Development, Working Paper No. 39.

Raiser, Martin, Christian Haerpfer, Thomas Nowotny, and Claire Wallace (2001): *Social Capital in Transition: A First Look at the Evidence.* London, European Bank for Reconstruction and Development, Working Paper 61.

Resunenko, V.I., and G. Maichel (1997): 'Reliable Supply of Yamal Gas to Europe'. In: OECD and IEA *Natural Gas Technologies: A Driving Force for Market Development*. Paris, OECD, 1047-1059.

Richter, Rudolf (1999): *Institutional Thought in Germany.* Report given to the ISNIE Annual Conference (Washington University, St. Louis, Missouri).

Roland, Gérard (2000): *Transition and Economics: Politics, Markets, and Firms.* Cambridge, MA, MIT Press.

Rose, Richard, William Mishler, and Christian Haerpfer (1997): 'Getting Real: Social Capital in Post-Communist Societies'. *Studies in Public Policy* No. 278, Centre for the Study of Public Policy, University of Strathclyde, Glasgow.

Rostow, Walt W. (1960): *Stages of Economic Growth.* Cambridge, Cambridge University Press.

Ryding, Helen (1998): *Electricity Restructuring in Ukraine: Illusions of Power in the Power Industry?* Heriot-Watt University, CERT Discussion Paper.

Sandler, Todd, and John T. Tschirhart (1980): 'The Economic Theory of Clubs, An Evaluative Survey', *Journal of Economic Literature*, Vol. XVIII, 1506-1508.

Sandler, Todd, and John T. Tschirhart (1997): 'Club Theory: Thirty Years Later'. *Public Choice*, Vol. 93, 335-355.

Schipanski, Dagmar (1997): '*Zur Lage der außeruniversitären Forschung'. Kurzstatement zur Festveranstaltung 'Forschung als Innovationsfaktor in den neuen Bundesländern'.* Jena, October 1.

Schmieding, Holger (1993): 'From Plan to Market: On the Nature of the Transformation Crisis'. *Weltwirtschaftliches Archiv*, Vol. 129, No. 2, 216-253.

Schmoller, Gustav (1900): *Grundriß der Allgemeinen Volkswirtschaftslehre.* München.

Schrader, Klaus (1999): *Ordnungspolitische Weichenstellungen für eine marktwirtschaftliche Entwicklung in mittel- und osteuropäischen Reformländern.* Kieler Studien 297. Tübingen, Mohr Siebeck.

Schröder, Rudolf (1999): *Konfliktbewältigung, soziokulturelles Erbe und wirtschaftlicher Fortschritt.* Tübingen, Mohr Siebeck.

Schumann, Jochen, und Andreas Meyer, Wolfang Ströbele (1999): *Grundzüge der mikroökonomischen Theorie.* Heidelberg, Springer.

Schumpeter, Josef A. (1942): *Capitalism, Socialism, and Democracy.* New York.

Seidel, Bernhard, und Dieter Vesper (2000): *Infrastrukturausstattung und Nachholbedarf in Ostdeutschland.* Berlin, DIW, Gutachten im Auftrag des Sächsischen Finanzministeriums.

Seidman, Ann, Seidman, Robert B. and Waelde, Thomas (eds) (1999): *Making Development Work: Legislative Reform for Institutional Transformation and Good Governance.* London, Kluwer Law International.

Siedenberg, Axel and Lutz Hoffmann (eds) (1999): *Ukraine at the Crossroads – Economic Reform in International Perspective.* Heidelberg, New York, Physica.

Sinclair, Alison (1997): *Liberalizing the Electricity Supply in Western and Eastern Europe: Lessons for Russia.* University of Potsdam, Institute for European Economy and International Relations, Discussion Paper No. 30.

Somlyody, L. (1994): 'Quo Vadis Water Quality Management in Central and Eastern Europe?' *Water Science and Technology*, Vol. 30, 1-14.

Spiller, Pablo T. (1993): 'Institutions and Regulatory Commitment in Utilities' Privatization'. *Industrial and Corporate Change*, Vol. 2, No. 3, 387-450.

Spiller, Pablo T. (1996): 'Institutions and Commitment'. *Industrial and Corporate Change*, Vol. 5, No. 2, 421-451.

Spiller, Pablo T., and Carlo G. Cardilli (1997): 'The Frontier of Telecommunications Deregulation: Small Countries Leading the Pack'. *Journal of Economic Perspectives*, Vol. 11, No. 4 (Fall), 127-138.

Spiller, Pablo T., and Ingo Vogelsang (1997): 'The Institutional Foundations of Regulatory Commitment in the UK: The Case of Telecommunications'. *Journal of Institutional and Theoretical Economics – Zeitschrift für die gesamte Staatswissenschaft*, Vol. 153, 607-629.

Spiller, Pablo T., and Mariano Tommasi (2000): *The Institutional Foundations of Public Policy: A Transactions Approach with Application to Argentina.* Paper presented at the Annual Meeting of the International Society for New Institutional Economics, Tübingen, September.

Stadelbauer, Jörg (1999): 'Suche nach Wegen: Stand und Perspektiven bei der Entwicklung räumlicher Infratrukturnetze im Verkehrs- und Kommunikationswesen des östlichen Europa'. *Osteuropa-Wirtschaft*, 44. Jhg., Nr. 1, 1-27.

Stahl, Silke (1998): *An Evolutionary Perspective in Transition Theory*. Jena, Max Planck-Institute for Research into Economic Systems, Discussion Paper 9804.

Steinherr, Alfred (1999): 'Russia After the Downfall: Should Europe Watch or Act?' In: Nuebler, Irmgard, and Harald Trabold (eds): *Herausforderungen an die Wirtschaftspolitik an der Schwelle zum 21. Jahrhundert (Festschrift für Lutz Hoffmann zum 65. Geburtstag)*. Berlin, Duncker & Humblot, 165-175.

Stern, Johnathan P. (1995): *The Russian Gas 'Bubble': Consequences for European Gas Markets*. London, The Royal Institute of International Affairs.

Stern, Jon (1994): 'Economic Regulation in Central and Eastern Europe'. *Economics of Transition*, Vol. 2, No. 3, 391-398.

Stern, Jon (1999): 'Styles of Regulation: The Choice of Appraoch to Utility Regulation in Central and Eastern Europe'. London Business School, *Regulation Initiative Discussion Paper Series*, No. 34.

Stern, Jon, and Junior R. Davis (1998): 'Regulatory Reform in the Electricity Sector in Eastern Europe'. *Economics of Transition*, Vol. 6, No. 2, 427-460.

Stigler, George J. (1971): 'The Theory of Economic Regulation'. *Bell Journal of Economics*, Vol. 2, 3-21.

Stiglitz, Joseph E. (1994): *Whither Socialism?* Cambridge, MIT Press.

Stiglitz, Joseph E. (1999): *Whither Reform? Ten Years of the Transition.* Washington, Paper prepared for the Annual Bank Conference on Development Economics, April 28-30.

Streit, Manfred (1997): 'Transformation von Wirtschaftssystemen'. In: *Gabler-Wirtschafts-Lexikon*, 14. Auflage, 3812-3814.

Streit, Manfred, and Uwe Mummert (1996): *Grundprobleme der Systemtransformation aus institutionenökonomischer Perspektive*. Jena, Max-Planck-Institut zur Erforschung von Wirtschaftssystemen, Diskussionsbeitrag 09-96.

Teubal, Morris, Dominique Foray, Moshe Justman, and Ehud Zuscovitch (eds) (1996): *Technological Infrastructure Policy – An International Perspective*. Dordrecht, Kluwer Academic Publishers.

Thanner, Benedikt (1999): 'Systemtransformation: Ein Mythos verblaßt - Der tiefe Fall Rußlands von der Plan- zur Subsistenzwirtschaft'. *Osteuropa-Wirtschaft*, 44. Jhg., Nr. 3, 196-225.

Thimann, Christian, and Marcel Thum (1999): 'Investing in Terra Incognita: Waiting and Learning'. *Economic Systems*, Vol. 22, 1-22.

Thünen, Johann Heinrich von (1842/1930): *Der isolirte Staat in Beziehung auf Landwirtschaft und Nationalökonomie. 3. Auflage.* Verlag Gustav Fischer, Jena. (1. Auflage: 1842. Rostock).

Timàr, Andràs (1992): 'Neue Autobahnen in Ungarn – Öffentlich-private Partnerschaft bei der Finanzierung'. In: Hauptverband der Deutschen Bauindustrie (ed.), 29-33.

Tirole, Jean (1990): *The Theory of Industrial Organization*. 3rd edition. Cambridge, Massachussetts, MIT Press.

Tjulpanov, Sergeij ([1969] 1975): *Politische Ökonomie und ihre Anwendung in den Entwicklungsländern. 2. Auflage.* Berlin, Verlag Die Wirtschaft. (Translation from the Russian Original of 1969).

Tollison, R.D. (1982): 'Rent Seeking: A Survey'. *Kyklos*, Vol. 35, 575-602.

Transport Infrastructure Needs Assessment (TINA) (1999): *Identification of the Network Components for a Future Trans-European Transport Network.* Brussels, Vienna.

Tullock, G. (1967): 'The Welfare Costs of Tariffs, Monopoly, and Theft'. *Western Economic Journal*, Vol. 5, 224-232.

United Nations Economic Commission for Europe (UN-ECE) (1998): *Reform and Restructuring of the Gas Industry in Economies in Transition.* Geneva, ECE Gas Centre Series No. 9.

Varian, Hal (2000): *Intermediate Microeconomics.* 5th Edition. New York, W.W. Norton & Company.

Vesper, Dieter (1991): *Ein öffentliches Infrastrukturprogramm für Ostdeutschland.* Berlin, DIW (Gutachten im Auftrag der Hans-Böckler-Stiftung).

Voigt, Stefan (1993): *Values, Norms, Institutions and the Prospects for Economic Growth in Central and Eastern Europe.* Institut für allgemeine Wirtschaftsforschung, Universität Freiburg, Discussion Paper, No. 93-01.

Voigt, Stefan, and Engerer, Hella (2000): 'Institutions and Transformation – Possible Policy Implications of the New Institutional Economics'. In: *New Developments in Economic Research.* Berlin, Expertise for the German Federal Ministry of Finance.

Voigt, Stefan, and Hella Engerer (2000): 'Institutions and Transformation – Possible Policy Implications of the New Institutional Economics'. In: *Neue Entwicklungen in der Wirtschaftswissenschaft.* Berlin, Gutachten im Auftrag des Bundesministeriums der Finanzen.

Voigt, Stephan and Daniel Kiwit (1996), *Black Markets, Mafiosi and the Prospect for Economic Development in Russia – Analyzing the Interplay of External and Internal Institutions.* Jena, Max-Planck-Institute for Research into Economic Systems, Discussion Paper 05-95.

Volckart, Oliver (1999): *Öffentliches und privates Wirtschaften: Zur Trennung von Staat und Gesellschaft im Verlauf der Vormoderne (ca. 12.-18. Jh.).* Jena, Max-Planck-Institut zur Erforschung von Wirtschaftssystemen, Diskussionsbeitrag 03-99.

Waelde, Thomas, and Christian von Hirschhausen (1999): 'Regulatory Reform in the Energy Industry of Post-Soviet Countries: The Third Way?' In: Seidman, A., Seidman, R.B. and Waelde, T. (eds): *Making Development Work: Legislative Reform for Institutional Transformation and Good Governance.* London, Kluwer Law International.

Waelde, Thomas, and James L. Gunderson (1996): 'Legislative Reform in Transition Economies – Western Transplants – A Shortcut to Social Market Economy Status?' *International and Comparative Law Quarterly*, Vol. 43 (April), 347-378.

Wagener, Hans-Jürgen (2000): *On the Relationship between State and Economy in Transformation.* Frankfurt/Oder, Discussion Paper of the Frankfurt Institute for Transformation Studies No. 14/00.

Welfens, Paul J.J. (1998), *Die Russische Transformationskrise: Monetäre und reale Aspekte sowie Politikoptionen*, Potsdam, European Institute for International Economic Relations, Discussion Paper 54.

Welfens, Paul J.J., and George Yarrow (eds) (1997): *Telecommunications and Energy in Systemic Transformation.* Berlin, Heidelberg, Springer.

Williamson, Oliver (1975): *Markets and Hierarchies.* New York. New York, Free Press.

Williamson, Oliver E. (1985): *The Economic Institutions of Capitalism – Firms, Markets, Relational Contracting.* New York, Free Press.

Wink, Rüdiger (1995): *Verkehrsinfrastrukturpolitik in der Marktwirtschaft – Eine institutionenökonomische Analyse.* Schriftenreihe des Rheinisch-Westfälischen Instituts für Wirtschaftsforschung (neue Folge), Heft 59. Berlin, Duncker & Humblot.

Wittkowsky, Andreas (1998a): *Fünf Jahre ohne Plan: Die Ukraine 1991-96.* Hamburg, LIT-Verlag.

Wittkowsky, Andreas (1998b): *Die Unterstützung langsamer Transformationsländer – Ansätze und Erfahrungen in der Ukraine.* Berlin, Deutsches Institut für Entwicklungspolitik, Berichte und Gutachten, 1/1998.

Woodruff, C. (1999): 'It's Value that's Virtual: Bartles, Rubles, and the Place of Gazprom in the Russian Economy'. *Post-Soviet Affairs*, Vol. 15, No. 2.

World Bank (1994): *World Development Report – Infrastructure and Development.* Washington, D.C., Oxford, Oxford University Press.

World Bank (1996): *World Development Report 1996 – From Plan to the Market.* Washington, D.C.

World Bank (1997): *World Development Report 1997 – The State in a Changing World*. Washington, D.C.

World Bank (1999): *World Development Report 1998/99 – Knowledge for Development*. Washington, D.C.

World Bank (2000): *Privatization of the Power and Natural Gas Industries in Hungary and Kazakhstan*. Washington, D.C., World Bank Technical Paper No. 451.

Wurzel, Ulrich (1998): *Natural Resources, Geostrategic Interests and the Necessity of a New Economic Policy for Kazakhstan*. Kazakhstan Economic Trends, 3rd Quarter, 16-32.

Wurzel, Ulrich (1999): *Eine neue Generation von Rentierstaaten: Bodenschätze, geostrategische Interessen und autoritäre Regime in Zentralasien – Der Fall Kasachstan. asien-afrika-lateinamerika*, Vol. 27, 543-568.

Yarrow, George (1997): 'Restructuring and Regulatory Reform in the Polish Energy Sector: An Assessment'. In: Welfens, Paul J.J., and George Yarrow (eds).

Annex: Macro-indicators for East European countries (1990–2002)

	1990	1991	1992	1993	1994	1995	1996	1997	1998	1999	2000	2001	2002(f)
Bulgaria (population: 8.4 m)													
Annual real GDP growth (%)	:	-11.7	-7.3	-2.4	1.8	2.1	-10.9	-7.4	2.0	2.0	5.0	4.5	3.5
Industrial production (%)	-16.0	-27.8	-15.0	-11.8	7.8	-6.3	-8.7	-9.1	4.3	-12.5	12.0	:	:
Indicator of market-oriented reform *	:	:	:	:	:	2.6	2.6	2.8	2.8	3.0	3.0	3.0	:
Czech Republic (population: 10.3 m)													
Annual real GDP growth (%)	n.d.	-11.5	-3.3	0.6	2.7	5.9	3.9	1.0	2.0	-0.8	3.1	3.6	3.5
Industrial production (%)	-3.5	-22.3	-7.9	-5.3	2.1	8.7	6.9	4.6	5.0	-0.4	5.8	7.0	:
Indicator of market-oriented reform *	:	:	:	:	:	3.3	3.4	3.4	3.4	3.5	3.5	3.5	:
Estonia (population: 1.5 m)													
Annual real GDP growth (%)	n.d.	n.d.	-14.2	-8.5	-1.8	4.3	4.0	9.0	6.0	-1.1	6.4	5.4	4.0
Industrial production (%)	:	:	-35.6	-18.6	-3.1	4.7	3.5	13.6	4.1	-3.4	13.6	7.0	:
Indicator of market-oriented reform *	:	:	:	:	:	2.2	3.3	3.4	3.4	3.5	3.5	3.5	:
Hungary (population: 10.2 m)													
Annual real GDP growth (%)	-3.9	-11.9	-3.1	-0.6	2.9	1.5	1.0	4.4	5.0	4.5	5.2	3.8	4.0
Industrial production (%)	-9.3	-18.4	-9.7	4.0	9.6	4.6	3.4	6.9	10.0	10.4	18.0	6.4	:
Indicator of market-oriented reform *	:	:	:	:	:	3.4	3.4	3.5	3.5	3.8	3.8	3.7	:

Annex continued

	1990	1991	1992	1993	1994	1995	1996	1997	1998	1999	2000	2001	2002(f)
Latvia (population: 2.5 m)													
Annual real GDP growth (%)	n.d.	n.d.	-34.9	-14.9	0.6	-0.8	2.8	5.9	5.0	1.1	6.6	7.6	5.0
Industrial production (%)	..	-0.3	-46.2	-29.8	-7.7	0.9	3.1	6.1	2.0	-8.8	3.2	..	..
Indicator of market-oriented reform *	..	..	..	..	..	2.7	3.1	3.1	3.1	3.1	3.1	3.2	..
Lithuania (population: 3.7 m)													
Annual real GDP growth (%)	n.d.	n.d.	-37.7	-24.2	1.0	3.0	3.6	6.0	3.0	-4.2	2.9	5.7	3.5
Industrial production (%)	-2.8	-2.8	-50.9	-42.7	2.0	5.3	5.1	3.3	8.2	-11.2	7.0	16.9	..
Indicator of market-oriented reform *	..	..	..	..	..	2.8	2.9	3.0	3.0	3.2	3.2	3.3	..
Poland (population: 38.6 m)													
Annual real GDP growth (%)	-11.6	-7.0	2.6	3.8	5.2	7.0	6.1	6.9	5.5	4.5	4.1	1.1	1.5
Industrial production (%)	-26.1	-11.9	3.9	5.6	13.0	9.7	8.5	10.8	4.8	4.4	7.1	-0.5	..
Indicator of market-oriented reform *	..	..	..	..	..	3.3	3.3	3.3	3.3	3.5	3.5	3.6	..
Romania (population: 22.6 m)													
Annual real GDP growth (%)	n.d.	-12.9	-8.7	1.5	3.9	7.1	4.1	-6.6	-6.0	-3.2	1.6	5.3	3.5
Industrial production (%)	-23.7	-22.8	-21.9	1.3	3.3	10.0	8.2	-5.9	-17.3	-8.8	8.2	..	..
Indicator of market-oriented reform *	..	..	..	..	..	2.4	2.6	2.8	2.6	2.8	2.8	2.9	..
Slovak Republic (population: 4.7 m)													
Annual real GDP growth (%)	n.d.	-14.6	-6.5	-3.7	4.9	6.8	6.9	6.5	4.5	1.9	2.2	3.3	3.5
Industrial production (%)	-3.6	-17.6	-14.0	-13.5	6.4	8.3	2.5	2.0	2.0	-3.4	9.1	4.6	..
Indicator of market-oriented reform *	..	..	..	..	..	3.2	3.2	3.3	3.3	3.4	3.4	3.4	..

Annex continued

	1990	1991	1992	1993	1994	1995	1996	1997	1998	1999	2000	2001	2002(f)
Slovenia (population: 4.7 m)													
Annual real GDP growth (%)	n.d.	n.d.	-5.5	2.8	5.3	4.1	3.1	3.0	3.8	5.0	4.7	3.0	3.0
Industrial production (%)	-10.5	-11.6	-12.6	-2.5	6.6	2.3	1.2	2.4	3.7	-0.5	6.2	2.9	..
Indicator of market-oriented reform *	..	..	..	..	..	3.1	3.1	3.1	3.1	3.3	3.3	3.3	..
Central and Eastern Europe (unw. average) (population: 97.0 m)													
Annual real GDP growth (%)	-7.8	-11.6	-11.9	-4.6	1.5	4.1	2.5	2.9	3.4	1.0	5.1	5.7	3.5
Industrial production (%)	-11.9	-15.1	-21.0	-11.3	4.0	4.8	3.4	3.2	2.7	-3.4	8.5	..	..
Indicator of market-oriented reform *	..	..	..	..	..	2.9	3.1	3.2	3.1	3.3	3.3	3.3	..
Belarus (population: 10.2 m)													
Annual real GDP growth (%)	n.d.	n.d.	-9.6	-7.6	-12.6	-10.4	2.8	10.4	8.4	3.4	5.8	3.0	2.0
Industrial production (%)	..	1.0	-5.2	-10.5	-18.9	-10.2	3.2	17.5	12.4	10.3	8.0	..	..
Indicator of market-oriented reform *	..	..	..	..	..	2.1	1.8	1.6	1.5	1.6	1.5	1.6	..
Russian Federation (population: 147.5 m)													
Annual real GDP growth (%)	n.d.	n.d.	-14.5	-8.7	-12.6	-4.0	-4.9	-0.4	-5.0	3.5	7.7	5.0	3.5
Industrial production (%)	-0.1	-8.0	-18.8	-16.0	-21.0	-3.3	-5.0	1.9	-5.2	8.1	9.0	4.9	..
Indicator of market-oriented reform *	..	..	..	..	..	2.6	2.9	2.9	2.5	2.5	2.5	2.4	..
Ukraine (population: 50.1 m)													
Annual real GDP growth (%)	n.d.	n.d.	-13.7	-14.2	-23.0	-11.8	-10.0	-3.2	-1.5	-0.4	6.0	9.1	4.0
Industrial production (%)	-0.1	-4.8	-6.4	-8.0	-27.3	-12.0	-5.1	-1.9	-1.0	4.0	12.9	14.2	..
Indicator of market-oriented reform *	..	..	..	..	..	2.2	2.4	2.4	2.4	2.5	2.5	2.6	..

Annex continued

	1990	1991	1992	1993	1994	1995	1996	1997	1998	1999	2000	2001	2002(f)
European CIS (unw. average) (population: 207.8 m)													
Annual real GDP growth (%)	n.d.	n.d.	-12.6	-10.2	-16.1	-8.7	-4.0	5.8	1.9	2.2	6.5	5.7	3.4
Industrial production (%)	-0.1	-3.9	-10.1	-11.5	-22.4	-8.5	-2.3	4.6	2.1	7.5	7.3	..	..
Indicator of market-oriented reform *	..	..	..	..	..	2.3	2.4	2.3	2.1	2.2	2.0	2.1	..
Total Eastern Europe and CIS (unw. average) (population: 305.8 m)													
Annual real GDP growth (%)	n.d.	n.d.	-12.0	-5.9	-2.6	1.1	1.1	3.2	1.8	0.8	3.8	5.7	3.4
Industrial production (%)	-9.2	-12.5	-18.5	-11.4	-2.1	1.7	2.1	3.5	4.9	-0.9	8.2	..	..
Indicator of market-oriented reform *	..	..	..	..	..	2.6	2.7	2.7	2.6	3.2	3.0	3.1	..

Notes:

*   Source: EBRD, values can vary between 1 (no reform) and 4 (market reforms accomplished)

.. :   not available

n.d.:   not defined

(p):   projections

Sources: National statistics, EBRD (forecast based on EBRD, 2002), BMWi Dokumentation No. 420, *DIW Economic Bulletin* March 1999

Author Index

Subject Index